The Folkways Omnibus of Children's Games

The Folkways Omnibus of

illustrated by
Alex D'Amato

Children's Games

Iris Vinton

STACKPOLE BOOKS

THE FOLKWAYS OMNIBUS OF CHILDREN'S GAMES
Copyright © 1970 by
THE STACKPOLE COMPANY

Published by
STACKPOLE BOOKS
Cameron and Kelker Streets
Harrisburg, Pa. 17105

ISBN 0-8117-0668-0
Library of Congress Catalog Card Number: 71-110479
Printed in U.S.A.

Contents

PART I   GAMES SHARED BY THE WORLD'S PEOPLES

PART II   THE SUN, MOON, AND STARS, AND THE SEASONS IN GAMES

PART III   OLD CULTURES IN TRADITIONAL GAMES AND PLAYWAYS

PART IV   GEOGRAPHY AND CLIMATE AS MOLDERS OF PLAY

Guide to Games

11

Guide to Lands and Peoples

AFRICA

EUROPE

LATIN AMERICA

MIDDLE EAST

Preface

THIS BOOK IS the result of over twenty years of close association with children and games. Its theme is that children's games are the common property of children throughout the world, and that they have imbedded in them folkways, playways and remnants of the past of all peoples. They are man's cultural residuals. Consequently, games provide a viable means for acquainting ourselves and children with other lands and peoples, of spanning the chasm between inhabitants of industrialized societies and those who still follow the agricultural cycle, and between the past and the present.

In the majority of societies today, children's games exist as forms of competitive fun or dramatic play, and have no particular significance. Some child-play is imitative of elders (for example, playing hospital or playing house), but that is merely informal play without the structure which is necessary in order to make it a game.

For the most part, children learn games from one another or are taught games that have been stripped of all meaning through evolution—the whole good, as it were, being in the games themselves: exercise, acquisition of skill, participation, social activity, fun. Games for their own sake are a recent development; in this respect, children's games are only a few hundred years old, having been ushered in by the discovery of childhood as we understand it today, along about the end of the seventeenth century. Before that time, people had no definite concept of childhood—children were simply little adults—and games were those which both children and adults played, just as they shared the same work. There was not the separation into age groups that marks modern society and that has tended to create the generation gap, communication gap, and the numerous other so-called gaps which have been the cause of concern to parents, educators, and public officials.

The games in this book range from those for children of nursery age through those for elementary school age, but they have in many instances proved to hold interest for older children and for adults and were chosen because of that quality.

Games derived from ancient folkways, customs, and mythology are presented in modernized variants for today's young players.

All games are informal, including the informal versions of sports games, such as baseball, soccer, and football. True games for children must retain that essential element of freedom to create within the framework of a particular game special rules, different requirements for winning, new ways of playing, or even freedom to evolve their own variations on the basic game in almost the same way as jazz bands used to embroider a simple musical phrase or tune until they had made it their own.

Although we can state with some certainty the time when childhood and children's games entered the life style of the Western world, we know almost nothing of precisely when a game became a game. Games like toys go back to the prehistoric past and become a part of magic. Like toys they are merged with ancient religions, customs, or events, and some of them, once they are understood, are a kind of historical document (for example, the game of London Bridge).

An exploration into the relatedness of children's games to the folkways—the new and the old—of the world's peoples discloses a vision of all mankind's work and play, hopes and fears. Children's games can indeed make the whole world kin.

Play and games are and should be an experience shared by all children every day of their lives. That experience enables each child to become aware of his own environment and culture and, at the same time, it can bring to his attention the richness and variety of the cultures which children in other lands and countries of the world share with him because the games they play are, more often than not, his games too. To that end, this book was written.

Part I

GAMES SHARED BY THE WORLD'S PEOPLES

Games Played
With the Hands

ALMOST AS SOON as a child becomes aware of anything, he becomes aware of hands—his and others'. Thus, games for children and mothers, and nursery-age play have ever and everywhere been associated with hand games.

The appeal of clap-hand games does not vanish with babyhood. It lasts through childhood during which an awakening occurs to the broader interest offered by folk songs and dancing accompanied by rhythmic clapping or drumlike beat of hands, which are used, like the voice, as instruments for making music.

CHANGE HAND CLAP   This game is played by children of the Nilotic peoples in Africa.

From across forty centuries, two little girls of Thebes in Egypt play Change Hand Clap for us on an antique vase found in a tomb. No record was left of the rules, but the game still looks the same today in Egypt, Ethiopia, and the Sudan.

The quickness with which the hands are changed is the secret. Three may play, though it's basically a game for two boys or girls, who stand opposite each other. They clap their hands, then each other's right hand; clap their hands, then each other's left hand. This is done faster and faster until one or the other misses.

PAT-A-CAKE   This is Change Hand Clap, accompanied by English words:

Pat-a-cake, pat-a-cake,
Baker's man,
Make me a cake
As fast as you can.

Pat it and prick it
And mark it with B
And put it in the oven
For baby and me.

It is the same game in Germany, Spain, and Italy (Sicily). Only the language and words are different:

German	English
Backe, backe Kuchen,	Bake, bake a cake,
Der Bäcker hat gerufen.	The baker called.
Wer will schöne Kuchen backen	He who wants to bake a cake
Der muss haben sieben Sachen:	Seven things he must have:
Eir und Salz,	Eggs and salt,
Butter und Schmalz,	Butter and lard,
Milch und Mehl,	Milk and flour,
Safran macht den Kuchen gul.	Saffron to make the cake yellow.

Spanish	English
Tortitas y mas tortitas,	Little cakes and more little cakes,
Para madre, las mas bonitas.	For mother, the prettiest.
Roscones y mas roscones,	Round loaves and more round loaves,
Para niñito (o niñita) los mas pequeños (o las mas pequeñas),	For the baby boy (or baby girl), the littlest,
Y para padre, los coscorrones.	And for father, the big lumps.

Italian (Sicilian)	English
Manu, manuzzi,	Hand little hand,
Pani e ficuzzi,	Bread and figs,
Vieni lu tata,	Here comes your papa,
Porta 'i cusuzzi.	Bringing candy.
Nuàtri nn'i manciamu	We eat it all up
Ea bambino Toni* 'un cci nni damu.	And to baby Tony* give none.

---

* The child's name, whatever it might be, is used here.

CLAPPING HAND   This is played the same way as Pat-a-Cake by Chinese children in Kwangtung Province, China, and throughout Malaya and Indonesia wherever the Chinese have settlements or communities. Usually they sit on floor or ground or squat on their heels while playing.

PEASE PORRIDGE HOT   This game is played to the familiar words, "Pease porridge hot, pease porridge cold, / Pease porridge in the pot, nine days old." It is an English variant of Pat-a-Cake, complicated with rhyme and varied claps on words, thus: on *pease, nine,* clap both hands on knees; *porridge, days,* clap both hands; *hot,* clap each other's right hand; *cold,* clap each other's left hand; *in the pot, old,* clap each other's hands.

The order of claps is reversed the next time round.

The game got to Britain by sea and land from the Mediterranean, but the rhyme came right out of that part of Ben Jonson's London commonly known as Porridge Island (St. Martin's Lane), which was "especially filled with second-rate cook shops."

Pease Porridge arrived in North America with the English colonists, then acquired new names: Slap Hands, Fall Tyrants (These are the days of Liberty, / Fall, tyrants, fall! / These are the days, etc.), and many more. Among innumerable versions heard here and there are these:

<table>
<tr><td align="center">Dingdong, Dingdong</td><td align="center">Pots and Pans†</td></tr>
<tr><td>

Dingdong, Dingdong,
There goes the gong.
Come along,
It's time for supper.
Wash your face,
Take your place,
Eat your food.
Do you good.
Go to bed
Or I'll smack your head.*

</td><td>

Pots and pans,
Dishes and glass,
Fought in a battle.
Bang, rattle went pots and pans.
Crash! Smash! went dishes and
   glass.
Who do you think won?

</td></tr>
</table>

---

* On the word "head," players must dodge quickly in order to avoid being smacked.

† In this version of Pease Porridge, players clap right hands, then left hands, each other's hands, and wind up clapping both hands.

And modern city versions heard here, there, and everywhere are these Pease Porridges:

Oh, sir, oh sir,
Where do I go, sir,
For a loaf of bread, sir?

Go to the grocer (gro-cer)
For a loaf of bread, sir.

Yes, sir, yes, sir,
I'll go to the grocer
And get a loaf of bread, sir.

Oh, sir, oh, sir
Shall I go to the grocer
For a polar bear, sir?

No, sir, no, sir,
Don't go to the grocer
For a polar bear, sir.

Oh, sir, oh, sir,
Where do I go, sir,
To find a polar bear, sir?

Go to the pole, sir,
For a polar bear, sir.

Yes, sir, yes, sir,
That's where I'll go, sir,
For a polar bear, sir.

Please, sir, please, sir,
Where do I go, sir,
For a pound of cheese, sir?

Go to the cheese store
There on the corner (cor-ner)
For a pound of cheese, sir.

Oh, sir, oh, sir,
Shall I go to the drugstore
For a ball and bat, sir?

No, sir, no, sir,
Go to a sports store
For a ball and bat, sir.

When playing in a group, children take turns asking round the circle or chant and clap all together.

FIST-HIDE GUESS   On the Tokaido Road or East-Sea-Way, between Japan's old capital, Kyoto, and Tokyo, the new capital, lies one of the world's most beautiful inlets—Surugo Bay. Fishing boats bob on the waters. From the cliffs, men and women dive, as they have dived for centuries, with sharp knives to gather abalone, clinging with suction feet to the rocks below. Among the pine trees on the side of the mountain where it comes down to the sea, children play at fist-and-shell games.

The game is suitable for any size group of small children and as a party game. All players except the hider, the player with the shell, sit in a row or circle with fists (backs of hands up) held in front of them. The hider with the shell in one of his fists, which he holds with backs of hands down, walks around touching fists, pretending to give the shell to someone, saying, "The shell is passing to you. You can't see it, but your hands feel it."

He actually leaves the shell in one player's fist. That player, as soon as he can, must try to pass it on to another player without anyone seeing. When the hider has touched all fists, he says, "Tell me, can anyone guess who has it?" and he begins to count, "One, two, three," etc.

Everyone guesses, including the one who actually has the shell. If no one can guess correctly before the hider has counted to twenty, the one who has it becomes the Hider.

CHAN, CHAN, SIKU, REMBAT   This was the Fist-Hide Guess as played in Korea, where the game well may have come from in the first place.

The Korean game differs in that as soon as the hider leaves the shell in someone's hand, that player must leap up and run around the circle or row and get back to his place before the hider catches him or he's the next hider.

Fist games were brought back to Europe by Portuguese and Dutch pepper and spice traders who ranged the China seas. As Hold Fast My Golden (or Diamond) Ring, and Button, Button, Who Has the Button? they were played in England and English colonies at social affairs.

Sacks (in which players pile fists one on top of the other and take turns striking them off) and the like (Socko, Sock-It, Chiddity Dick) were considered fist feats of strength and endurance rather than games, and were activities reserved for "rough boys."

Finger changing games and mathematics have a common basis: the fingers and toes, which are used in various counting systems. Thus, the quinary system is based on the numeral 5, and, ultimately, on the fingers of one hand; the decimal system is based on the numeral 10, and, ultimately, on the fingers of both hands; and the vigesimal system is based on the numeral 20, and, ultimately, on the digits of both hands and both feet. Measurements are sometimes still made in terms of hands and feet (so many hands high, so many feet long, etc.).

The games are many thousands of years old. The Frenchman Jean François Champollion, who deciphered Egyptian hieroglyphic writing from the famous Rosetta stone, translated descriptions of how to play them which he found on ancient vases, bowls, and other artifacts. Men, women, and sometimes children were shown playing Guess How Many? with written descriptions close to the pictures rather like captions in a modern cartoon strip. Archeologists have seen the same finger games on Egyptian, Grecian, and Cretan pottery any number of times, and there is apparently little difference between those of antiquity and those of today. The big difference is in the players. Gods and goddesses as well as mortal men and women were habitually engaged in such games, playing for money or prizes, and sometimes for fun. Children are shown playing for fun and sometimes for prizes.

Finger changing games arrived with Greek merchant ships in Roman ports, where they became popular as Flashing Fingers (Micare) or Mora with Roman and, later, with Italian boys. As Uno, Cinque, Sette, and sometimes Mora, they crossed the Atlantic to the United States and got off the ships with Italian immigrants in Boston, Massachusetts.

UNO, CINQUE, SETTE   Two players, or as many pairs as want to, can join in the quick eye, quick hand, quick say competition. Spectators also enjoy this game of chance and skill even in its simplest forms. It makes a good travel pastime.

Players sit or stand facing each other. They say rapidly, *"Bucca, bucca,* how many is this?" and extend the fingers of one or both hands at the same time. Each player tries to guess the number of fingers "thrown out" by his opponent, and quickly shouts the number. The winner is the one who guesses correctly the most times out of ten.

ODD OR EVEN   This is played the same way as Uno, Cinque, Sette except that the player has only to guess whether the fingers "thrown out" are an odd or an even number. This is varied by hiding one hand inside the other, doubling up some fingers on the hidden hand and asking opponent to guess how many fingers of the hidden hand are not doubled up.

MATCHING FINGERS   In this finger changing game from Northeast Africa, six play; one pair of partners plays against another pair, each pair having a watcher who calls out the results. Two players sit back to back, so that one cannot see the other's fingers. Each must try to guess how many fingers his partner will "throw," and match that number. The pair's watcher calls out the results, as, for instance, "Willie, three; Wilma, four." If both Willie and Wilma stretched out four fingers or any matching number, the watcher cries, "They match!" and scores 25 points for his pair of players. The pair that scores 100 first wins. (Note: Players may decide upon any number of points for match and game they wish before the start of play.)

JAN-KEM-PO   The Japanese play a finger changing game which involves not only chance and skill but also quick thinking. Hand, fingers, and fist are used. It can be played by any size group of various ages, with one player called the changer.

In this game, the hand represents a piece of paper when all the fingers and the thumb are stretched out. The fist represents a stone. With index and middle fingers extended and the others held by the thumb in the palm, the hand represents a pair of scissors.

The changer is chosen by lot, or any player may volunteer for the part. He stands in front of the group, doubles his right fist, and moves it three times slowly from the elbow as though pushing against something, and says each time, *"Jan-kem-po."* On the third *"Jan-kem-po,"* he quickly spreads his hand wide for paper or holds his fist still for a stone, or shows index and middle finger thrust out for scissors.

The others must counter quickly whatever he does: if he comes up with paper, they must display scissors in order to cut the paper; if he shows scissors, they must show fists, for stones break scissors. If the changer comes up with a fist, they must show two fists for two stones can crack one stone.

The player in the group who overcomes the changer twice is the winner and becomes the changer. Since it is often hard in a large group for the changer to observe who comes up first with the correct counterplay, players can take turns as observer, calling out the name of the one with the correct counterplay.

FIVE FINGERS   The Chinese play a game like the Japanese Jan-Kem-Po. It is for two or for one player who is the leader and a group. Each finger and the thumb represent something, beginning with the thumb which is the sun; index, clouds; middle, wind; ring, smoke; little, eyes. The leader or finger changer must be countered in these ways:

Sun is hidden by clouds; clouds are dispersed by wind; wind chases smoke; smoke gets in eyes and causes tears, and one rubs the eyes and can't use sun, clouds, wind, smoke, or eyes. (Fingers must rub the eyes.)

In another version, the thumb is not used. Change fingers into metal, water, wood, fire, and earth, which is palms pressed together. The finger changer calls out as he puts up each finger what the finger represents. Play and counterplay go like this:

Metal splits wood; water extinguishes fire; fire burns earth (and goes out). Metal is countered by the fingers representing wood and fire (two fingers can go up in this game), since wood, or charcoal, fires were used in ancient times to melt metal.

A variation using finger puppets (make them of fingers from old gloves, yarn to form heads, and rice grain) is this five-finger game of finger changer and players who counter his changes thus:

Grain is eaten by Pig.
Pig is eaten by Tiger.
Elephant subdues Tiger.
Monkey rides Elephant.
Elephant with his trunk takes Monkey off his back.

Substitute Mouse for Monkey if desired, for Mouse frightens Elephant. With the two toppers on the end, the victor is the quick player who can at once come up with the second counterplay.

More than one response is not correct in Five Fingers; the conventional powers of the different fingers must be firmly established at the beginning of the game. If players wish to make up their own conventions, giving their own powers to the different fingers, that is fine. Children should be encouraged to change, rearrange, and create in their games.

Roman and Spanish Games Brought to The New World

MUCH OF THE early diffusion of games, particularly of ball games, was the work of the Roman armies whose soldiers played them in camps and took them everywhere they went as conquerors, police, or pacification forces—north to Gaul and Britain, west to Spain, south to Africa, and east to Asia.

Romans had five different types of balls, from stone to grass and feather, and far many more ways of playing games with them. When the Roman legions brought their games into Spain in the second century B.C., the Spanish acquired them, and Spaniards, in turn, brought them to the New World.

There, children of Aztec *caciques* and Indian nobles learned them from Spanish teachers in the schools established not long after the Conquest. The games became a part of the life of children in New as well as Old Spain.

One of the earliest educators taught Latin through games. He was Francisco Cervantes de Salazar, a graduate of the University of Salamanca, who had come to Mexico to seek his fortune. He wrote a textbook for the study of Latin, containing descriptions of four old Roman games, popular with children in Spain. Salazar taught them, of course, under their Latin names: *Pilae Palmariae Ludus* (Palm or Hand Ball), *Ludus Spherae per Anulum Ferreum* (Ball Through Iron Hoop),

Obeliscorum seu Lignearum Pyramidularum (Obelisks or Wooden Pyramids—a kind of Bowls), *Saltus* (Hop Leap or Hop, Step, and Jump).

SALAZAR'S PALM BALL   The game, also known as Salazar's Hand Ball, is for two or four players. The rectangular playing area may be marked off indoors or outdoors. Vary it in overall size to keep it within the striking abilities of the players. Divide the area across the middle with a rope, drawn taut.

A tennis ball is the proper substitute for the Latin stuffed-leather ball. Players should wear thick gloves and tennis or other kind of ground-gripping play shoes.

"*Ludileges variari volant,*" Latin teacher de Salazar told his pupils, meaning "vary rules as players wish." The game is usually played according to the following rules:

Points are 15, 30, and 45. The game is won either by a player or team being ahead in games and tying the score, or by obtaining high score and game.

The game is started by a player standing just back of the boundary line on his or his team's side of the area and striking the ball with the palm of his hand, over the rope into the bounds of the other side. The striker must cry out, *Excipe!*" as he hits the ball to warn the receiver. If he doesn't, he scores nothing even though the ball falls inside the opponent's boundary line.

A ball touching or going under the rope or beyond the boundary line is a fault and 15 points are added to the opponent's score. This rule does not apply to the serve, however. If the ball touches the center rope on the serve, the serve does not pass to the other side unless that rule is made at the game's start. The server simply continues until a fair ball is served.

The ball should be hit back while on the fly, but can be returned after one bounce. Whether returned on the fly or on the bounce, the ball may be caught and thrown back on the fly or from one bounce.

PELOTE   This is a villagers' hand ball game from the land of the Basques on the border between France and Spain, where, in the misty Pyrénées, caring for sheep is the way of life for most. From time to time a few of the famous Basque sheep herders left their mountains to go to the United States as herders in the high Sierras of Nevada. In their adopted land, the children of their descendants play Pelote, Pelotte, Pilota, and Hand Ball—it's all one to them. They often increase the number of players to a dozen or more. The striker gets only one chance to serve the ball across the rope. If he fails, the ball goes to the opposite side. With these exceptions, the game is played the same way as Salazar's Palm or Hand Ball. (Note: The game of Pilota is thought to be the origin of the sport of Jai Alai.)

SALAZAR'S BALL THROUGH IRON HOOP This game suggests an early form of croquet and has an element of golf. It is played on a large level place or playing green by two or more players. A large group may divide into teams.

An iron hoop is placed in the center of the green and boundary lines drawn at both ends. The hoop has a front and back indicated on it in some way.

Each player has a medium-size ball—a croquet or similar wooden ball is satisfactory—and a mallet or any strong stick with a solid head for striking.

Objective is getting the ball through the hoop in the fewest number of strokes. Game may be set at so many "hoops," such as nine, and the winner or winning team is the first to drive the ball through the hoop that number of times without touching the sides and in the fewest strokes.

If the ball is struck or rolls through the back of the hoop, it is an error and adds two strokes to the player's score. An extra stroke is also added to his score if his ball is struck or rolls out of bounds.

Two to eight will find one hoop adequate for a fast enough game, but more than eight should have two or more hoops placed at various spots—not lined up—about the area. Playing then is ordered as in golf matches: the first pair or foursome plays, then the second, and so on. Some kind of recognition can be given for "a hoop in one."

When more hoops are used a different "par for the course" has to be set.

Salazar's Ball Through Iron Hoop can be fun for a group of four to ten, playing indoors on a carpet that is rolled up and put away after the game. Use old golf balls, improvised sticks, and small wooden blocks piled up to form arches; several are better than one. Gentle, careful putting is needed in playing.

SALAZAR'S OBELISKS This game is also known as Salazar's Wooden Pyramids. Although usually played outdoors by children of Spain and Mexico, it can be played either indoors or out. Needed are seven or nine pins or small wooden pyramids and a large indoor baseball or, for young children, a small bag filled with sand.

Two or more may play. If three play, the players take turns acting as referee.

Set up the pins about a foot apart in two rows, 8 or 10 inches apart. In front of the pins about 3 feet, draw a line, and place the odd or queen pin (call it king pin, if you like) either in the middle, or on the left or right end of it. The starting line is drawn 12 or 15 feet in front of the pins, and another line 6 or 7 feet in back of them.

Each player in turn bowls the ball (throws or tosses the sandbag) from the starting line at the pins. Each pin knocked down counts 1 point; the queen pin counts 4 points. If a player bowls and fails to pass the queen's line or bowls beyond the back line, he is penalized 1 point, which goes to his opponent. The game is 20 points.

Each player quickly sets up the pins he has knocked down.

When as many as ten or more children play, they may divide into teams with, for each team, a pin boy who resets the pins as soon as they are knocked down and a ball boy who quickly calls out the number of pins knocked down, retrieves the ball, and throws it back to a teammate at the starting line. A referee to rule on plays and a scorekeeper are also required.

MAZATE This is the Guatemalan variation of Salazar's Obelisks or Wooden Pyramids. It may be played indoors or out, with few or many players. Softballs and a wooden bowling pin (sometimes called a jack) or big wooden peg for the target are all that's required. Of course, children may like to make their own bowls (balls) of sun- or oven-baked clay and decorate them with Maya-Quiche designs as the Indian boys and girls of Guatemala used to do.

Each player tries to get his ball closest to the pin or touch it without knocking it over. The ball is rolled, but a player may stoop, kneel, or bend over in delivering it from the starting line. Distance from the starting line to the target depends upon the age and ability of the group. The player wins whose ball rests closest to the pin when all have bowled.

Players may or may not be permitted to knock another's bowl out of the way in aiming to get close to the pin. Make the rule at the start of the game.

If a large group is playing, one may find it best to use one ball and have the players write their names on pieces of masking tape (if the game is indoors) or on small cardboard disks (if outdoors). Each player then marks the place where his ball came to rest, as a golfer does on the putting green, and hands the ball to the next player.

SALAZAR'S HOP LEAP   Also known as Salazar's Hop, Step, and Jump, the game is usually played outdoors by two or more boys and girls. An object some distance away—tree, post, fence, anything at hand—is selected as goal. In turn all jump with both feet or hop on one foot, or proceed by hop, step, and jump from a starting line to the goal. The winner is the player who reaches it in the fewest number of hops, leaps, or jumps.

In variations, players hop sideways or backwards, or hop to see who can hop nearest to the goal or reach it while holding the breath.

In returning to the starting line, the game may be varied. Each player tosses a stone or stick in the air and must try to pick it up from where it falls each time in one hop or as few as possible as he proceeds back to the starting line. The winner is the one who takes the fewest tosses and hops or jumps to get there.

HALF-HAMMER   English boys adapted the game of Hop, Step, and Jump from the pentathlon of the Olympic Games. The high jump, broad jump, vaulting, and javelin and hammer throws were all part of the Olympics in ancient Greece as well as of the Games today; at the same time, they are basic elements in countless children's games around the world. Boys were admitted to the Greek Games, but only allowed in such events as running, jumping, and the hop, step, and jump.

To play, two or more in turn hop on one leg, then take a long step, then jump with both feet. The winner is the boy or girl whose distance is greatest. (In Sparta in old times, women and girls participated in athletic contests.)

KANGAROO-HOPPING   There is a modern astronaut version of Salazar's Hop Leap. American astronauts strap on a harness attached to a 19-foot piston, nicknamed "pogo," which extends from the ceiling of a big room. They crouch, then leap forward on both feet in imitation of a kangaroo. They soar up about 12 feet and land 12 or so feet away. Scientists developed kangaroo-hopping as a good way to get around the surface of the moon, where the pull of gravity is one-sixth that on earth.

Omitting the giant pogo, two or more can compete in kangaroo-hopping races and imagine themselves on the moon.

HOP BALL   This a combination of Salazar's Palm Ball and Salazar's Hop Leap enjoyed by most children under ten years old in large groups, indoors or out. Players gather in a circle. One player begins the count.

"One," he says and steps outside the circle. The next player says "Two" and steps outside. The third player says "Three" and remains in the circle. The count goes on around, with every third player staying put and the rest going outside the circle.

A "squashy" basketball or similar ball is tossed by Outside players at the feet of the Insiders, who are scattered about within the circle made by the Outside ball-tossers. Insiders try to avoid being hit by hopping or jumping over the ball. As soon as a player is hit, he changes places with an Outsider. Insiders must not be hit above the knee.

The game may be played with three teams of six or more players on each team. Team One, known as the Hoppers, occupies the area between the throwing lines of Team Two and Team Three. Members of Teams Two and Three throw a large soft ball back and forth, attempting to get all members of Team One out of the game by hitting them below the knee as quickly as possible. Each team takes its turn being Hoppers.

The team that remains longest in the center is the winner. Players take turns being timekeeper.

LA HERRADURA   A tragedy which took place during a game of La Herradura, or Horseshoe Quoits, almost three hundred years ago changed history and became one of the great legends of Peru. The story goes this way:

After his defeat by the Spanish conquistadores, the Inca Manco Capac II fled with his family, including his three small sons—one of them six-year-old Titu Cusi—and some followers. The Inca took refuge in the Vilcabamba, among the highest peaks of the eastern Andes. There he built cities and established a secret fortified capital of an empire among the clouds, the highest ever known.

Over the years, one by one, a few Spaniards found their way to the Inca in his mountain realm and pledged him allegiance. Finally, there were seven of them in the Vilcabamba. They instructed the Indians in the use of firearms and in horsemanship, and taught the Inca Manco, his sons, and the nobles how to play bowls and horseshoe quoits.

"Then one day," wrote twelve-year-old Titu Cusi, "we were playing at horseshoe quoits—just the Spaniards, my father and me—and, as my father was raising the quoit to throw it, they all rushed upon him with knives, daggers, and some with swords. He fell to the ground covered with wounds. They turned furiously upon me, and hurled a lance which only just failed to kill me also. I fled into some bushes and down the rocks. They looked for me, but could not find me. However, the Spaniards went out of the gate in high spirits."

Twenty years later, it was seen that the seven did not get far away. An envoy sent on a peace mission to Titu Cusi, now the Inca, saw the skulls of the seven Spaniards exposed on the city walls beside the gate.

Today, visitors can take guided tours to Sacsahuaman, above Cuzco, Peru, in the Andes. There somewhere is the lost Vilcabamba, the fabulous secret city where the fatal game of horseshoe quoits took place.

The game of Horseshoe Quoits or Horseshoe Pitching is enjoyed by all ages and can be played almost anywhere. Equipment needed is four horseshoes (any kind of iron or heavy rubber rings may be substituted), and two pegs, standing 6 inches above the ground. The pegs may be set 20 to 40 feet apart, according to the pitching ability of the players.

Games may go on for a designated period of time and the player or the team scoring the most points may be declared the winner; or a goal of so many points, say, 50, may be set.

"Ringers" usually count 5 points; "leaners", 3; and the quoit closest to the stake, 1, but any number of points may be assigned as players wish.

American Ball Games
That Went Around the Globe

FIRST TO GO from the New World to the Old were rubber-ball games. Rubber was perhaps the only thing known in common by all the many groups, tribes, and nations of South America, Central America, and the most southern part of North America.

Plants containing some rubber are found almost all over the earth, but to the Indians of the Amazon Basin goes the credit of discovering the weeping wood of Brazil, the *Hevea brasiliensis,* or rubber tree. They could scarcely not have found it, for its fruit, a pod about the size of a bird's egg, gets drier and drier until one day the capsules explode with the rattle of gunfire and seeds are shot sometimes as far as a hundred feet.

Indians of the region were the inventors of the first rubber process. They gathered the creamy latex, falling like tears to the foot of the tree, coagulated it into *caoutchouc* (raw rubber) in the smoke from a fire of ouricury nuts (large, oily nuts from the Brazilian feather palm), and molded it into moccasins, bottles, and syringes with which they squirted latex on feather cloaks for waterproofing and on themselves for protection against insects. And they made all kinds of solid and molded balls for games.

BAMBOULA This may have been the game seen by Christopher

Columbus on his second voyage to the New World which included Puerto Rico, Hispaniola (modern Haiti and the Dominican Republic), Jamaica, and Cuba. This game was played all over the Caribbean.

Upon his return to Spain in 1496, Columbus told King Ferdinand and Queen Isabella that he saw native peoples playing a game with a "ball made of the gum of a tree which though heavy would fly and bound better than those of leather filled with wind in Spain."

Bamboula is a noisy, romping kind of game, played on a field that permits much running by opposing teams of from five to twelve or more on each side. In the center is a pole, the *bamboula*. Goals of 5-foot-high boards are placed at the ends of the field. In Bolivia, narrow sheets of tin often serve for goals and make an exciting sound like peals of thunder when the ball strikes them.

A rubber ball somewhat smaller than a tennis ball is used. Each player has two rackets, one for scooping up the ball from the ground and another for throwing it. Either table tennis paddles with lengthened handles or badminton rackets are suitable.

The ball is tossed up at the center pole to start the game. One point is scored whenever a team succeeds in hitting the goal at its end of the field with the ball. There won't be much scoring, but excess energy will be worked off in a short time. At the start of the game set the points necessary to win.

TLACHTLI   This game, pronounced tel-lach-lee, was described by a Spanish conquistador about twenty years after Columbus had told the King and Queen of Spain about the Caribbean game of the flying, bounding ball of tree gum. The conquistador had seen Indians in Mexico playing in a 30-foot wide and almost 200-foot long, narrow court, with a big, bounding ball. High up on two sides of the high, decorated walls were "stones with holes in them as big as the ball," he said.

Players wore carved stone "U"-shaped (like horse collars) or closed belts, low on their hips, turning and twisting so that the ball would strike one of the knobs on the stone belt and fly with tremendous speed across the court and through a stone ring, if they were skillful or lucky enough. The player who could strike the ball through the ring won the game. Often two opposing teams also played the game.

When played by the Olmecs, Mayas, and Aztecs as a ceremonial game honoring their gods, the loss of the game cost the losing team's captain his head, literally. When played for amusement, the losers always flew away as fast as they could after the game, for the winners, if they could catch them, had the right to claim their feather cloaks and all other valuables.

BUMP BALL   This is Tlachtli for today's boys and girls in large or small groups playing on the beach or playground, or in a gym.

A large lightweight rubber ball is needed. Mark out a space about the size of a basketball court, and draw three parallel lines across the court, separating it into four fairly equal parts.

Players are divided into two teams and the teams divided into an equal number of centers, middies, and ends. Players on each team take places near their respective lines—center, middle, end. To start, the ball as in basketball is put in play by tossing it up between the centers. Centers must try to bump the ball with hips, backs, shoulders, or let it bounce and then bump it to a teammate. The ball must not be kicked, thrown, or batted.

Each time a middie bumps or bounces the ball to an end teammate, he scores 3 points for his side. The end who bumps or bounces it over his end line scores 2 points. Winner is the first to score 25 points.

TLATLICO   This kind of Tlachtli was played by the Olmecs in the vicinity of Vera Cruz, Mexico. The word "Tlachtli" was Aztecan. The Aztecs used the same name for several varieties of rubber-ball games.

Hernando Cortez, conqueror of Mexico, was back in Spain early in the sixteenth century with a group of Indians from Mexico and Central America. A German artist, Christoph Weiditz, happened to be visiting at the royal Spanish court, and he made tinted pencil drawings of the gymnastics and games, among them a version of Tlachtli, demonstrated by the Americans.

"The Indians play with a blown-up ball, hitting it with legs and hands. . . . they wear hard leather over the thighs and lower back and hips so that they receive the impact of the ball, also leather gloves," the artist wrote on one of his drawings.

The ball was large and was kept in the air as long as possible by two contending individuals or teams. The ball could be returned only with hips, buttocks, knees, hands, and heads. (Players in other forms of the game wore wooden belts shaped like horse collars or yokes, helmets, and knee pads. The right hand was bound with rope, forming a sort of gauntlet for hitting the ball.)

The Indians amazed the Europeans with their physical feats. Their fascinating rubber ball was not solid but hollow and was made over a mold of clay or wood which was later removed.

The variety of Tlachtli they demonstrated was a kind of informal soccer. In this version, players advance the ball toward their team's goal line at the end of the field by bunting with knees and legs, thrusting with hips and backs, butting with heads, and batting with gloved right hands.

At the start of the game, a player must bat the ball with the palm or bump it by twisting his hip when the ball is tossed up among the players. Despite shoving and pushing, he must get the ball going toward his team's goal. The game is exhausting and raises clouds of dust on playing fields and showers of sand on the beach. It does afford a wonderful scramble for a short period, with definite rules about no tripping, no strong-arming, and no kicking the ball. Points may be set for a game, if desired.

HULAMA   This form of Hip Ball is a variation of Aztec Tlachtli played by Tarascan Indians around Mazatlán, Mexico. A player wears a wide, thick, rounded belt at the waist and a heavy leather band around the hips and bounces a 12-pound rubber ball off his hip. In this variation *only* the hip may be used to strike the ball; otherwise the game is played like Tlatlico, described above. Use any lightweight ball of soccer size, for, obviously, only skilled young men, such as the modern student archeologists who tested it, are able to hip-bounce a 12-pounder.

BOIRI   The people of the Gilbert Islands, which lie north and south of the Equator in the Pacific, play this kind of informal soccer. To the north are the Marshall Islands and to the northwest, the Marianas—all of them in seas teeming with fish and all of them reflecting the passage of foreign peoples, sometimes the settlement for brief or long periods, from the west and from the east.

For playing Boiri, native boys use a round, resilient ball, slightly larger than a softball, woven of coconut leaves (a soft rubber ball may be substituted). They attempt to keep it in the air by kicking and bouncing it on head or shoulders. Players are not allowed to use the hands at all. If the ball gets lost, the player who spots it doesn't point to it with his finger; he turns his head and points with his nose.

Games Carried
Throughout the World
By Colonists and Settlers

BECAUSE SO MANY games have been transported around the world by settlers, most people can travel to strange shores and far-away places and find children playing the same games that they see back home.

STOOLBALL English settlers brought this game to North America. From Fort Hill lookout on November 20, 1621, Pilgrims of Plymouth, Massachusetts, watched the English ship *Fortune* enter the harbor. She came with thirty-five new colonists. The newcomers were not steady, level-headed Pilgrims, but boisterous, happy-go-lucky strangers who had "nor pot nor pan to cook any meat in."

The reason for this was that the *Fortune* had a "long tarry" in old Plymouth while awaiting clearance. The emigrants, waiting around for the ship to sail, had sold all their belongings and most arrived in the New World with nothing but the clothes they had on. But they were hard workers, and the Pilgrims had no complaints on that score.

Then "on the day called Christmas-day" this happened, according to the first history of Plymouth Colony: Governor William Bradford "called them out to work as usual, but the most of this new company said it went against their consciences to work on that day." The Governor excused them and went off with the others to work.

When he and the men came home at noon, they "found them—the

Strangers—in the street at play openly, some pitching the bar, and some at Stoolball, and such like sports." So Bradford went over to them and "took away their implements, and told them it was against his conscience that they should play and others work. If they made the keeping of the day a matter of devotion, let them keep to their houses, but there should be no revelling in the streets."

During free time on week days, however, ball games went on "without let or hindrance."

England's national game of Cricket is said to be derived from Stoolball, which was played at first mostly by milkmaids when they returned from milking the cows. The milking stool on which they sat and those used in the house by the hearth were called "crickets."

Stoolball is a game for outdoors, but it can be enjoyed just as well by small children in a large indoor area. Few or many may play, either individually or divided into two teams. A soft ball and a stool or large carton are the equipment. Instead of using the hand to bat the ball, a short, stout stick may be substituted.

The game consists simply in setting a stool upon the ground or floor and choosing a defender who takes his position beside it. The other players, called "bowlers," take turns toeing a line 10 or more feet away, and pitching the ball at the stool, trying to hit it. The defender bats it back if he can. Anyone who succeeds in hitting the stool becomes the defender, or batman. Any player, including the bowler, who catches the ball when it is batted back, also becomes the defender.

The winner of the game is the player or the team that hits the ball the most times before it touches the stool.

To vary the game, add another stool ("wicket") and have defenders run from one to the other. Add fielders to field the ball, and give the bowlers more "overs," or "balls," that is, chances to try to hit the first stool or carton, or whatever is being used for a "wicket." Only the first stool is pitched to or bowled to by the pitcher. The other stool is a base to which a defender runs when he bats the ball back to the pitcher, and he must wait for a good ball batted back to the pitcher by another player at the first stool on which to run back. A defender can, of course, be tagged with the ball by the pitcher or fielders while running.

PASS AND CATCH   Groups of small children enjoy this game either indoors or outdoors. Young Princess Elizabeth I of England and her ladies-in-waiting played it in palace gardens, while other children were playing it in country lanes and pastures. The English colonists brought Pass and Catch over to New England and children of the Puritans played it on Boston Common.

To play, make two lines about 6-10 feet apart—one for a pitchers' line, the other for a catchers'. (Distance between lines is determined by age and ability of players.) Players are divided into two or more teams, each team with a pitcher, who takes his place behind the pitching line, with a softball. At the signal, "Ready! Go!" the pitcher of each team throws to his team's first catcher, standing in line behind the catching line. Pitchers throw so that their catchers will be sure to get the ball. Upon receiving the ball, the catcher runs quickly to the pitching line and the pitcher to the end of his team's line, and the ball is thrown quickly by the new pitcher to the next player in his team's catching line. This goes on until all have pitched and caught. The team to finish first wins.

CIRCLE BALL   This is a catch-and-throw activity for the younger ones and is a little more complicated than Pass and Catch. Older players will enjoy it, too, by complicating it further with a number of points for games and rules for errors, making a more formal game.

Players divide into groups of four or more each, depending upon how large the whole group of children is. They stand in circles which are six or so feet apart. Each circle has a soft ball, of the right size for small hands to grasp easily. Each circle takes a name of a city, river, country, or whatever. Or it may take a number.

To start the game, the player with the ball in each circle throws to the player opposite him in the next circle, in the order that has been previously agreed upon. The player receiving the ball throws it on to the player opposite him in the next circle, calling out, as he throws, the name or number of the circle.

Everyone should have a chance to throw and catch before the game is declared over. Circles of children may play as pairs, if they wish, rather than from circle to circle all around. If desired, a player may be appointed to give the signal to throw each time.

FOX IS THE WARNER   This tag game was played in the Old Dominion by the children, grandchildren and great-grandchildren of the Negroes brought to Virginia in August of 1619 by a Dutch ship whose captain had hijacked a Spanish trader carrying them from the western horn of Africa to the West Indies. References to the game by chroniclers usually remark that it was enjoyed by small children in the kitchen yard or near the fields where the adults of the families were working.

The player chosen to be the Fox stands in his den or hole which is marked out for him. When he is ready to come out he cries a warning:

This is the morning,
The fox gives warning.
I'm coming out!
So watch out!

With that the Fox hops out of his hole, rolled-up paper, handkerchief, or small, leafy branch in hand, ready to hit the others who gather around the hole to try to prevent his getting out. If the Fox can hit a player without putting a foot outside his hole and without ceasing to hop on one leg, that player must be caught by the others before he can run away. He must be chased into the den to be the new Fox.

The game was shunted around a great deal, for the same game is played as Fox in the Hole (or Den, His Earth, etc.) in Greece and Italy, where instead of rolled-up paper or handkerchief, the Fox has a soft leather ball tied to a string. The same game, as Tod (Fox) in the Hole, is played in Scotland.

NINEPINS   This game, also known as Kegelspiel, was one form of Bowls brought by the people of the Netherlands to Nieuw Amsterdam (renamed New York by later English settlers) and to the Mohawk River Valley of North America.

By the middle of the seventeenth century, the little Dutch town at the mouth of the Hudson River had grown so big, a town planning committee was necessary. The committee at once set up certain ordinances. Among them was one which prohibited erecting hen coops, tethering goats, throwing rubbish, or playing games (such as Kolven, a kind of golf, and Bowls) in the streets.

For instance, Ninepins could only be played on the Bowling Green at the end of the street where "on the left you espy the town pump facing the north wall of the fort." And Bowling Green it remains in the modern city of New York, although no one has bowled there in over two hundred and fifty years.

Nonetheless, the sounds of bowls striking pins can still be heard all up and down the Hudson River. The long, rolling peals like distant thunder are often mistaken for a summer storm in the Catskill Mountains.

Actually, as New York author Washington Irving related in his story of the good-natured Hollander Rip Van Winkle in *The Sketch Book,* the thunderous rumbling and crashing are caused by Hendrick Hudson, discoverer of the river, and his crew of the *Half-Moon.* They are playing at Ninepins in a hollow of a mountain in the Catskills, and people hear the bowl hitting the pins and the pins tumbling about. In this way Hendrick Hudson can pass the time happily while keeping a guardian eye upon his river and the once Dutch city.

To play the game of Ninepins, two wooden balls and nine pins and a level surface indoors or out are needed. Two or more of almost any age may play.

Pins are set up in two circles, one inside the other. Players line up behind a line 25 or more feet away. First player bowls, attempting to knock over as many pins as possible, each pin counting for 1 point.

He rushes forward after play, picks up the ball, replaces the pins, returns to the line, gives the ball to the third player while the second player is bowling, then goes to the end of the line.

Second player does the same, and so on, until everyone has had a good workout. This is a fast game and good fun for a short time.

Highest score in the time allowed for the game is the winning score. All players take the same number of turns at play.

TENPINS   This was a form of Balspel, or Bowls, enjoyed by children in Holland and brought to Nieuw Amsterdam. The pins were small and stumpy, with a bulge in the middle. Because they resembled hand-dipped candles in shape, they were sometimes called "candlepins." There are ten of them and they are lined up close together against a wall.

Players stand in a line at a distance from the pins and take turns throwing a hard ball underhanded at the pins. Each pin knocked over counts 1 point, and the first player to make 20 points wins the game.

A pin boy is chosen by lot or counting-out rhyme (see Part IX) for the first game. Thereafter, the player with the fewest points becomes pin boy for the next game.

The same game was played by Belgian children, who often used small pins resembling little wooden dolls, having a short cylinder for a body and a round knob for a head. It is one of the many games played by children of the Low Countries (the Netherlands) depicted in the world-famous painting *Les Jeux d'enfants* ("Children's Games") by the great Flemish painter, Pieter Breughel the Elder. Most of the games can be seen in most parts of the world, for the people of the Netherlands took them along everywhere they went, and there were few places in the world they did not go to at one time or another. The sixteenth-century French author François Rabelais in his book *Gargantua and Pantagruel* describes Gargantua playing many of them.

KINDER KAATSEN   This was a kind of Children's Tennis popular in Dutch villages. When families of Holland emigrated to Java, Sumatra, the Timor Laut archipelago, Moluccas, and other islands in the Indian

Ocean and the China Sea, they played this game as well as various kinds of Balspel (*met den bal spelen,* or games with bowls or balls) in their new homes. Soon both native and immigrant children were playing them.

Kinder Kaatsen may be played by two or more. Either the hand or a stick-bat may be used to hit with. Draw a line down the middle of a playing area, inside in a room or outdoors. Players divide into opposing teams and scatter about their side of the area.

A chosen player tosses up the ball (any kind of hollow rubber ball) and bats it across the line. Player on opposite side hits it back on the fly or on the first bounce. Players must be cautioned to stay within a small space which they have selected and try to hit the ball back across the line only when it comes nearer to them than to their teammates. No one can hit the ball when there is interference. There are no "outs," "errors," or "fouls" in the game; it's just for fun and recreation.

WINDSPEL   The people of the Frisian Islands and along the German North Sea coast, in Denmark, and all around the Kattegat, played this game before it was taken by Dutch settlers to North America and to the South Seas. Two or more can play.

In one version, a stone is placed on the end of a piece of wood and the other end struck with the foot or a stick, making the stone fly up in the air. The player who can make a stone fall farthest away is the winner.

In another version of Windspel, a piece of wood, a ball, a stick, and a brick are needed. The wood is balanced on the brick (a flat stone will do as well) and the ball placed on one end of the piece of wood. With the stick, the player strikes as hard as possible the other end of the wood.

The ball flies up and the player shouts, "Windspel, Nicholas" or whatever the name of the player is who is to catch the ball on the fly or the first bounce. If that player fails, the stick-hitter tries again, calling out the name of another player, and so on until someone catches the ball and becomes the hitter.

MALIEN KOLF   Malien Kolf and Kolven traveled with Dutch families to Nieuw Netherlands in North America, where they were played daily in the streets of Nieuw Amsterdam until street play was prohibited. In Java and Sumatra, however, Dutch and native children played them anywhere.

Two or more play. If more than four play, divide into teams. Almost any age enjoys these games.

Both Malien Kolf and Kolven require a fairly large area outdoors on which to play. Each player needs a long stick with a solid wooden head and a leather grip (wind with cord or tape for the same effect) for a *malien-kolf* (a golf club or stick), and a small wooden or hard rubber ball. (A discarded modern golf club which a child finds easy to use is suitable for a *malien-kolf*.)

To play Malien Kolf set up two 16-inch poles opposite each other, about a foot or so apart, near the end of the playing area. Six to 8 inches beyond and in line with the poles, place a metal hoop.

The ball is hit from a starting line 20-30 feet away (distance depends on age and ability of group). The ball must hit both poles in going between them and go through the hoop, to score. After each hit, players must play their balls from wherever they lie, going toward the poles and hoop. Winner is the player or team getting the ball through in the fewest hits.

KOLVEN   To play Kolven, base lines are drawn at both ends of the playing area. It is most fun with two teams of four each. Each team tries to drive the ball with a golf club or stick to or across the opponent's base line. First to do so ten times wins the game.

When Japanese children played the game, they called it Mari Uchi.

PALE-MAILLE   This game was brought to England by seventeenth-century French Protestant refugees—Huguenots—many of them silk weavers who settled in Spitalfields in the east of London between Bishopsgate and Bethnal Green. It was one of the most popular of French children's games and it soon became equally popular with the English, who called it Pail-Mail at first, then settled for Pall-Mall, because that was what the mallet used—a sort of hand or palm maul or mell—was called.

The name Pall-Mall, pronounced pell-mell, was also given to a different game (see Jeu de Paume below).

Pale-Maille is played with a ball, mallet, and an iron ring or hoop that is affixed to a swivel base, through which two or more players drive the ball.

One side is marked, "Entrez!" and the other "Sortez!" There is a penalty for the player whose ball rolls or who knocks his ball through the exit side.

The game is a simple form of Croquet, which was also introduced by the Huguenot refugees, and was called Crooky by English children.

PALE-MAILLE-GRELOT   This was a modification of Pale-Maille by the people in Vietnam, Laos, and Thailand (formerly Siam), especially in the vicinity of Bangkok. French families carried the game with them when they settled in the Southeast Asia peninsula.

The game is played like Pale-Maille, with this difference: the ring or hoop has a tiny bell suspended by a string from the top of the hoop and it signals the errors with its ringing. The objective is the knocking of the ball through the hoop without hitting the bell. The lower the little bell hangs, the harder it is to get the ball through without at least a tinkle.

JEU DE PAUME   The French palm ball game and simple forerunner of Tennis (popular with French and English kings and queens), began its travels so early with the people of France to England, North America, and Asia, there's no record of them. The game not only went everywhere with them, but it also remained there from generation to generation.

As a matter of fact, Palm Ball was shunted back and forth between Europe and the British Isles. As Palla (from Germanic and Middle English related words "bal" and "ball"), the game came into Italy from the Germanic Longobards. As part of the game Pallamaglio (Hand Ball) it found its way back to Germanic countries and on to England as Pall Mall (in this case the words meant "ball alley").

Whether one calls the game Jeu de Paume, Palla, Pallamaglio, Palm Ball, Hand Ball, or Pall Mall (say "pell-mell"), it can be played almost anywhere by two or more or by teams of boys and girls who have a ball and a clear expanse of wall or a sloping roof.

The best kind of roof is one that slopes down to about 8 feet from the ground. Both roof and wall should have plenty of clear space in front of them.

Each player takes his turn serving the ball from any place and at any speed at the sloping roof or wall. The ball must roll or bounce within the boundary lines previously set in order to count a point. Service passes to the next player if the ball falls or bounces outside the lines. The serve passes to a player's opponent when the latter catches a ball that is properly within boundary lines. In order to score, the receiver must catch the ball before it touches the ground or on the first bounce if the children are small fry. Game is usually 5 points.

For the adaptation made by city children see Stoop Ball in Part IX under Typical Street Games.

CALL BALL   In this English version of the French Jeu de Paume, players stand some distance away from a blank wall. The first player, as he throws the ball against the wall, calls out the name of another player who tries to catch the ball on the rebound. If he succeeds, he throws the next time. If he fails, the first player throws again and calls out another name.

JINKER BALL   This was what the Scots made of Call Ball. Someone tosses the ball against the wall. Whoever catches it on the rebound becomes the Jinker. All the rest immediately run and hide. The Jinker tries to touch one of the players before he succeeds in hiding. Whoever is touched starts the game again by tossing the ball.

LA LONGUE PAUME   A slight variation on Jeu de Paume, this game is played against a wall or sloping roof, but the ball is bounced on a *tamis,* or bricklayer's sand sieve, and then struck with the hand. English and American children usually bounced the ball off anything handy or on the ground before hitting it.

Usually two teams of five each play.

Part II

THE SUN, MOON, AND STARS, AND THE SEASONS IN GAMES

Games Suitable for the Hours From Sunup to Sundown

"LOVE THE DAY and the night. Be glad of the dark and the light," sang Euripides, the Greek. Poets sing in many languages of the daily cycle, and there are countless poems about work that follows the sun from dawn to dawn.

Games have always been linked to the daily round, often with their own songs and dances. The following are games especially for daytime hours.

GAZELLE STALKING   The Bushmen of Africa live mainly now in the Kalahari Desert, although they once roamed most parts of Africa south of the Zambezi River. They were the first people to speak the famous click languages, so called from the clicking sound made by the tongue against the palate and roof of the mouth. The four clicks are sounds of consonants found only in their languages and those of the Zulu and the Bantu who adopted them.

Before dawn, the Bushman sets out to hunt the springbok, a South African gazelle. His clicking song appeals to the sun: "Come out, sun, come out. Sun, rise that we can see to find the springbok."

Although only two players at a time take part, it is much fun for the Watchers too. Both Gazelle and Stalker are blindfolded. They are taken to opposite sides of a bush or, if indoors, a long or large round table. Watchers cry, "The sun's out!" and someone signals with a clicker or ratchet-rattle for the players to move round the object.

The Stalker must catch the Gazelle to end the game and select the next Gazelle. Both need to move as quietly as possible and Watchers to be very quiet. If, within a certain time limit, the Gazelle succeeds in escaping the Stalker, he is declared free and selects the next Stalker.

Called Deer Stalking, the game is played in England and Scotland. The American and Indian version, Buffalo Hunt, has a ring of children holding hands. Buffalo and Hunter drape jackets or coats over their heads instead of being blindfolded, and must go around within the circle, bent over in imitation of the plains buffalo being stalked by an Indian in a buffalo hide.

COCK-A-LOO   This game comes from Ethiopia (historical Abyssinia). Hundreds of years before the Christian era, Homeric poems in Greece attracted attention to the *Aethiopes,* the Ethiopians, in whose land, so the poets said, the sun set and the gods attended banquets in the evening. Ethiopia has never since failed to hold interest for peoples of other lands.

It drew explorers, searching for the source of one of the world's great rivers, the Blue Nile. And, among the northern highlands at Lake Tana, the source was found at last. The river's course runs past dwellings of the Amharas ("mountain people"), Coptic Christian monasteries carved out of stone, down the mountains past coffee (our word "coffee" comes from Kaffa province) plantations to the Galla farms, then to lowlanders' villages of round huts topped with conical roofs like straw hats. Along the river from highland to plateau to lowland, children can be found of a morning playing Cock-a-Loo, though they may have their own name for it in the local language.

The game is a kind of hide-and-seek. Cast lots for one to be the Mother and another to be It. Mother sits on a low stool or on the ground, feet straight out in front, and It, putting his hands over his eyes, hides his head in her lap. The other players run away and hide.

While they are hiding, It asks the Mother, "Cock-a-loo?" She answers, "No, it's not yet dawn." It keeps on asking, "Cock-a-loo?" as though he were crowing. The Mother keeps on telling him that it's not yet dawn or the sun isn't up yet until all the players are hidden.

Then she says, "Now the sun is up." And It goes to look for the hiders. As he finds them, they race back to the Mother. If they can touch her before It can, they may go hide again.

ANIMAL KEEPERS   This game comes from the Kikuyu (or Gikuyu) people of Kenya. According to a Kikuyu myth, the ancient fathers of the Kikuyu, the Masai, and the Kamba peoples were given their choice of a spear, a bow, or a digging stick. The father of the Masai chose the spear and was told to tend the herds on the plains. The father of the Kamba chose the bow and was sent to the forest to hunt. When the father of the Kikuyu chose the digging stick, he was taken to the top of Mount Kenya and shown the rich land below. In the middle of the land where fig trees grew in a great cluster, he was told to make his home, farming and raising sheep, goats, and cattle. And so he did.

There the Kikuyu lived in such harmony between work and play that they could scarcely tell the one from the other. They needed no numbers because they gave every single creature and thing a name. The Kikuyu believe that people must observe, name, and describe, not put numbers on beings and count them.

Girls and boys can name and describe the different birds, plants, animals, insects, and all the things around them. A boy learns to recognize each one of the family's herd of cows and flocks of sheep and goats by name and by its size and shape, special markings and color, or the way the horns grow. Fathers and sons make games of observation and remembering.

Every once in a while several farmers bring their herds together and mix them all up. A boy from each family then picks out the animals of his father's herd from all the animals. At midday, which is watering time, the herds are separated. Each boy inspects the cows, sheep, and goats (*gothorima*) and says whether or not all his herd is there. Usually one or more animals are missing that have been purposely hidden. If the boy observes this, he is asked to name and describe them. When the boys make mistakes, they aren't scolded. The whole thing is simply repeated, fathers and sons enjoying it a second time.

If small children want to pretend to be the various herds, flocks, and the observers, then an imitative game grows naturally out of the Kikuyu's special kind of observe-and-remember roundup. Animal Keepers, an adaptation of it, however, makes an excellent getting-acquainted activity.

Players are told that they are taking animals to a new zoo that is all ready for them, and each player is the keeper of one animal to see that it arrives safe. A self-sticking label with the name (or picture) of a wild animal is placed on the back of each player, without his knowing what it is.

Players then circulate, giving hits to one another to help each keeper learn the name of his animal. The hints should be accurate but misleading, for the idea is to keep the players guessing as they move about and get to know one another. A player gives only one hint before moving on to the next person. For instance, a player says, "Your animal has feet like stumps." The other may say, "Elephants have stumpy feet."

If he has guessed wrong and he's the keeper of a hippopotamus or rhinoceros, the other can say, "I didn't say it was an elephant. I only said it had feet like stumps."

As soon as a player has guessed the right animal, he removes the label from his back and puts it on his chest.

LOOK AND REMEMBER   This is an old American game that fits into the same class as that of the Kikuyu's, for a small space indoors. Cover a table with many different things: scissors, books, pencils, a small toy, a wooden figure, a dish with a carrot in it, a big button, etc. Children walk around three or four times, looking but touching nothing. Spread a cloth over the objects, give children pencil or crayon and paper, and ask them to write the names or draw as many things as they can remember seeing. Winner is the one with the most correct names or recognizable drawings, and may be awarded a prize from the objects on the table.

Different leaves and plants are more interesting for identification at camp or in the country than a collection of miscellaneous objects.

CLOWN TAG   This game was played by the Indian children of Mexico, Guatemala, and other lands along the South American west coastal flyway. There the chachalaca greets the sun in the morning and the moon at night. About the size of a bantam, and dark grayish brown, the chachalaca announces sunup and sundown by repeating, "Cha-cha-lac-á, cha-cha-lac-á, cha-cha-lac-á," the song from which it received its name.

When the chachalaca begins his evensong, children seem to think it's time to play tag. Like children of many lands, they find that period between the dark and the daylight when shadows lengthen and fade, just right for games of tag.

Some in Guatemala say that the mischievous trickster Chiltic does his most outlandish acrobatic dances on stilts about dusk or during the twilight just after sunset. Sometimes for no reason at all a sudden hush comes upon the children playing a clownish kind of tag in the streets. They look up and there, dancing along the telephone wires on his stilts, is Chiltic. He dances to enchanting music which no one can hear but him and the children. At one point he lifts his stilts and hovers in the air like a hummingbird over a flower. The next instant he is gone and the children are back at play.

In the game of Clown Tag, all players are chased by It, who tries to touch or tag one of them on the shoulder, arm, head, or leg. When chasing and tagging a player, It must hold one hand on the place he has been tagged. The first It has no tagged spot.

Essentially the same simple tag game is played along the United States-Mexican border and in the Rio Grande Valley, where it is sometimes called Payasada. English-speaking children call it Spot Tag and Japanese Tag.

CHAIN STOOP TAG   This game resembles a pantomime of Australian aborigines. *"Ngkinjaba iturala albutjika"* means in the Aranda language to turn homeward in the afternoon when the sun is bright and hot. Women and children of the Aranda, aborigines who live in the wastelands of central Australia, start back to their home camp then. They have been digging since early morning about the roots of acacia trees for witchetty grubs, the larvae of white ants (termites), one of their main foods and much prized as a delicacy.

Men whose totem (symbol of their common ancestor) is the witchetty grub perform ceremonies in the hope that the grub will multiply and there will be plenty for the community. One ceremony consists of a pantomime of the fully developed insect emerging from its chrysalis. For this, the men build a long tunnel of branches to represent the chrysalis, through which they shuffle hunched up, singing. The pantomime is so like Chain Stoop Tag played by English-speaking children in Australia and elsewhere as to make little difference.

Here's how to play. All players except It link arms and squat facing one another in two lines, leaving an open lane between them. Stooped over, It runs down the lane and tags a player, who must run stooped over through the lane and try to get back into his place before It catches him.

If It catches the player, the two join hands to tag a third, and so on until all players have been caught and the chain is complete, at which time they all hunker down in a circle and are ready to continue with Squat Tag.

SQUAT TAG   One player is chosen to be It. A brightly colored handkerchief is given a player in the circle, who must try to pass it to the next or across to another player before It can tag him.

As soon as a player is tagged, he becomes It. The handkerchief is tossed to a squatter in the circle, and the game continues with the new It trying to tag a squatter who has had the handkerchief passed to him. The former It is free to run at will and also try to take the handkerchief from a player squatting in the circle. The idea is for squatters to become runners until all are runners being chased by the one who is It.

Ostrich Tag is a variation of plain Squat Tag in which a player, when about to be caught by It, can remain free if he puts his arm under his knee and holds his nose.

CAROMS   This game—as well as Name Tag and Farmer and Thief— is played by the children of Yemen in the Middle East. Most Yemeni are farmers whose gardens and orchards grow on irrigated terraces in tiers about the mountainsides or along wadis, the narrow watercourses, where rain has been caught during the winter. Grapes, pomegranates, apricots, sweet lemons, melons, carrots, onions, and many other fruits and vegetables are cultivated in walled orchards and gardens.

Thursday is usually thought of as the day to go to market. Boys help their father load camels with produce and one camel with a tent and cooking utensils for the family's overnight stay.

Father puts his *jambiyyah* in his belt, for no man goes anywhere without his curved dagger. Boys too young for the real thing carry toy copies in their own wide belts into which they cram as many different things as other boys stuff into their pockets.

The mother and the girls mount camels; the father and the boys, donkeys. With pack animals strung out down the line, the caravan sets off for the market town.

From a distance, the town, bristling with slender stone towers, ancient one-family fortresses, has a skyline resembling a modern skyscraper city. But there the resemblance ends, for it is undoubtedly many centuries old, walled, and has gates that may have been closed before midnight and not opened until dawn.

The *suq,* or market-place, is a mixture of new and old; taxis and bicycles jostle camels, donkeys, and ox-carts; small boys drive a flock of sheep; hawkers sell black bread, cinnamon, saffron, and sesame-and-honey pastries; a radio sounds and somewhere a troubadour plays a flute.

As soon as children finish helping their parents, they scamper off in the direction of the reedy sound. There they are sure to find two or four boys seated on the ground around a board, playing Caroms, while a crowd of young kibitzers look over their shoulder and the flutist makes music.

Caroms is a simple, informal kind of pocket billiards, played on a square or rectangular board having a pocket in each corner. The game is a favorite everywhere in Yemen and is the same as that of Americans, Europeans, Scandinavians, Italians, and Spaniards, some of whom say that it was first played by Egyptians, others by the Persians or the Ethiopians, and still others that Caroms came from India or from the "Land of Sheba," as Yemen was called in biblical times.

Players snap disks with thumb and index or middle finger, trying to hit other disks into the pockets. Each carom (disk) hit into a pocket counts one.

There are slight variations in the arrangement of a certain number of disks on the board and the position of the snapping line at the start, but players usually decide those things for themselves. Children can make their own boards from 16-inch by 24-inch scrap lumber and glue paper or plastic cups at the corners, or they can draw a rectangle on the ground and dig out holes for pockets. One-inch plastic disks or tiddlywinks make good caroms.

NAME TAG   Seven o'clock in the afternoon is just before lunch, Yemeni time. The Yemeni count the hours beginning at sunset, for they keep lunar, or moon, time instead of solar, or sun, time. This makes midnight and noon about six o'clock. At noon the market is busiest, but by mid-afternoon everything has almost come to a halt. It is too hot to work; so parents rest and children sleep. When time comes for the evening meal everyone is alert again. Afterwards children play until bedtime.

For the game of Name Tag someone is chosen It. He locates the others by calling their names. The player called must answer very softly and not move until he is found by the sound of his voice and by touch.

FARMER AND THIEF   Two good runners are chosen to be the Farmer and the Thief. Other players make as big a circle for the orchard wall as they can by standing at arm's length. At the start, the Thief is inside the circle and the Farmer outside.

"Get out of my orchard!" the Farmer cries and takes after the Thief, who runs in and out between players, crawls between their legs, and leapfrogs over their backs as they bend down. The Farmer must do · exactly as the Thief does. When he skips an action, the children cry, "He got away!" and a new Thief is selected. If the Thief is caught, he becomes the Farmer and must chase a new Thief.

Games for Nighttime Hours

A NUMBER OF games played in twilight or darkness help children overcome fear of the dark, enjoy special stimulation to the sense of hearing and touch, and develop keener night vision.

BURNING STICKS   Many peoples in many lands—including Scotland, England, Ireland, and Australia—played games after dark with lighted broomstraws, firebrands, flambeaux, or candles. Safety demands that all fire hazards be avoided and the safe, just as much fun though less dramatic sparklers, punk sticks, dowel sticks whose ends are decorated with night-glow paints, pencil flashlights, and the like, be substituted.

Scottish children sit in the dark making whigmaleeries and ingrydoories, that is, rings and pictures, with the red end of a burnt stick. One only at a time makes pictures, and the others try to guess what they are. The successful guesser becomes the next maker of ingrydoories.

Jack's Alive (England), Dingle Dousie Stick (Scotland), and The Church Cat (Ireland) vary but little in the way they are played. Children sit around in a circle or facing rows on the grass or indoors on the floor. A lighted punk stick or sparkler is handed to a player who twirls it and recites:

Jack's been alive for many a day;
Keep him alive or a forfeit pay.

The player hands the stick quickly to the next child. If the punk or sparkler goes out while anyone is twirling it and reciting, that one must pay a forfeit—such as tell a joke or riddle, sing a song, whistle a tune, or tell a ghost or scary story in the dark. Actually, in Scotland in bygone days a dingle dousie was a little bell softly tinkling. One told a story while another dingled the dousie very, very softly. When the dingling stopped, the story teller stopped, and story and dousie went to one's partner, proceeding clockwise until the story and tellers were exhausted.

GECKO GECKO   When an Arnhem Lander, of Arnhemland, Australia, wants to warm himself on a chilly evening, he often holds or carries a firebrand in his hands. Children play Gecko Gecko, Shadow Tag, and other running games in the flickering lights from firebrands of grown-ups, sitting or moving about a lonely campsite in northern Australia.

Gecko Gecko can be played by any number. Players form two groups. One, calling themselves Geckos, have two small blocks of wood which they keep clapping together in imitation of the sound "gecko," from which the little nocturnal lizard got its name. The other group, calling themselves Beetles, are chased by the Geckos, who try to catch them. Captured Beetles are sent to The Tree, where they stay until all Beetles are caught. Geckos capture Beetles by touching them.

This is a good game for equalizing efforts of good runners and poor runners. Constantly clapping blocks together provides a handicap for the good runners. A dimly lighted room or an outdoor area with lanterns affords appropriate background for this game.

WHAT ARE YOU DOING?   This is played sitting in the dark with one player, It, having a flashlight, which substitutes for a firebrand. Whenever the light is turned on a player, that person must be doing something—such as pretending to wash the hands or face, fishing, looking in a mirror, etc.—which the other players must guess. Anyone caught not doing anything must try to get away before It can touch him, or he is It.

LAND CRABBING   This is a nighttime activity of the Tahitian Islanders of the South Pacific, whose children play by the light of the moon and the stars. Many youngsters around the world have a tradition of playing at night. English, Canadian, and American children had a general shout for calling out their friends on a bright night:

Joe, Sally (or whatever the name), come out and play,
The moon is shining as bright as day.
Lose your supper, lose your sleep,
Come out anyway and play in the street.

In the South Seas, cocks greet the rising of the moon as well as that of the sun, and often become a raucous crowing chorus on a starlit night. Among the nocturnal creatures of the South Pacific islands are the land crabs of Tahiti.

Englishman Robert Louis Stevenson, author of *Treasure Island, Kidnapped,* and other childhood favorites, found Tahiti all that he had ever dreamed of. The island was "loved of the moon and the sun," he said,

> Where the brown children all the day
> Keep up a ceaseless noise of play . . .

He wrote friends at home in England, telling them he swam in the lagoon every day, attended local feasts and "had four helpings of pork," ate roasted crabs, and went land crabbing with the Tahitians.

Young and old arm themselves with pails, fishpoles, and lines and go into the gardens to catch land crabs. The fishline is baited with a bunch of green leaves from the hibiscus tree.

Everyone walks very quietly so as not to send the crabs scurrying off. The rustling sounds the crabs make as they search for food can be clearly heard.

Fishermen stand still, cast, and wait for the crabs to fasten their nippers in the leaves. They then pull the creatures toward them, pounce on them, and pop them into pails.

Children who live where land crabs are there to be caught can do as the South Sea Islanders do. Others who live where there are no crabs can have fun playing the following fishing game.

ANGLERS For small children indoors and as a party activity, this is a fine game. Crabs and fishes are cut from pieces of 8½-inch × 11-inch cardboard. Make a V-shaped slit near the head and fold down so that each fish or crab can rest on the tip of the V. A line with a bent pin is attached to a 3-foot stick for the fishpole.

Children can make their own poles, cut and color as many crabs and fish as they like. They sit on chairs around a "pond" or along the banks of a make-believe stream and try to pick up fish and crabs by angling. Players take turns keeping the flaps on the undersides of the cardboard creatures so that their heads will be off the floor and the children fishing can hook them.

Fishlines, baited with tiny magnets with which to catch plastic fish having scales of steel filings glued to them, make good fishing too.

The fisherman who catches the most or, if different size fish have been made, the largest fish, is the winner.

THE CAT THAT WANDERS BY NIGHT   This game comes from the Chinese of the Chiang-nan region of South-of-the-River Yangtze, China. Moon-gazing is a traditional pastime of the Chinese. Mountain shelters were built, leaving one end open so that host and guests could sit at the table, have refreshments, and gaze at the moon.

A twelfth-century painting of the Han Palace at Hang-Chou shows the empress and her retinue climbing to a tower high on a rock to enjoy the moonrise. Below in the palace courtyard are oxen, carts bearing theatrical trappings, and people getting ready for a pageant celebrating the full moon of midautumn.

Children—the boys wearing appliqué cloth tiger caps for good luck—do the dance of the Dipper Star and play games by the light of the full moon.

The game, The Cat That Wanders by Night, is a lighthearted bit of nonsense for a large group either indoors or out. Before the start, tell the players that Cat borrowed Monkey's Horse while Monkey was up the river saving old Mr. Kao's Pig from the Dragon. Horse ran away and now Cat is trying to find him before Monkey returns. Cat doesn't search during daytime, of course, for he's a night prowler.

A player is chosen for Cat. The other players then select Horse, without telling Cat who it is. Some object or place is called Monkey's Home. Cat closes his eyes and pretends to be asleep while the other players scatter and hide. At the words, "Wake up, Cat," Cat opens his eyes, gets up and begins to wander about looking for Horse. At the same time he tries to find someone who may have seen Horse.

When Cat finds a hidden player, he asks, "Have you seen Monkey's Horse?"

The other replies, "Yes, but I don't know where he is now."

"Will you wait for Monkey at his home and tell him I'm looking for his Horse?" asks Cat.

"I'll do that for Monkey," replies the player and goes off to wait there.

If the player happens to be Horse, he says, "I'm Horse, you Silly Cat. I'm on my way home, so stay away from me, Cat."

The dialogue is only suggested. Players make up any words they wish, just so they don't give away to Cat the secret of who Horse is until Cat actually catches him. As soon as Horse is caught, he at once becomes the next Cat.

GATHERING STARS   This game comes from the Pygmies of Gabon, Africa. Full of poetry and dancing are the Pygmy myth and miming of star gathering. The Milky Way is stardust made of broken stars, they say. Little gods travel the road in the sky, gathering up stars in armfuls like Pygmy women gathering piles of locusts and putting them in baskets until the baskets are filled and spilling over. The gods must gather stars in order to provide fuel for the sun to burn.

For Gathering Stars two lines are drawn 15-20 feet apart. Three or four children, depending on size of group, are chosen Catchers. The rest stand on one of the lines. Catchers chant,

> Star bright, star light,
> How many stars are out tonight?

The others answer, "More than you can catch and carry." Then they run to the opposite side, trying not to be captured while crossing by the Catchers. Captives joint the Catchers and help to catch the rest. Last one caught becomes the first Catcher, who chooses two assistants, and the game continues.

A similar game, Blackberry, is played by Americans of the Middle Atlantic states and in the Middle West, and by Canadians. The method is the same as that of Gathering Stars except the chant, which goes:

> Fugitives challenge: Blackberries, blackberries on the hill,
> How many pails can you fill?

> Pickers reply: Briers are thick and briers scratch,
> But we'll pick all the berries in the blackberry patch.

KULIT K'RANG   A form of Pick Up Stars, this game has been played by girls all over Southeast Asia, but most particularly by those of Malaya and Indonesia.

Two or more may play, sitting in a circle on the floor or grass. A bowl for losers' shells is placed in the middle. Each player has twenty cockleshells in her lap or in front of her. Any kind of small shells or pebbles will answer the purpose. In turn, each player puts a shell on the back of her hand, tosses the shell up in the air, snatches one from her lap, and catches the tossed shell as it comes down. If she fails to snatch or to catch or both, she loses one shell to the bowl in the middle. Game continues until all are out of shells.

Sometimes the bowl, rather than each player, is supplied with twenty or more shells in the beginning, and every time a player wins her snatch-and-catch, she may take a shell from the bowl. Final winner is the girl with the most shells.

Sun Myths
Transformed into Games

READERS ACQUAINTED WITH Mark Twain's *The Adventures of Tom Sawyer* are familiar with American boys' recipes for getting rid of warts, one of which called for spunk water and another for a bean and some magical words. Tom's spells for wart riddance were small magic. He seemed to have no great magic such as the Indians up and down the Mississippi River possessed for slowing down the sun and holding back sunset. They in common with many peoples over the earth knew what to do when the day was growing too short.

For instance, a traveler in the Fiji Islands of Melanesia, who wants to make sure he gets to where he's going before dark, looks for a sunny patch of reeds. He ties a handful of them together, thus tangling up the sun's rays. By the time the sun has untangled his rays, the traveler has arrived at his destination.

In North America, Cherokee and Osage Indians tied a knot in the top of tall grasses and held back the sun.

To keep the sun from going down too soon, the traveler in Yucatan and the Australian Outback places a piece of sod in the fork of a tree so that it exactly faces the sun, who has to stop to dry the grassy sod so it falls out of the fork and releases him.

Hurrying home, afraid they'll be late for supper, African boys and girls pluck some grass, put it in the road, and place a stone on it. That done, they feel sure Mother will keep the meal waiting for them.

Now, if you want to make the sun go faster, take some sand, face the sun, toss the sand up, and blow hard. That's the way it's done along Australia's Roper's River.

As for sun traps, people in all lands, from earliest times, have speculated about the daily journey of the sun across the sky. Myths, legends, and sacred pantomime games tell how the sun was trapped or snared and made to run its course.

According to the Incas of pre-Conquest Peru, the sun was held captive and "must be tied like a beast who always goes round and round in the same track. If the sun were free, he would visit other parts of the heavens where he has never been."

Modern man does not attempt to trap the sun, but giant reflectors and other devices are made to trap its heat and energy for men's houses and for other purposes.

TYING THE SUN TO THE HITCHING POST   This game is derived from a pantomime ceremony of the Indians of the Andes from Colombia through Peru, Ecuador, Argentina, and Chile.

A gigantic stone sundial can be seen today at Machu Picchu, the fortress city built by the Incas in the Andes of present-day Peru. The city was dedicated to the Sun God and the sundial was used in the ceremony of *Inti-Huatana,* "the tying of the sun to the hitching post." On each side of the dial iron hooks held a net that was stretched to catch the sun. When caught, he was tied there. The sacred pantomime of the ceremony remains as a children's pantomime game.

Whether the game is played indoors or out, small children enjoy it. They join hands and stand in a semicircle. One player is It, who chases another, the Sun. As the Sun runs around outside the semicircle, It tries to catch him and pull him inside through the open half. When It succeeds, the children quickly close the circle, trapping the Sun inside. Players part to let It in and out between two players, but not for the Sun. A new It and new Sun are chosen each time a Sun is trapped.

SNARING THE SUN-BEAST   This game is suggested by the solar mythology of the Hawaiian Islanders and other peoples of Polynesia. Many in the world know about Hercules, hero of Greek and Roman myths. But not as many know about Maui, the great hero of Polynesian legends and tales, whose feats were even more amazing than those of Hercules.

For example, Maui went fishing with his brothers one day. After a while he felt a twitch at the end of the line. Thinking he had a bite, he began to pull. He pulled and he pulled and he pulled.

"Maui, you must have caught a very big fish," said his brothers.

Maui pulled and pulled and pulled some more. And he couldn't pull the fish in.

"You must have caught a whale," said his brothers.

With that, Maui gave a tremendous tug and pulled up a whole island right out of the bottom of the sea.

Another example turns into a game: Maui decided that the Sun-Beast was galloping across the sky too fast and should be slowed down. Farmers needed more time to work in their fields and gardens. Vegetables and fruits needed more sunshine in order to grow better. So one day Maui and his brothers made some snares, ropes with running nooses at the ends. They placed the nooses in the Sun-Beast's path, then hid on each side. Soon the Sun-Beast came galloping up. His forefeet came down in one noose, then his hind feet in another. Quickly, Maui and his brothers pulled the ropes taut and the Sun-Beast was caught. Ever since then the ropes have been kept tight on the Sun and he is allowed to run just so fast and no faster.

The game suggested by Maui's feat is a competition for all ages and an aid to acquiring nimble feet. Hawaiian children dig a series of shallow holes to form an obstacle course. Individuals or teams run the course, stepping into each hollow.

When enough space is available, a course can be made anywhere by taking ten to fifteen shallow corrugated cardboard or wooden boxes and laying them out by ones and twos, short and long steps apart, in much the same way as a course of wooden frames is set up for players to run in football practice. Old automobile tires may also be used.

If the group is large, players are divided into teams. The team wins that has most players who succeed in running the course without failing to step in a box or has fewest misses. For small groups, the course is run as individual competition and the winner is the one who has fewest misses in three tries.

Knocking a box out of place or stepping outside it counts as a miss. With older participants, time taken to complete the course counts too, and a timekeeper with a stopwatch should be appointed.

BADGER THE SUN   This game comes from a legend of the Japanese, especially on the main island of Nippon and the north sea district of Hokkaido. Long, long ago in Japan, the Sun Goddess grew so angry with the earth's peoples for cheating, lying, killing one another, and generally bad behavior that she hid in a mountain cave and left the earth in darkness. Mankind thought of first one way and then another to lure her from the cave.

Finally, they hit upon asking the badger to lure her out. He was only too willing to fall in with their plan, for he was a great tease. Badger went at once and began to pester the Sun Goddess. When she could stand his teasing no longer, she came rushing out to catch him, but instead she herself was caught by the people waiting beside the entrance to the cave. They set her upon the road in the sky and held her there by ropes which are the sun's rays. Never again was she let go free.

To play the game, children stand in rows radiating from a center at which Badger stands. At the start the Sun is outside the rows and must chase Badger down the various rows and round the outside, trying to catch him.

"Here comes Badger, down this way!" "There goes Badger over there!" the children cry out from time to time to tease and mislead her.

As soon as Badger is caught, he grasps Sun's hand. Another player quickly grasps her other hand. Still another player takes hold of Badger's other hand, and with Badger and the Sun in the middle, players join hands to make a long rope, then begin pivoting about Badger and the Sun faster and faster, chanting nonsense words or rhymes which they themselves make up on the spur of the moment, until, one by one, they have to let go.

It is to be noted that in this legend and game, it is the badger who teases and is not teased. The badger gave his name, it is said, to teasing, because in the Western world men at one time enjoyed watching a tied-up badger being teased, that is, "badgered," by dogs that were set upon him as in bull and bear baiting.

Myths and Play
Based on Seasonal Changes

ANCIENT IDEAS OF the solar calendar often concerned families of sun gods who were responsible for shortening and lengthening days, for heat and cold. A Finnish myth tells of the family that cares for the sun-lamp which is extinguished at sunset by the young daughter and lighted at dawn by the young son. When the father rests, then it is winter.

People today know that seasonal changes are caused by the 23½-degree tilt of the earth's axis of rotation to the plane of the earth's orbit. The four seasons unfold at about 18½ miles per second as our spinning planet goes on its journey of almost 600,000,000 miles in space around the sun—that journey called a year.

Lands of no seasons exist at the equator, where the effect of the earth's tilt is hardly noticeable. "But by the equator, they know not autumn and they know not spring, neither the change of seasons or of sorrows," wrote Herman Melville in *The Encantadas or Enchanted Isles*, the name he gave the Galápagos in the South Pacific. Equatorial lands lack the kind of seasonal games found in temperate lands, where one season contrasts sharply with another.

At the top and the bottom of the world occur the long day and the long night, for, at its most noticeable, the effect of the earth's tilting is the difference between day and night—the six-month day and six-month night in Arctic and Antarctic lands. Various peoples see this as a battle between the two seasons of winter and summer and act it out in games.

PTARMIGANS AGAINST DUCKS   This is a game of the Eskimos of the Alaskan and Canadian Arctic. When autumn storms announce the approach of the long winter, a community of Eskimo parents and children divide into two groups for a mock battle. All those with birthdays in the winter are Ptarmigans, northland birds whose winter plumage is white and whose feet, clad in feather snowshoes, never leave a print for enemies to follow. Those born in summer are Ducks, the southern migrants. A line is drawn on the ground. Ptarmigans grasp one end of a long sealskin rope, Ducks the other. Each side then tugs to drag the other across the line over to its side.

If the Ducks, who represent summer, win, the Eskimos expect mild weather throughout the winter.

Tlingit, Haida, and other Indians in the American Northwest and in Canada play this game, but simply as Summer-born Against Winter-born.

Children in the United States know the game as Tug-of-War or Pom Pom Pull Away and play it without its having any significance whatever for them, although in all the many lands from which they, their parents, or their ancestors came to America, this tug-of-war was a calendar custom.

SHOVE WINTER OUT   This game comes from the Indians of Patagonia, of Tierra del Fuego, and other islands in the cluster at the southern tip of South America. Some scientists say that no people in the world adapted themselves so well to living in a cold, hostile land as the native peoples of this far-southern glacier region. They hunt, fish, collect mollusks and limpets, and know the seasons by the kinds of fungi to be found. A tuniclike garment and shoes of guanaco (wild llama) skin are worn in the coldest winter weather in June.

When a bundled-up explorer asked an almost naked native how he could stand the cold, the latter pointed to the explorer's bare face and said, "I am all face."

Windbreaks of hides and boughs serve for shelters against the rains and sleet of a December midsummer as well as July's snow and wintry blasts. Because of year-round fog and damp, fires are kept going constantly, never allowed to go out. Explorer Fernando de Magellan, while finding the westward sea route to India, saw the fires burning and named the place "Land of Fire"—Tierra del Fuego.

The game is a vigorous one for older children, in large or small groups, indoors or out.

Draw a circle that can hold half the group, whose foreheads have a streak of black crayon or watercolor to represent Winter Weather. The other half, Summer Weather, have green streaks on their foreheads.

All players fold their arms and keep them folded. Summers attempt to shove Winters out of the circle and occupy it themselves. Shoulders and backs only are used in shoving and pushing. Winters must not step outside the line, for once they step or are shoved outside, they must remain there, joining the Summers to shove out the rest of the Winters. Winters may sit down to make it more difficult for their opponents to shove them out of the circle.

Games to Accompany the Growing
And the Hunting Seasons

ALMOST SINCE man's invention of the wheel it has been a symbol of the classic monotony of the yearly cycle of vegetation, turning as a wheel. Temperate lands generally observed the agricultural year with "in spring we plant and sow, summer we weed and hoe, autumn we reap the harvest, and in winter we with all things rest." Different games followed the cycle, often alike in lands far removed from one another.

OATS AND BEANS AND BARLEY The game is suggested by the old "hiring fairs" of the English countryside which were known as "wakes." The young plowman and the dairy maid, for instance, who wanted more wages, better working conditions, or simply needed a job, waited for early spring when the hiring fairs opened, then hurried off to the nearest market town holding a wake. There they stood or wandered about with a straw or green twig in their mouth to show they were ready for hire.

Such fairs came to be held at various dates between March and October, depending upon the local crops. Late in August in Derbyshire, England, a flower show and country fair took place. At Bunbury wakes ryegrass and clover should be ready to cut. At Wrenbury wakes early apples were about ripe and pickers were needed.

Resemblance to present-day practices, in the United States and some other countries, in hiring workers for harvesting various crops, is obvious.

The game employs a circle-and-chanting rhyme for boys and girls. All join hands around the Farmer in the middle, and walk around chanting:

Oats and beans and barley grows
In fields and rows, in fields and rows.
And this is the way the farmer sows:
He stamps his foot (children and Farmer stamp feet),
He claps his hands (children and Farmer clap hands),
And turns around and views the land (all turn around),
Waiting for a partner,
Waiting for a partner (children and Farmer fold their arms and stand
   still).

The Farmer then chooses a partner, who takes the Farmer's hand. The rhyme and action are repeated, the partner choosing a partner this time, and so on until all are chosen and have joined hands.

This is also a game for July in the Grecian countryside about Athens and on the island of Crete, when the barley is harvested. Usually three or four children are chosen for Farmers and stand in the middle, and the rhyme goes something like this:

This is the way the barley grows, the barley grows,
And bows its head when the wind blows.
This is the way the farmers reap:
They swing their arms,
They stamp their feet,
They clap their hands
And turn around
And turn again
And point to one
To cut the barley down.

Throughout the rhyme, the children and the Farmers suit their actions to the words. On the word "bows," children and Farmers bow to the right and the left; on the word "point," Farmers point to those they want to join them in the center.

CHERRY CHOP   In France and England an old and widespread custom was the holding of cherry fairs or cherry feasts in July, when cherries were ripe. Orchard owners had families with their children come from miles around to pick, eat, and buy to take home or to sell. Girls peddled them through London streets, crying, "Six pence a pound, fair cherries."

It was a short but merry feast. Children stuffed themselves and played Cherry Chop and other summer games. French and English poets compared the shortness of life to a cherry fair, and Americans had a saying from a popular song that "life was nothing but a bowl of cherries."

The game is suggested for picnics and outings. A shallow hole is dug in the ground. If weighed so as not to tip easily, a shallow bowl will do as well.

Each player has a supply of from five to ten pebbles or small stones. At the fairs the glutted children used cherrystones.

To start, one pebble is placed in the hole and the first player (chosen by lot) tries to knock it out. If he succeeds, he keeps it, and another is put in the hole to replace it. If he fails, he loses one of his pebbles to the hole. Players keep all stones they knock out. Winner is the one with the most pebbles at the close of the game, and is given some small prize.

NORTHLAND SOCCER BALL   Danes, Eskimos, and other peoples of Greenland, Iceland, and various northern countries play this game.

Since Viking days, Iceland and Greenland have been visited and settled by Scandinavians of Norway and Sweden, the Irish, Danes (Greenland is part of the nation of Denmark), and others who live and work among the native Eskimos. In those northern lands people harvest the sea and look forward in the autumn to the fishing season in preparation for the long winter.

Most Eskimos catch whale in the old ways of their ancestors, and when the white-whale season opens early in the fall, the fishermen set their nets. Each owner of a whale net sets it every year in the same place, a spot all recognize as his.

When a catch is netted, the cry of *"Kilaluvak katortak!"* (white whale!) goes up and everyone rushes down to the shore to watch the fishermen in a boat untangle the whale from the net, and secure it with rope. The crowd then help haul it up on the beach. There half a dozen or so men begin to cut it up for food, and men, women, and children begin to celebrate the catch, eating pieces of whale skin, singing, dancing, shouting, and playing games together.

The game is vigorous, and is suggested for teams of small or large groups, outdoors. It is played in the Arctic with a ball made from a small bladder, stuffed lightly with grass or moss and partially inflated so that it is left limp. A football with well-used, well-softened leather, partially inflated, is much the same thing.

Both boys and girls play, and are divided into two teams (half the boys and half the girls on one team, the other half on the other team). The side of a building, a fence, or some large upright surface is selected for the goal. A large circle is drawn, with whatever surface is selected for the goal at a point on the perimeter.

Boys of each team must stay within the circle, kicking and pushing the ball with their feet, throwing and catching it, in order to advance the ball toward the goal. Girls of each team station themselves outside the circle and throw or kick the ball back to their teammates in the circle. Girls must play outside the circle, boys within. For overstepping bounds, players have a time penalty of two or three minutes during which they must not play, or they must drop out of the game until an opponent (either boy or girl) oversteps bounds.

To start, a girl selected by lot, throws the ball to a teammate in the circle who runs forward to receive it. The game proceeds as a kind of soccer with players kicking, catching and throwing the ball to advance it. Either boys or girls may run with the ball and score for their team by touching the goal while in possession of the ball. Each goal counts 1, and game is 10.

TOUCH-POLE TAG   Filipinos around Manila, and on the islands of Luzon and Mindanao play this game.

When the North Pole is tipped farthest away from the sun, the Northern Hemisphere has winter, and the Southern Hemisphere summer, generally speaking. But there are places in the Northern Hemisphere that are tropical, such as the Philippines, an archipelago of 11 large and 7,000 small islands, lying south of Taiwan and north of Indonesia. Early in December when the United States is ready for winter weather, the Philippines are enjoying springtime temperatures in the 70's and 80's. Farmers watch the skies at evening and, when the constellation Orion appears at seven o'clock, they begin to clear their fields for sowing and planting. They raise much rice and hemp.

In olden times, farmers had a magic formula of words and steps which they performed in the belief that it helped make the crops grow. From the custom came a children's game played just for fun. Ordinarily, they use the English language, for that is the *lingua franca* of the islands.

The game can be played by small or large groups. A tall stake is driven into the ground for the touch-pole. (Use a stanchion for play in play streets, a chair for indoors.)

Count out for It, who stands at the touch-pole. Others make a big circle around It and the pole, hands joined. The following dialogue and action take place:

IT. Would you know how the farmer plows?
OTHERS. Yes, we know. This is how the farmer plows. He holds
the plow and his *caraboa* pulls. [*They mimic a man with hands on plow handles, leaning forward and pushing to help his water buffalo.*]
IT. Is that so?
OTHERS. Yes, that's so.
IT. Would you know what the farmer does when plowing's done?
OTHERS. Yes, we know. This is what the farmer does when plowing's done. He bows low. He bows low. [*They bend to It, turn and bend low in other direction, then turn back to face It.*]
IT. Is that so?
OTHERS. Yes, that's so.
IT. Would you know what the farmer does when his work is done?
OTHERS. Yes, we know. This is what the farmer does when his work is done. [*They shout.*] He runs with his *caraboa* to the river.

The players quickly scatter, and It must catch one of them to take his place as It. When chased by It, a player tries to reach the touch-pole, for he can't be tagged if touching the pole. A player is not allowed, however, to stay "safe" at the touch-pole. Also, It must immediately take off after another player and not continue to threaten the one who has just touched the pole.

CHUKE   This is a game played by the Charoti Indians of Grand Chaco, South America. About March the rainy season ends, edible fruits are almost gone, and winter begins in Chaco. Then in every village young and old begin to carve the wooden blocks for the game of Chuke. As soon as each player has carved four for himself, all start playing and the game goes on for the whole month of March, but it is never played at any other time of year. Every winning fall of the blocks is announced in a loud voice, so it can be heard a long way.

The game is one of chance and a bit of skill for anyone from five to seventy-five. Two, three, or four may play. Each player has four wooden blocks, about 1 inch x 1½ inches, flat on one side and rounded on the other, which he makes himself. Flat sides should have the same color or design painted or carved on them, rounded sides another color or design. These are his "dice." He provides himself with four pebbles, buttons, or disks, which are his "men."

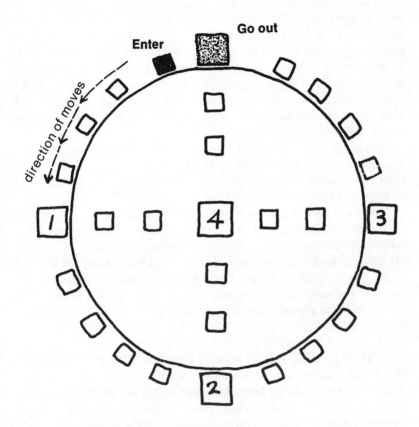

Then on the ground or on a large sheet of paper draw a big circle and divide it into quarters, placing large and small squares (29 in all) as in the diagram. Players hold all their blocks in the palm of one hand and turn palm over, letting the blocks fall, and, according to the fall, move their men around the circle to the Go Out point. When two or three play, each player (unless players decide to use just two or three men) must try to get all four of his men around and out before the others. Winner is the one who does so first.

When four play, they pair off and play as partners, using four men to go around and out.

These are the number of counts to move for the various falls:

4 round sides or 4 flat sides facing up: move 5 squares
3 rounds and 1 flat up: move 4 squares
2 rounds and 2 flats up: move 3 squares
1 round and 3 flats up: move 2 squares

All players start from the Enter point on their first fall and move as many points counterclockwise as the fall calls for. Any fall that places a man *exactly* on any one of the large squares (1, 2, or 3) allows the player to move his man to the big center square (4) and move to Go Out without having to go clear around the circle, and in addition gives him an extra fall. Players may divide falls and move two or more of their men, provided none comes to rest on a square occupied by another man. There must be only one man resting on a square at a time, although a player may move a man past *one* of his own men or *one* of those of another player. Thus, although it might be one square less to move from big square 3 round the circle to the Go Out point, it is often better strategy to use the cross squares, especially if there are a number of men all trying to use the shorter round-the-circle route.

A player does not have to wait until he gets the exact count in a fall to land on the Go Out square before taking a man out. He may take a man out on the exact or any count over the number needed.

Chuke is the kind of game of chance found throughout the world. It is like Nyout, which is widely distributed in the Orient, and is in turn basically the same as those games played with wooden blocks, often carved with the player's totem, by Indians all the way from Alaska to Antarctica.

CATCH OLD MRS. WINTER AND THROW HER IN THE RIVER

The Czechs, especially of Bohemia, Czechoslovakia, play this game. Winter has had a special historical meaning for the people of Bohemia since the days of "the King and Queen of Hearts," when 17-year-old German Frederick and 16-year-old English Elizabeth were married on St. Valentine's Day, 1613. He was King of Bohemia for a single winter before he was forced off the throne by his rival, "The Knave of Hearts" of the Mother Goose rhyme. Ever afterwards, Frederick was called "the Winter King."

That this "Winter King" had particular meaning for Americans has been forgotten long ago; yet it was his son, Prince Rupert, who was the original Yankee Doodle who "stuck a feather in his hat and called it macaroni" at a battle during the Great Civil War in England. Those words became a part of the song, "Yankee Doodle," which the English, then the Americans, sang so lustily during the American Revolution.

Macaroni was another name for a gay blade who made fun of conventional people and customs and was *not* a kind of Italian pasta. And the old Bohemian custom of getting rid of tiresome and dull winter with a romp and a revel found its way into a lively, harum-scarum children's game.

The game is one good runners and poor runners can enjoy playing, since wits can be used to decoy pursuers and to invent ruses for preventing the capture of Mrs. Winter.

Players are divided into two sides, Old Mrs. Winter and her Friends, and the Catchers.

Old Mrs. Winter is a stick with a piece of white cloth on the end, and is carried by one of her Friends. The two sides line up facing each other. The Catchers start the game by stepping forward and saying, "We've come to get Old Mrs. Winter. It's time to throw her in the river."

At this, the Friends all dart off in different directions, pursued by the Catchers. Friends of Mrs. Winter pass her from one to another, try to hide her, and use all kinds of ways to keep her from being taken away from them.

Once a Catcher has hold of Old Mrs. Winter, however, she must immediately be given up. When this happens, the game continues with Mrs. Winter's Friends trying to get her back from the Catchers. This back-and-forth struggle, so typical of early spring weather, can go on until children are bored or tired.

Instead of Old Mrs. Winter, the Swiss have Old Man Winter. And late in April, they usher in the new season of spring by the Burning of the Boogg, that is, getting rid of Old Man Winter.

Part III

OLD CULTURES
IN TRADITIONAL GAMES
AND PLAYWAYS

Traditional Sliding
And Hurling Games

IDEAS OR WAYS of doing things, transmitted from ancestors, grandparents, and parents to their children crystallize into traditions of a family, clan, a nation, or a whole people.

Much about the differing traditions and customs in the world can be learned from games, especially those of children, imitating the institutions of the past of their own and neighboring people. Laws and rituals often disguised, exist too in children's games and sometimes afford the only vestiges of very ancient laws and customs. People become what their traditionalists pour into them, even in their game ways.

Rock slides are the ancient forerunners of pool and playground slides of Europe and the Americas, and the playground sliding boards as in Hong Kong. They are also the prototypes of the amusement park shoot-the-chutes with toboggans or other flat-bottomed coasters for riding down a steep incline and splashing out onto the water.

Long ago in a ritual, probably connected with initiation ceremonies for boys, Nigerians slid down the great rocks at tribal ceremonial sites of their land on the gulf of Guinea, west coast of Africa. Children today slide there for amusement, sitting on leather pads or mats.

A snowy hill in winter, a grassy one in summer, or a high, hard-packed sand dune are suitable slides for children anywhere who may lack the wonderful rock slides of the African West Coast. Banged-up lids of discarded refuse cans or big trays make good seats on which to go scooting down. The more sliders, the more fun. Individual or team competition should have a starter at the top who sends sliders down at intervals as in the Olympic Games' toboggan races.

Winner is the one who goes farthest, or the team with best general score for distance.

Sticks of every kind, according to the material available in the environment, were fashioned into digging sticks, spears, javelins, lances, and a variety of tools. They were people's way of getting food in every land. The stick-tool was even held in common by man and animals, such as gorillas, chimpanzees, and others that poke out juicy grubs or ants from their nests in earth or rotting trees and logs.

Later peoples used sticks in warfaring, either in defense or offense, and, more important, in gaining their food through hunting on land and in the water. Skill in throwing sticks was a necessity. Practice in it began as soon as a child could hold a stick and there was no better way of learning than in games and contests of stick-throwing.

THROWING THE JAVELIN CONTEST   The tall Tuaregs of the mountains between Ceuta and Oran in North Africa compete in an ancient Arabic contest, the objective of which is seeing who can throw a spear or javelin the farthest or highest. The high throwing is accompanied by hopping; the number of hops between the throwing of the spear and its landing provides the basis for judging the winner.

Throwing a spear, javelin, or long pointed stick to see who can throw farthest is a contest common throughout the world. The Sioux Indian children of North America added feathers to the end of the long sticks to help guide them, and held the throwing contest on ice or hard-frozen snow. They held the stick near the middle and swung it back and forth over the shoulder, then threw it down along the ice or the hard snow. The player whose stick went farthest was the winner.

STICKS IN A MOUND   This is a kind of spear-throwing or stick contest played by children almost anywhere there are sandy or earthy mounds, river banks, or levees like those along the Mississippi River. In wintertime snowbanks may be used for the contest.

All that is needed to play are long sticks such as broom handles with one of their ends whittled down just enough to stand up or hold in sand or earth when thrown.

Children play as individuals or teams, throwing at the mound from a toe line some distance away, then running up, retrieving their sticks, coming back down the other side, or by a previously determined route, and taking their places again on the toe line. Winner is the person or the team who does so in the shortest time.

There are countless variations on this game that one may see children playing all the way from Bechuanaland, Africa, to Turkey and Jordan and other countries of the Middle East. Sioux Indians used grassy mounds and, later, white and black migrants to North America from across the Atlantic tossed pointed sticks at the levees. These embankments built along the rivers in southern states of the U.S.A. made exciting places to run and play games, like Bank Go Up and Bank Go Down (Sticks in a Mound, transplanted to America).

Games on Foot
And on Ice

VARIATIONS OF THE same basic game of polo are traditionally played in Iran, Afghanistan, Turkey, Tibet, China, Japan, India, Arabia, Russia, England, Ireland, Canada, Argentina, and the United States of America. Polo is a word that comes from the Tibetan *pulu,* meaning ball.

Afghanistan's national sport of *buz kashi* (goat-drag) with riders mounted on big polo horses, trained to bite and kick, and modern-day international polo matches with world-famous teams riding specially bred and trained polo ponies, seem a far cry from stick-and-ball with players afoot. But polo, the sport that became international, is only a kind of hockey on horseback. And there are at least a dozen varieties of hockey that are really polo on foot and traditional in countries around the globe.

Polo afoot and on horseback had their beginnings in Persia (Iran) long ago and spread east and west. Following are several Eastern variants and a children's version of polo played by the Georgians in the U.S.S.R.

PERSIAN STICK BALL This is a polo-afoot game for two teams with four to six on a side, played outdoors or in a large indoor space. Needed are paddle-shaped sticks and a bag filled with wads of wastepaper or anything lightweight.

Draw a goal line at each end of the playing area. Teams stand in semicircles back of their captains in the center of the space. To start, the ball is tossed up between the captains, who try to hit it to a team member. The ball is advanced to a team's goal line by paddling it along the ground or floor, or lifting it and throwing it with the paddle to a teammate or across the team's goal. The ball must not be hit or batted except in the toss-up between the captains at the start of the game.

First team to make five goals wins.

CHINESE BAG-HOLE BALL   Teams of four to six, outdoors or in, can play this lively polo-afoot competition.

A special kind of goal must be constructed—a metal screen fastened securely to two posts. Midway and about three inches from the bottom of the screen cut a round hole about ten to twelve inches in diameter. Attach the mouth of a bag around the hole. The goal is placed at the end of a rectangular playing area whose size depends upon space available and abilities of players.

Play with a light ball such as a ping-pong ball and stick curved at the end. Use hockey sticks if they are available.

The side that hits the ball through the hole into the bag wins. Outdoors, when plenty of space is at hand, set up two goals, one at each end of the field. Each team defends its own goal and tries to hit the ball into its opponent's bag-hole.

Mouse Down a Hole is Chinese Bag-Hole Ball, played with one goal by individuals or teams of English-speaking children. Competition consists of players trying to make a certain number of goals first.

DAKIU   This Japanese game is similar to Chinese Bag-Hole Ball and is played outdoors with two to four on a side and a scorekeeper.

The goals are screens or boards with a round hole fourteen inches in diameter in the center and a bag behind it for catching the ball. A goal is set about five feet from the ground at each end of the playfield. Opponents face off at center of field, and the scorekeeper tosses up the ball to start play.

A small, light ball is used, and players are equipped with long-handled rackets (sticks with paper plates or heavy cardboard disks tacked or stapled on the ends serve very well).

Objective of the game is lifting the ball up on the racket, carrying it, and placing it in the bag of the opponent's goal. Hands and feet cannot be used, only the paddle. Teammates lift the ball from one another's rackets as well as from the ground, in order to advance it toward the goal. Opponents attempt to intercept the ball by lifting it off ground whenever it falls from players' paddles. Only players on the same side are permitted to lift or transfer the ball from one another's paddles.

Each ball holed is 10 points. Game is 40.

ROL   In this Indian game, also known as Dribble Stick Ball, teams of four to eight on a side stand back of their goal lines at opposite ends of a field or large indoor space. It is another kind of polo afoot. A round, light, bouncy ball and ping-pong paddles or anything similar are used to play.

To start, captains stand in center field. The ball is bounced and each captain tries to hit it with his paddle toward his team. This is the only hit allowed. Thereafter, the ball must be dribbled by tapping it quickly with the paddles, with the objective of dribbling it past the opponent's goal line.

A team scores 5 points for each goal made. Winner may be the team with either the most points scored within a certain time limit, or the first reaching a certain number of points.

TSKHENBURTI   Because this traditional polo of Georgia in the U.S.S.R. is played on horseback by teams of men or teams of women with long-handled rackets and a ball somewhat smaller than a volleyball, it is also called Horse-Ball.

Small children imitate the adult sport in an informal game played outdoors. Skipping ropes or lengths of stout cord are used for reins. One player pretends to be the horse and grasps the ends of the rope which another player, the rider behind him, holds as reins. A light plastic or nonbounding ball, about the size of a baseball, is the best kind to use. Sticks with disks or small blocks of wood nailed to the ends are good substitutes for mallets. Two poles are driven in the ground about 6-7 feet apart at each end of the area to serve as goalposts. At the start, the ball is placed on a small mound of earth in the center of the playing area. Teams line up to each side of the ball, facing the goalposts of their opponent. Upon signal, the center player-rider on each team tries to hit and drive the ball toward the goalposts he faces. As soon as the ball is in play, opposing team's players are free to try to intercept it and hit it toward the other team's goalposts. That team's players try to prevent it.

Objective is hitting the ball through opponent's goalposts for 2 points. Game is 10.

The secret of the game lies in the ability of the makebelieve horse and rider to act as one, and the different horses and riders to play together

Goal Posts Team A

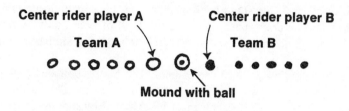

Center rider player A   Center rider player B

Team A   Team B

Mound with ball

Goal Posts Team B

as a team. Riders rather than horses should guide the progress of the ball toward and through the goalposts, as in the sport of polo.

DISK PITCHING ON ICE   This game is part of a tradition that is almost universal among children in lands where the winter season brings snow and ice. The tradition includes making a snowman or Old-Woman-Winter, building forts, sliding on the ice, and carrying on snowball battles. In addition, children have their own versions of their country's adult games. This particular game is a variation of Curling, which is traditional in Scotland, Ireland, Germany, the Netherlands, Flanders, Cornwall in England, and certain northern states of the U.S.A. It's an outdoor game for all ages.

A tee or peg is set up near the end of a strip of ice or hard-packed snow. With the tee as a center draw a circle about 5 feet in diameter. Mark a pitching line 20 to 25 feet away from the tee. If various ages play, use several pitching lines to give all a fair shot at the tee.

For the flattened, polished stones with handles used in Curling, substitute wooden disks 6 inches in diameter, making them of 1½-inch board or anything similar.

Each curler has two disks, and players compete either as individuals or teams, aiming their "stones" at the tee.

One point is scored for each tee shot, that is, for each disk that lies within the circle. Another point is scored for being nearest the tee. Curlers also try to knock opponent's disks out of the circle or away from the tee.

Rock collectors substitute stones—large and flat enough to skim the ice well—for the wooden disks. They initial them for easy identification. Knocking about the ice helps polish stones, although it is not comparable to polishing them in a regular rock tumbler. Flat polished stones with notches for thumb and finger were used in the original Scottish game.

BROOM HOCKEY This vigorous, competitive team game is a variant of Ice Hockey, traditional with Canada. Hockey on ice is also a tradition in Ireland, Scotland, U.S.A., and in most northern countries in both Europe and Asia.

For Broom Hockey a strip of ice or packed-down snow from 40 to 50 feet in length is required. Near each end is a goal post with a semicircle (called "striking circle") drawn 3 feet in front of it. There is a line across the middle of the ice strip.

There are usually 6 players on a side, one of whom is a goal keeper. Players use old brooms for hockey sticks, and a wooden puck, painted a bright color. Ice creepers, that is, some kind of play shoes with nonskid treads should be worn.

Objective of the game is sweeping the puck inside the opponent team's striking circle. Goal keepers operate just outside the circle and strive to prevent the puck from entering it. To start, the puck is placed in the center between two players of the opposing teams. Points required for goals and for game should be set before the game starts.

Myths, Legends, And Spectacles Transformed into Play

SHAKESPEARE IN *The Tempest* has the sprite Ariel tell Ferdinand, Prince of Naples: "Full fathom five thy father lies; / Of his bones are coral made; / Those are pearls that were his eyes; / Nothing of him that doth fade, / But doth suffer a sea-change / Into something rich and strange."

So it is with myths many times. They undergo marvelous transformations not only into other myths that reveal mankind's web of interlocking beliefs, but also into play for a child's world.

GO TELL AUNT NANCY This game of African origin is played throughout the Caribbean as far south as Cartagena, Colombia, and in the Gulf Coast states of the U.S.A.

Among the Hausa and other peoples of West Africa, the Spider is known as Anansi, the most clever of animals. (In the Old Testament of the Bible one reads, too, that: "The spider taketh hold with her hands, / And is in kings' palaces.")

Anansi appears in some myths as an assistant to the chief of the gods and in others as a trickster so clever that he frequently outtricks and outwits himself. In fact, the reason he is so small is because he played a trick on a poor chameleon who got the better of him because Anansi outsmarted himself.

Anansi suffered a sea-change when he sailed with the West Africans

96

for the West Indies. He became Annancy and the Aunt Nancy of song and rhyme: "Go tell Aunt Nancy, / Go tell Aunt Nancy, / Go tell Aunt Nancy, / Her old gray goose is dead. / The one that she's been saving . . . / For a feather bed."

Rhyme and song turned into various games, one of which is played by small children in groups of a dozen or so. In this game, one is selected to be Aunt Nancy, another the Fox, and another Mother Goose; the rest are goslings.

At the start, the Fox is in his den, and Aunt Nancy is telling Mother Goose to look after herself and the goslings while she (Aunt Nancy) is down at the river washing the clothes.

No sooner is she gone than Fox comes in and entices Mother Goose away and takes her to his den.

The goslings then form a ring and chant:

> Go tell Aunt Nancy,
> Her old gray goose is gone.*

Aunt Nancy comes back, scolds them, then tells them to take care of themselves while she is down at the river doing the washing. And she leaves. The ring of children chant:

> She left nine little goslings,
> Behind the barn alone.

The Fox comes in and entices a gosling away. The ring of children chant:

> The Fox, he came and took one,
> And now there's nine less one.

Aunt Nancy returns, scolds as before, then returns to the washing, after cautioning them again.

The Fox comes and entices another away. Children chant:

> He took two little goslings,
> And now there's eight less one.

Aunt Nancy keeps coming to see the goslings, scold them, caution them, and returning to the wash. The Fox continues to entice goslings away. Children remaining chant:

---

* Note: In all verses of the rhyme, the first line is chanted three times.

He took three little goslings,
And now there's seven less one.

He took four little goslings,
And now there's six less one.

And so on until the Fox comes for the last gosling, who chants as she or he goes off, "Who will tell Aunt Nancy, / The Fox took every one? / And now there's [*very loud*] none!"

"None" is the signal for Aunt Nancy to appear and Mother Goose and her goslings to rush out of the den and chase the Fox, who must try to get back to his fox-hole without getting caught.

If a number greater or less than twelve play the game, the numbers in the rhyme are changed accordingly. A large group should be broken up into smaller ones, for too many goslings make the game tiresome.

CATCH IT, CATCH IT, PUT IT IN THE BASKET   This is an on-going tag game among the children in Louisiana, who are American Indian, Spanish, French, black African, and English. It was no doubt a myth of the Kono people of Sierra Leone, Africa, at one time. But it underwent a change when it arrived in the bayou country, where the magic of children turned it into a tag-and-hide.

The myth as told in old times in Louisiana went something like this:

The Bat was sent to the moon with Night shut in a basket. He was told to leave Night there so that it would be always Day on earth. Well, on the way to the moon, Bat saw some delicious fruit growing on a tree near the path and, putting the basket down, he stopped to pick and eat it. Cat, who happened to be passing by and who, as everyone knows, is the most curious of animals, saw the basket on the ground and Bat eating fruit. Cat wondered what was in the basket and, making sure that Bat didn't see or hear him, he crept over and began to sniff.

Night, hearing the sniffing, knew it was Cat and she said in a tiny voice, "Let me out, Cat. It's me, Night."

And Cat, who everyone knows loves to prowl in the dark, let Night out.

And that's why there's Night and Bat has to sleep and rest all during the daylight so that he can catch Night and put her back in the basket.

The game of Catch It, Catch It, Put It in the Basket goes like this: Supplied with a bouncing ball, children stand in a circle. Bat is selected by some counting-out method, such as pointing to a player on each word of:

> Oysters grow on live oak trees;
> Patates in the ashes for Old Brother Silas.
> Old Brother Silas, the patates are done.
> Old Brother Silas, choose you one.

The player "one" falls on is Bat, who is given the ball. He walks round the outside of the circle, bouncing the ball. Suddenly he steps inside and quickly bounces it in front of a player, saying, "Catch it, catch it, put it in the basket." That player must catch the ball on a bounce and throw it to Bat, who must catch it and tag the player with it before the latter can run away and hide. If Bat succeeds, the player becomes Bat, and Bat takes the player's place in the circle. If Bat fails to tag the player, the latter goes off and hides. (Bat must tag within the circle or within a previously agreed upon distance from it.)

Game continues until only Bat and one player, now called Cat, are left; all the others have hidden. Bat then quickly throws ball to Cat and runs off. It doesn't matter whether Cat catches it or not; he must chase after Bat and try to tag him with the ball. But Cat must not permit Bat to lead him so far away that he will not be able to find any of the others. Cat must tag someone other than Bat, either by touching that player with the ball or tossing it at his feet. The first player tagged, whether Bat is or not, must help find and tag the others until all are captured. If Bat is tagged, he must help too. Last one caught is the next Bat. Only Bat and Cat may use the ball to tag.

CHO-CHO-CHUCKIE   "Cho-cho-chuckie" sings out the Afro-Brazilian farm child, calling the chickens to her, to feed them. Cho-Cho-Chuckie is also the name of a kind of circle tag, one of the various sea-changes which an old legend of the Fon people of Dahomey in Africa underwent when it came to Brazil. The legend goes like this:

The Fon noticed that the Portuguese who came from Europe to trade were always the first ones in the marketplace in the morning. They sat there all day long and stayed until after everybody else had gone home. No matter how early in the morning the Africans came or how late they left in the evening, the Portuguese were sitting there in the same place in the market.

Finally, the Fon decided to stay up all night and find out when the Portuguese merchants came and when they left. So, late one night, the

Fon went to the market, but, alas, only to find that the Portuguese had gone, leaving hollows in the ground where they had been sitting. The Fon filled the hollows with black warrior ants and hid behind the trees to see what would happen.

Just before cock-crow, the merchants arrived. They sat down, then jumped up and ran off with loud cries. And that made the Africans laugh, because they looked just like frightened chickens scattering with noisy wings and raucous squawks, in all directions.

Small children enjoy the game of Cho-Cho-Chuckie either indoors or outdoors. One is It, who carries a large sponge. The rest are players who sit in a ring, legs out, facing one another.

It runs or skips around behind them. Now and then It says, "Cho-cho-chuckie," as though calling chickens. On one of the cluckings, It drops the sponge behind a player. That player must get up, pick up the sponge, run after It, and try to hit him before he can take the player's place.

If It reaches the player's place safely, he stands there on one foot, holding the other up with his hand. The player becomes It. (Players may change from one foot to the other as often as they like, but if It sees anyone not standing on one foot, he calls out the name, and that person is It.)

When all players are on one foot except the last It, he shouts, "It's raining!"

Players at once raise an arm as though holding an umbrella and scatter in all directions, with It chasing them. The first one It catches is It for the next game, which may be either Cho-Cho-Chuckie or any tag game the children elect to play.

DOS Y DOS   In Spain, and in some parts of Portugal too, small boys pursue little bulls through the streets with hootings and clappings in a kind of game. But little boys and girls, not only in Spain but also in Latin America, take part in Dos y Dos wherever *corridos de toros* (bull-fights) are held.

This game is an imitation of a pass (*al alimon*) or waving of the cape between two bullfighters. To play, children march around, saying, *"Al alimon. Vamos a enfilar y dos y dos."* (Let us line up, make two rows.) They stand in two rows, facing one another, holding hands.

The Spanish and English words for the game follow:

Dos y dos, toreros,	Two by two, bullfighters,
Dos y dos enfilados,	Two by two in a row,
Al alimon, al alimon.	The pass, the pass.*

---

* During the first verse, the children step backward and forward.

Al alimon, al alimon,
Vamos a saltar;
Vamos a saltar, dos y dos,
Al alimon, al alimon.

The pass, the pass,
Let us hop;
Let us hop, two by two,
The pass, the pass.†

Al alimon, al alimon,
Vamos a correr;
Vamos a correr, dos y dos,
Al alimon, al alimon.

The pass, the pass,
Let us run;
Let us run, two by two,
The pass, the pass.‡

Al alimon, al alimon,
Vamos a volar;
Vamos a volar, dos y dos,
Al alimon, al alimon.

The pass, the pass,
Let us fly;
Let us fly, two by two,
The pass, the pass.§

Al alimon, al alimon,
Pasen los caballeros;
Pasen los caballeros, dos y dos,
Al alimon, al alimon.

The pass, the pass,
Let the gentlemen pass through;
Let the gentlemen pass through,
    two by two,
The pass, the pass.||

THE FIGHTING COCKS   This is a game played by children the world over and is as traditional as the raising of chickens and breeding of fighting cocks. The bloody spectacle and gambling sport may have almost disappeared from most lands, but children still go on with their cockfight game in the Philippines, Peru, the West Indies, American Indian reservations, and other places.

Players divide into pairs each of which draws a circle five or six feet across. If there are many players, they take turns playing in several circles.

Each player of a pair in a circle clasps his hands underneath his knees, with his fingers entwined. Hunkered down on their heels, players jump and bump against each other, mimicking cocks fighting. Each tries to push, bump, or force the other player out of the circle and win the match.

---

† During the second verse, the children hop, let go hands, whirl about, and grasp hands.
‡ During the third verse, the children drop hands, run standing still, whirl about, and grasp hands.
§ During the fourth verse, the children step backward and forward, thrusting their hands and arms upward.
|| During the last verse, the children raise their arms to form an arch, and two by two, peel off from one end of the rows and go through with quick glide-steps.

Sometimes the game is complicated by having players match rhymes or give opposite terms. When a player in a pair fails to come up with the rhyming word or the opposite term at the count of five, the other may shove, push, or bump the player and he must not return the action. Thus in a matching rhymes cockfight, one player says, perhaps, "Sister," and unless the other comes up quickly with a rhyming word, such as "Blister," the first has the right to give him a push or a bump with his shoulder to force him toward the edge of the circle. In using opposite terms, the first player may say, for instance, "Pull," and the second player must say before the count of five, "Push" or any other word that is the opposite of pull.

Kites as Mythical Creatures
And as Playthings

KITE CONSTRUCTING AND flying is an ancient activity still carried on around the world. In the West, the kite is simply a toy to fly on a windy day in big, clear, open spaces or from big, flat rooftops in town and city.

Kites have different names in different countries. "Kite" is an English word. In France the kite is called *cerf-volant* (flying stag); in Japan it is *tako* (octopus); in Germany it is *drache* (dragon); in some places in China it is *feng-cheng* (wind bird); and in India it is given the name *patang* (feather).

In the East, kites have mythological, legendary, and historical associations, represented by different shapes, colors, and ornamentations that are traditional with a locality, country, or people.

FANCY KITE CONTEST Fancy kites are traditional with the Chinese, Koreans, Japanese, Siamese, Malays, and others throughout the East, where professional kite makers construct them to represent birds, fish, or mythological and legendary creatures, or create new forms and designs that are individual works of art. In Honduras, Central America, the tradition is to build big kites, some of them six or more feet high. Children are experts in flying them. But it is the young—sometimes old—amateurs who, in the East as in the West, make a

103

hobby of kites and create their own fancy varieties for the springtime kite-flying contest.

Kites may be square, rectangular, triangular, box, or any other shape, but they must all fly. They are painted to resemble different things: hawks, carp, tigers, dragons, monsters, and so on. Or they may be just funny-looking people with movable arms and legs which flap in the wind. Fancy kites are painted with glaring colors and the figures on them as large as possible, so that they may be seen from a long distance. In the United States, when contests are held in connection with local drives for funds for any community cause, the kites carry slogans, cartoon figures, and ingenious eye-catchers of all sorts.

Often hummers are added. They are made with a bow or a strip of thin wood or bamboo, and a string of nylon cord or even a rubber band. One is fastened to the kite top to make it hum when flying.

Judges award prizes (different colored ribbons) for the most beautiful, most unusual, funniest, most original, best singer (among kites with hummers), highest flier, etc. The more prizes the better.

KITE FIGHTS   These contests are traditional in Japan, Korea, and China, among other lands. For a fight, or "gathering" as the Koreans call it, sturdy, simply constructed kites are needed. The strings partway down from the kite are brushed with glue mixed with some sharp substance, such as powdered glass paste, or the pounded up bits from a broken flowerpot or cup, making the string like rough sandpaper. When strings on fighting kites rub together one can cut the other.

The gathering is held in an open field on a sunny, breezy day with just the right amount of wind to keep the kite flying vigorously.

The rule is that any kite may be cut down by any other. Fliers maneuver their kites so that strings are crossed, often several of them. The moment a kite falls, it is recovered, fixed, and put back into the gathering. As in automobile races, kite-fliers should have standby crews who make repairs quickly.

KITE BIRD, FLY UP AND TAKE MY TROUBLES AWAY   A tradition among some people of Korea and Malaya is writing the year's misfortunes on a kite, in the form of a bird, and flying it as high and as long as possible. In this way, the kite-bird carries troubles away and the kite-flier can start afresh.

Any group of children can try setting down some things they wish would go away on portable, roll-up kites and sending them up. This kind of kite is made of two slender pieces of wood, attached together at a common center in such a way that they may be closed to lie one atop the other, or opened out to form a cross. The covering of thin cotton material is fastened to the crosspieces with adhesive tape. Kites can be carried easily to any flying place. If transparent plastic film such as that used for garment bags is the material, writing may be done on adhesive tape and affixed to the film.

KITES WITH FANUS   Fanus are little lanterns. Children in Iraq make them of two wire hoops to which the corners of thin translucent colored paper squares are pasted. They place tiny candles in them and hang them on a return string alongside the regular kite string.

Steps in Making Fanus

Overlap corners of squares and paste them together. Then paste one hoop (hoops can be made of light picture wire) on the overlapped corners to form the bottom of the lantern. Cut a circle from the aluminum foil and, if necessary, paste that down inside the hoop, letting it overlap the hoop's edges. Turn down the corner of one square over the second hoop and paste in place. Do the same with the other square. Put paste along edges of both squares of paper to hold them together, thus forming the lantern. Take the candle and stick the four pins in it to make a candle holder. Place candle in lantern, and tie lantern to kite return string by handle made of string or light picture wire.

Kites with fanus are flown at night, and they make a lovely slight. When ready to fly such a kite, carefully light the candle and pull the lantern up toward the flying kite. Several lanterns can be attached to one kite return string. Let them hang there until the candles go out.

Because fanus are a fire hazard, they must be handled with great care and flown only in safe places. Less hazardous fanus can be made

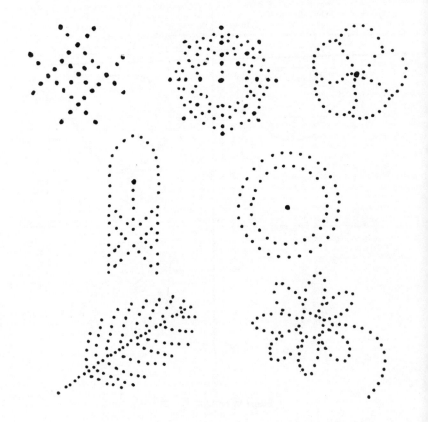

entirely of aluminum foil. It will probably be sufficient to fold them rather than paste them. Prick designs in them with pins. Make the designs on paper first; then lay paper on foil and prick through the paper. Foil makes handsome lanterns, resembling the beautiful punched tin lanterns of Mexico and other Latin American countries. The illustration shows several designs.

For absolutely safe kite-flying with paper fanus, paint them with colors that glow in the dark.

Kite-flying has spurts of popularity which die down rather quickly, but it remains an on-going activity with some children in practically every nation.

The following safety rules of the Detroit Edison Company should always be observed:

1. Construct the kite frame of lightweight wood. If nails or pins are used, be sure they are covered to eliminate the chance of cuts, scratches, or torn clothes.

2. Control the kite with stout, dry, all-fiber cord. Avoid metallic threads or wire—they can cause shocks if touched against electrical equipment.

3. Change altitudes by letting out or reeling in the cord. Prevent trips and falls by keeping the cord off the ground, wrapped tightly on a spool or stick.

4. Pilot a kite with alertness. Sudden gusts of wind may cause loss of balance or pull the control cord quickly through the hands, leaving a bad burn.

5. Select a kite-flying site away from trees, highways, railroad rights-of-way, and overhead lines. Kite flying is most fun without all these obstacles.

6. Abandon any kite that gets tangled in a high tree or overhead wires. No attempt should be made to retrieve it.

7. Never fly kites near electric wires and television antennas.

8. Never use metal or metallic string.

9. Never climb poles.

Traditional
Ball Games

MANY BALL GAMES, such as Hurling and Baseball, have venerable traditions. Certainly, ball games are universally popular.

HURLING   This ancient Irish game is still a tradition in Ireland, and in Cornwall and Devon in England. It is a fast, running, highly competitive game that few or many may play as individuals, or as teams.

Two goals are established at considerable distance from each other, in order to allow for much running. A 3-inch ball of wood (or regular softball) is advanced toward the team's goal by catching and throwing it among teammates, and by carrying it. The ball must not be kicked.

Players are not tackled by opponents, but caught. A player, upon being caught by an opposing player, must try to throw the ball to a teammate before the opponent can grab it. As soon as an opponent touches the ball, he claims it and puts it into play for his own team.

Players agree upon points for goals and winning score before game starts.

For play streets and playgrounds and the like, children prefer using a football smaller than regulation size instead of a softball.

ONE OLD CAT   This game—like Stick Ball, Scrub, and Long Ball— is an elementary form of the traditional Baseball of the U.S.A. that has spread to most of the world's lands.

One Old Cat can be played indoors or outdoors by boys and girls of around ten or so. Space required is approximately 30 by 50 feet. No boundary lines are needed, for all balls hit are considered fair. Equipment needed is a ball and a regular baseball bat or a broom handle.

Fielders are scattered over the whole playing area. At one end of the field is the base; at the other, home base. About two-thirds of the distance from the home end of the field is the pitcher's box.

Players cannot be run off the base as long as one player is up at bat at home plate. Three strikes are "out," but there are no foul balls. As soon as a player hits a ball, he must run for base. Batter is out when the ball is caught on the fly, or is picked up after it falls and carried to base before batter reaches it.

BASEBALL IN PANAMA   Children of Panama play a version of the formal U.S. game of Baseball. In an outdoor area, mark four bases and baselines—a diamond. For two teams of six or more players on each team, it affords a good game.

First team up to bat stands by home base. The other team has a player on each of the other bases and scattered about the field. Batter throws the ball in the air and tries to hit it well out in the field, but inside the baselines. The opposing players try to get the ball and tag the runner by throwing the ball and hitting him. (Use a soft ball.) The runner is safe if he is on a base when tagged.

The next player hits the ball and runs. First player tries to run to the next base, or on around to home base, if he can. When three players are out, the teams change places.

A run is scored when a player succeeds in running around and touching all the bases without being tagged. Each inning requires that both teams have a turn at bat. A game has nine innings. The winning team is the one with the greater number of runs at the end of nine innings.

ROUNDERS IN NEW ZEALAND   This is an outdoor game for two teams with the number on each side depending upon how many players there are. A tennis racket and ball are used. A fairly large play area is needed, with four bases marked as in a regular baseball diamond. The pitcher's box is in the center. A pitcher and catcher are chosen for each team.

First team up to bat stands behind home base. The other team's pitcher takes his place in the pitcher's box, the catcher behind home base, and the fielders scatter about the playing field.

First man to bat stands by home base. Pitcher throws ball underhand over home base at a height between knee and shoulder of batter. This is a fair ball, which batter tries to hit. If he does, he drops the racket and runs to first base, on to second, third, and home if he hits the ball far enough. Fielders try to catch ball in air as this puts the whole opposing team out and the teams change places. If they cannot catch the ball before it touches the ground, they stop it and try to tag the runner out with the ball in hand, unless he is safe on a base. If he is tagged out, he may not come up to hit again during the current time his team is at bat. Unless a ball is caught on the fly, a whole team must be tagged out before teams change places.

A batter must run to first base on every hit, fair or foul. If the pitcher fails to throw a fair ball, the batter may walk to first base. As no two players may be on the same base, a player already on one must move to the next base, or on around until he reaches a free base, or home. Players may not be tagged out while doing this.

Objective of game is running safely around all three bases and reaching home. Each player who does so scores one run for his team. Winning team is that with greater number of runs at end of a certain number of turns at bat by teams, the number of turns being set before the start of the game.

Part IV

GEOGRAPHY AND CLIMATE AS MOLDERS OF PLAY

Beans, Peas, and Marbles As Universal Playthings

THE SAME TYPES of topography are found all over the world. Hot, sandy deserts exist in North America as well as in South America, Africa, Asia, and Australia. There are mountains, grasslands, and watersides everywhere on earth.

Whether dwellers sought to change their geography (there is growing concern today over the changes man has made and is making in planet Earth) or simply accommodated themselves to it, the regional elements, which include climate, suggested and often largely determined how they worked and lived and, indirectly, the games their children played.

Beans and peas are of many kinds. Some are so very tolerant of soil and climate that few lands, regardless of geographical region, are without their beanstalk or pea patch. Linked to peas and beans is the game of marbles.

Marbles is a children's game so old that its origin is lost in the distant past, and so widespread that it is known from one end of the earth to the other. Nuts, small spheres (⅓-2 inches in diameter) of stone, glass, baked clay, hollow steel, or other material are used to play with. The common name of the game, however, is derived from the fact that at one time the spheres were generally made from chips of marble.

Growing out of common natural materials, utilized with skill and imagination, bean, pea, and marbles games occur in infinite variety.

112

MANKALA   This favorite African game owes its popularity to Shamba of the Bonnet, who was king of the Bushongo people of the Congo and one of the great rulers of historical times. He was famous not only as a man of peace for his abolition of cruel weapons and efforts to abolish warfare, but also as author of inventions. He traveled widely for the sake of his people, bringing back to them useful crafts and new products, plants, and foods, and, not least, the Arabic game with the Egyptian name of Mankala, to replace the gambling to which they were much addicted.

The game is played by two people, young or old, with beans and two rows of six or seven holes dug in the ground or carved in a 3-foot-long board. Large circles drawn on paper may substitute for the holes.

Players sit opposite each other at the sides of the rows. Before the start, five beans are placed in each of the holes when fourteen holes are used. (Four beans are the usual number for a twelve-hole game.) Objective of the game is acquiring the most beans.

Each player in turn begins by taking the beans out of one hole in his row and distributing them, one in each hole, clockwise around the holes as far as the beans will go. The game continues with players in turn picking up beans and distributing them clockwise until a player finds—after he has deposited all the beans of a hole—that the hole in which he put the last bean contains two, three, or four beans. When this occurs, the player removes those from that hole and the beans from all the holes back of it until he reaches a hole which contains one bean or five or more beans, whereupon he must stop.

Caution: While collecting beans, a player makes sure to take beans only from holes on his opponent's side or row of holes, even though he (the one playing) has just deposited them.

When a hole contains more beans than can be distributed around the holes without repeating a hole, a player distributes them, starting with the hole at the end of the row at his opponent's right, and removes beans according to the general bean-hole rule above.

Other rules include:

1.   When a player finds two, three, or four beans in each of the opponent's row of holes, he ordinarily would take them all. But in this case, because it happens so rarely, the player *cannot take any beans at all* from his opponent's hole, but must continue to distribute the beans he has.

2.   Beans may not be taken from only one or the other end holes of an opponent's row.

3. A player's turn consists in his distributing the beans of only one hole.

4. A game ends when there are six or fewer beans in the two rows.

5. Winner is the player who has beans remaining after distributing five beans in each of the seven holes on his side.

BEAN HOLE TOSS   Since the climatic limits to growing beans and peas are very flexible, the game is played by children wherever these legumes are plentiful in both temperate and tropical regions.

From the northerly areas of West Africa comes an indoors-outdoors version for three players. On flat ground dig a cup-size hole; for a cement or wood surface, use a small metal bowl which makes a delightful sound like splashing rain when the beans hit it. A weighted paper container serves well, too. A small brush and paper plate are needed for collecting scattered beans.

Scratch a tossing line 3-5 feet from the hole or bowl (distance depends on age and ability of players). Each of two players has fifteen beans; the third player has the brush and paper plate.

First player holds the beans in his hand and throws them underhand at the hole, trying to get as many in it as possible. Those that fall outside the hole are left; those inside, the player picks up. Second player follows. Third player brushes up the scattered beans and tosses them. If he gets all in the hole, he's the winner. If he fails, the player having the most beans at the end of four or more rounds is the winner.

HABA GABA   The name of this beanbag toss for two to six players means literally "French bean" from *haba,* a Spanish word for bean, and *gaba* (short for *gabacha,* "Frenchy"). It became popular in Sierra Leone ("lion mountain" region in West Africa), which was settled by the British for black Africans who had fought on Britain's side in the American Revolution. They called themselves Creoles, and developed their own language, Krio, a form of English with many Spanish, French, and Portuguese words. The game was also played in neighboring Spanish and Portuguese Guinea and French Senegal.

To play, one or more beanbags are needed, and a board or a large piece of corrugated cardboard with three holes numbered 1, 2, 3 of different sizes (2, 3, and 4 inches in diameter) at top, center, and bottom of it. Set the board so that it slants away from players at about a 45-degree angle.

Make a throwing line ten feet or so from board. If different ages play, have several tossing lines. Players take turns pitching the bags through the holes for one, two, or three points, according to their numbers. When four or more play, they rotate keeping score and picking up and throwing back beanbags to tossers.

An inning consists of eight to ten tosses for each player, and game goes to the player with most points scored after three innings.

BEANS AND PEAS ESTIMATING   This is a guessing game for old and young. It is likely to turn up almost anywhere: Puerto Rico, Mexico, Australia, Jamaica, Italy, Spain, Venezuela, which has scores of varieties of red, black, and white beans, or at a school carnival or fair in England, Canada, or the U.S.A.

Needed are pint-sized containers of glass or other transparent material. Fill them with six to ten different kinds of dried beans and peas, both domestic and foreign, which are locally available. Coffee beans, red and white kidney beans, lima beans, peabeans, soybeans, chick peas, field peas, and sugar peas may be used. Number the filled containers and place them on a table.

Prepare cards for the guessers with the following column headings: Container Number, Kinds of Beans or Peas, and How Many Guessed. Give each guesser a card. Guessers then pass around the table and fill out their cards. They should not take too long over their guesses.

Small prizes may be given to those who come nearest to the correct number in three out of five guesses, three out of six, etc. Other prizes for identifying correctly the kind of bean or pea also may be given.

Children in cities and towns usually don't know the names of the different beans and peas; so it is a good idea to list the varieties and then help the players identify them before the contest.

Children who will not be participating in the guessing enjoy helping to prepare for the event by estimating the number with which they fill each container. They may use any method they choose to obtain an accurate estimate. For example, fill a 2-ounce measuring cup, count the beans or peas, then see how many cups it takes to fill a pint container. The resultant count will be accurate enough.

BEAN GO   This Japanese game for two is played with soybeans and green beans, peanuts (unshelled) and red kidney beans, or other distinctive pairs. A board, piece of paper, flat ground, or cement is ruled into squares, 29 squares up and down and 31 squares across (fewer or more in odd numbers may be used if desired). Players in turn place one bean at a time on any square they wish. The objective is enclosing opponent's bean in a diagonal square. Each bean as it is enclosed is removed from the board.

When one player has board covered with his beans, he wins the game.

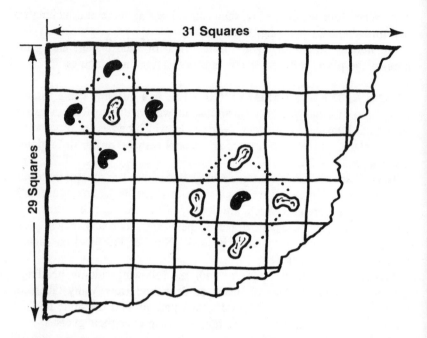

One rule only must be observed: first encircler keeps opponent's bean and his own beans cannot be retaken in that grouping.

When Bean Go flags, play Five Beans in a Row on the same squares. Each player's objective is getting five of his beans in a row in any direction—vertical, horizontal, or diagonal.

FIVE CURD-BREAKERS CUTTING THE BEAN CURD   In a series of poems, Fan Cheng-Ta gives a picture of country life during "a golden year" in olden days in Soochow district, China. When autumn brings a good harvest and the "day of double brightness" (fall equinox about September 23) comes, the big clay storage jars are crammed full of beans and corn, and little children play at cutting the *taofu* (soybean) curd. Actually, this favorite bean curd is cut with "breakers" in ½-¼-inch cubes for use in stews and soups.

Children play in groups of five, one of whom in each group is the "caller" as in a country reel in England or square dance in the U.S.A. or Canada.

Four Curd-breakers make a square, standing one at each corner, with the Caller in the center. Before the start of the game, the Caller explains what to do when the different instructions, or calls, are given. Here are some suggested calls, with their corresponding actions:

1. Cut the bean curd from corner to corner. (Players skip diagonally and change places.)

2. Cut the bean curd up and down. (Curd-breakers go bouncing tiptoe along four sides of the imaginary square until each Curd-breaker is back where he stood at the beginning.)

3. Two by two, back and forth across the river. (One pair then the other on opposite sides skip forward, pass each other, skip backward to their places.)

4. Fetch your clogs, it's raining. (Players run diagonally to opposite corners, then walk back to their places as though they were wearing clogs.)

5. Frost on the ground, slide across. (Players sit down, clasp hands around knees, and don't budge.)

Any Curd-breaker that the Caller can drag to the center of the square becomes the next Caller.

Once they get started playing, children like to make up their own calls and actions.

BEAN FEAST   The annual dinners, called "bean feasts," held by employers for their workmen in England and in almost every bean country of Europe and North America, gave way to such feasts and feeds for any occasion for jollification. There is no better way of winding up camp time, a games tournament, day camp, or neighborhood playground season than with a children's bean feed. Boys especially like them.

ENGLISH NINE HOLES   In this game players bowl marbles at a cardboard bridge with nine arches. Each arch has a number, and the Owner of the Bridge pays that number of marbles to the player who shoots through it. Marbles that miss the arch aimed for are taken by the Bridge Owner. Objective is winning as many marbles as possible during play, which continues as long as the players wish, or until all but one or most of them are out of marbles.

The game also may be played without a Bridge Owner by having a common pool of marbles, players taking their winnings from the pool.

In the United States, boys formerly called the game Immies after the marbles which were cheapest.

INTERNATIONAL AIRPORT   This is a current version of English Nine Holes played in the United States, Mexico, Chile, Bolivia, and Venezuela. Method of play is the same, but the bridge with its nine arches is replaced by a long box with different sizes of gates cut in the long side. Each gate is labeled with a destination—London, Paris, Rome, Damascus, Amsterdam, Prague, etc.—and the price of the flight. Most expensive is above the smallest gate, least expensive over the largest gate. Instead of a Bridge Owner, there is an Airport Controller.

Usually "migs," "immies," or other cheap marbles are used for money, a mig representing, say, fifty American dollars, so many English pounds, or so many thousand lira, or whatever currency players choose after deciding upon the location of the International Airport.

NUREMBERG MARBLES ALLEY   The name of the game comes from Nuremberg, once the marbles manufacturing center in Western Europe.

The alley should be raised about 18-20 inches from the floor, but any hard, dent-free surface or a long table will do as well. Enclose it with a rim to prevent marbles from rolling off. Draw a ring in the center of the alley, 3-4 feet in diameter. Everyone playing puts in the same number of marbles known as gibs, mibs, migs, hoodles, immies, ducks, etc. (These are only some of the names given marbles that cost little and are to be shot at. Marrididdles are homemade marbles which anyone can make by rolling and baking common clay.)

"Shooters" are marbles variously known as taws, moonies, chinas, glassies, agates, aggies, steelies, etc. Each player may use any kind of shooter he pleases.

Players when shooting must knuckle down fairly, that is, place the knuckles of the shooting hand on the surface so that the flip of the thumb is not aided by a jerk of the wrist.

All first shots must be made from any point within a hand's span of the rim. Subsequent shots are made by the player from the spot where his shooter comes to rest.

Objective of game is shooting the marbles out of the ring. Winner is player who shoots most out in any one game.

RING TAW   This is a version of Nuremberg Marbles Alley played in Thailand, Burma, Laos, and Vietnam, where the children usually toss or pitch marbles instead of "shooting" them with thumb and index finger. They pitch them from a pitching line around the outside of the marbles' ring.

MARBLES TOURNAMENTS   For a boys' and girls' marbles tournament, a playing alley 20 feet by 12 feet on hard smooth ground, cement, or other hard surface, is needed. A ring 10 feet in diameter is drawn in the center and 13 marbles arranged in a cross within the ring. Six play at a time in the preliminary eliminations and two only in the championship matches.

Each player in turn knuckles down and shoots from outside the ring line at any point, trying to knock one or more marbles out. He continues shooting from the spot his shooter comes to rest each time until he fails to knock out a marble. Then he picks up his shooter and waits for his next turn to shoot. He is credited with the marbles knocked out of the ring. Then they are replaced in the ring as at the start of the game, and the next player comes up to shoot.

For tournaments, two officials are needed: a referee and a scorekeeper.

TEARING UP THE PEA PATCH   This is a U.S. version of Ring Taw for 10-12 players, each of whom puts two marbles, usually steelies or chipped glassies in the pile or "pot" at the center of a small ring about 3 feet in diameter.

Players stand toeing the ring line around the pile of marbles and in turn drop from eye's or arm's length high their shooters on the pile. A player claims any marbles that he knocks out of the ring.

ZULU MARBLE GOLF   Four, six, or more holes are made in the ground at a distance from each other. Players take turns bowling a marble along the ground in regular succession into all holes. The player who completes the round of holes in fewest bowls is the winner.

SCOTTISH GOING-TO-SCHOOL MARBLES   The game received this name from the fact that it was most often played by two children on their way to school. At the start, each player bowls his marble to any distance he wishes. His marble then becomes the target at which the other player bowls. Second player must either hit it or come near enough to it for him to span the space between them with his thumb and little finger. He wins in either case and his marble remains to be bowled at by the first player. Players continue alternately until the game is won by the player who has most hits or spans when school is reached.

In England and Ireland the game was also known as Hit and Span.

GUDE   This is a marbles game played in Brazil. Before they start to play, players decide what will be won, say, two marbles from each loser. They dig three holes in the ground, four feet apart to form a triangle.

One shoots for the first hole about a foot away. If his marble goes in the hole, he shoots for the second. If he misses, his marble stays where it stopped rolling. If it came to rest in a direct line with the hole, the next player, while aiming for the first hole, tries to hit the first player's marble so that it rolls as far as possible from the hole; then he shoots again for the first hole, playing his marble as it lies.

Players go around the holes three times. Winner is he who first does this successfully. After collecting his winnings, he starts the next game.

NORTH, SOUTH, EAST, WEST, AND BIRDS IN THE BAMBOO

This Chinese marbles game is played with two marbles, usually glassies or chinas. These are placed on the ground, and several players kick them in turn so that one marble hits the other and sends it in the direction that the player names: north, west, etc.

A turn lasts until a player kicks "birds in the bamboo," which means he fails to hit the other marble at all or to make the hit marble go in the direction named.

Pastimes of the Hot and The Cold Desert Dwellers

ALTHOUGH THE SAHARA is the biggest desert by far in the world, and the Atacama, stretching along the west coast of South America, the driest on earth, they are basically part of an immense belt of deserts—rocky, sandy, mountainous—that encircles the globe. The belt extends eastward from Cape Verde on the coast of West Africa, across Arabia, to the end of the Gobi Desert, through Australia, and clear around to, and including parts of, the Americas.

The tundra, a treeless plain characteristic of northern Arctic regions, runs across the top of the earth from Alaska to Labrador, from Lapland across Siberia to the Bering Strait. Its soil is black and musky, but the permanently frozen subsoil, permafrost, contains thick masses of roots of mosses and lichens, the chief food of reindeer and caribou that dig it up with their hoofs.

In this cold desert of the north, conditions are severe and, until recently, ways of life changed little, but the land is vast and beautiful. Here live northern nomads: Eskimos, Lapps, Khanty, Mansi, Nentsy, and many other peoples.

Almost inevitably, desert conditions impose the nomad's way of life upon people. Wherever grass grows, there goes the desert family in search of pasture for its flocks and herds. A way of life for thousands and thousands of years, nomadism is as scientific an adaption to natural environment as seasonal agricultural migrations are to modern man-made conditions under which families go where the crops are ready for harvesting.

From ancient until present times there has been continued conflict between nomadic and settled peoples. Feuding went on between peasants of Iran (Persia) and nomads of Turan; between roving tent-dwelling people of the camel and the farmers in Syria, Palestine, Lebanon, Afghanistan, Arabia, and Algeria; between the Indians of North America and the white settlers and homesteaders encroaching on the red man's hunting grounds, and among countless other groups over the earth where feuds grew out of natural geographic conditions.

Children's games reflected these feuds. Here is a vigorous outdoors game from Iran that is typical, suggesting the basic conflict of land and crops to be protected from nomads and their foraging animals.

NOMADS AND SETTLERS   Children choose up sides—Nomads and Settlers. The latter gather as many sticks and stones as desired and place them within a large circle drawn on the ground. Then, clasping hands, they station themselves all around inside the circumference to prevent the Nomads from entering and obtaining any. Nomads draw an outer circle around the Settlers' circle at a distance of ten or more feet between the circumferences. Space between the two circles is No-Man's-Land. Nomads station themselves behind the line of their circle and charge the closed circle of Settlers, with the aim of making off with as many sticks and stones as they can. Settlers attempt to prevent their entering the circle by keeping tight hold of hands. Nomads may not use hands but must try to push through or dodge under, using heads and shoulders.

When a Nomad succeeds in entering the Settlers' circle and grabbing some sticks and stones, he must be allowed to leave without hindrance. Once outside No-Man's-Land, however, he may be chased and captured there. A "capture" consists of tagging the Nomad with the palms of both hands.

Settlers learn to be cautious about chasing Nomads, since it takes a moment for the other Settlers to close the circle, and that gives some quick, clever Nomad a chance to dart inside. A captured Nomad is out of the game, which continues until all the sticks and stones have been taken by the Nomads, or all the Nomads have been captured by the Settlers. This is a fast game, so no player is out of a game for long.

RAZZIA   The name of this game means "raid." It is a variation of the game of Nomads and Settlers. As soon as a Bedouin boy of the

Arabian Desert is seven or eight, he helps herd the sheep and goats. In the past, he also had to help guard them against raiders, who were once a constant threat like the rustlers in cattle country of Argentina, Australia, Canada, and the United States.

Razzia is a rough-and-tumble for two teams, called Raiders and Protectors, of a dozen or more. Sides do not have to be even; there may be fewer Protectors than Raiders. One or two sticks represent the flock of sheep or goats, around which the Protectors form a circle. Upon signal, the Raiders rush up and form an outer circle four to five feet away, standing back of a previously drawn ring. Raiders' objective is obtaining possession of the stick by first "cutting out" or enclosing Protectors in order to take it without interference.

Two or three Raiders enclose one Protector by joining hands and keep him enclosed until they can get him past the boundary of the outer circle and out of play. A Protector must keep arms at sides in struggling to get free. He may push, shove, and try to duck under Raiders' arms, but he is not permitted to strike or kick.

Protectors cut down the number of Raiders by grabbing both hands of any Raider before he has a chance to join hands with another Raider for an enclosure. A Raider who is thus "unhanded" cannot play. It takes only one Protector to unhand a Raider, for Raiders are not permitted to grab, only to enclose.

As soon as the ring of Protectors is broken up and the stick seized, the game is won and Raiders become Protectors. If, however, Protectors succeed in cutting the number of Raiders down to one or two, Protectors are declared winners.

GOATS AND CAMELS   This is a kind of Ninepins often played by Bedouin and other desert children during an encampment on the journey to new pastures. It helps them pass the time while herding the kids and lambs.

If the camp is beside a stream, they make goats and camels and lambs of mud which they let dry in the sun. If it is a dry camp, the children gather small round stones. Each child has ten or more goats and camels, kids and lambs, with which he makes a ring in the sand.

In turn each player says to the others, *"Taal shûf"* (come and see), and the others go and try in turn to "buy" one of the animals by tossing a stone and dislodging it from the ring. A player continues to "buy" until he fails to knock a beast from the ring. Winner is the player who succeeds in buying the most.

WILD HORSES   Little boys and older girls of the Berbers, who live in northern regions of the Sahara, play this in the cool of the moon-light evenings. The girls find a high rock upon which to climb, and there they sit, clapping hands and chanting some refrain such as:

> Wild horses,
> Wild horses
> Run, run away!
> Wild horses,
> Wild horses,
> Run, run around,
> Run fast today!

And they shout, urging on the boy-horses and boy-jockeys, who course hand in hand in pairs round and round. The boy of a pair who runs in front is the horse; the boy behind, the jockey. Horses are per-mitted to kick out to try to prevent another horse passing them. The horse and jockey ahead after rounding the course three or four times is the winning pair.

DOWN COME THE TENTS   After the evening meal when the moon is shining bright this game is played by many small children of the nomadic Berbers, the Tuaregs, of the Sahara. This people, called "the veil wearers" because the men wear veils, are tent-dwellers of the Hog-gar mountain range and sandstone plateaus, who travel great distances, making their living by trading and raising sheep and goats and one-humped (Arabian) camels. As soon as the grass gives out, families strike their tents and move to new pastures.

At the start of Down Come the Tents boys are seated in one part of the area, girls in another. Upon a clap of someone's hands, they all stand up, join hands, and form rings of three or four in each ring. Then they begin to whirl with long, gliding steps toward the center of the area. They whirl faster and faster until they break apart, at which point they quickly sit down, letting arms hang loosely and heads droop.

WINDING ROUND THE REEDS   The *kella,* or water tower, is the tower of strength of the old Semitic phrase to the nomads and travelers of the sandy belt that crosses Asia through central Iran and the Gobi Desert. There, in some of the driest and hottest land in the world, water is a priceless gift. And a well, its drum turning and buckets spilling water into a cistern, is an object of ancient worship. A game known to different peoples by different names links the drawing of water with the water-elder tree, reeds, and rushes that live by the waterside.

To play Winding Round the Reeds, any number of small boys and girls stand in a line, holding hands, with the two or three tallest, who represent the reeds or turning drum, at the end of it. The rest, beginning with those behind the reeds, start to wind around, encircling them. They say as they wind, "The reeds grow thicker and thicker; the reeds grow thicker and thicker."

When all have wound round tightly, they peel off one by one, all except the reeds, and scatter to hide. The reeds must then hunt and find them.

DRAW A PAIL OF WATER FROM LAME TIMUR'S WELL   An ancient well, looking like half an enormous orange, stands beside the old road into Samarkand in the Hungry Steppe region of the U.S.S.R., where, with the help of modern irrigation, the scorched plain produces grains and other crops. The legend is that the Tatar-Mongol conqueror Timur the Lame, known as Tamerlane, had such wells built a day's journey apart for caravans on the old road from Samarkand to Tashkent. They were really fortresses in which were a spring or well and shelter for a caravan with as many as fifty camels. People and animals were allowed to drink their fill, but there was so little water in the parched land that no other use was permitted.

People came to regard the wells as sacred, as people tend to regard most wells in dry, hot lands. Rituals and games related to wells were practiced and became widespread, with the result that children in places as far away from Tamerlane's fourteenth-century well as England and Scotland or as close as Afghanistan, Turkey, or Greece play Draw a Pail of Water in one or another of its many variants.

To play, small boys and girls (those nine or younger seem to enjoy the game most) gather in small or large groups that are multiples of four. To start, four players stand in a square, grasping hands across corners (arms and hands form an X), with other players standing around them in a circle.

The four pull backward and forward, chanting:

> Send a lady's daughter
> To draw a pail of water.
> Father's a king and mother's a queen
> And two little sisters dressed in green.

They repeat this a number of times before they raise their hands and sing out: "One in a rush," "Two in a rush," "Three in a rush," etc., then suddenly name a player in the ring around them.

The player named must rush under the raised hands and stand next to two of the players, as in the diagram.

Chanting continues until another name is called and a second player rushes under and stands opposite the first rusher, with whom hands are joined (see diagram). Successive twos grasp hands, and join in pulling backward and forward, and chanting until no more can possibly grasp hands, whereupon they all shout: "One rush, two rush, three rush, four rush, and all under the bush rush!"

And everyone sits down quickly.

MOJAVE DESERT CYCLE HOUNDS   This is a modern adaptation for desert sands of the old English chase game of Hare and Hounds. It is a motorcycle competition run on the sands of the Mojave Desert in California, but boys and girls who are good bicyclists can have fun competing wherever plenty of space with sandy dunes is available.

The "hare" is whichever player is in the lead of the race at any particular time; all other players are "hounds" trying to overtake and pass him. First to pass is then the hare; first to overtake that hare becomes the hare, and so on.

They follow a double-loop marked trail, with checkpoints, which is laid out as in the diagram. The markers which mark the course are

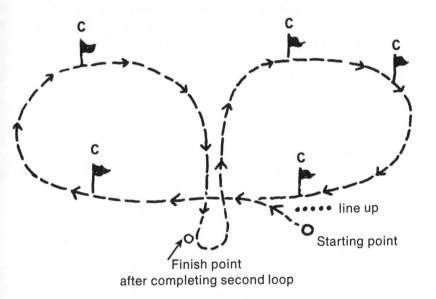

Finish point
after completing second loop

white pennants on sticks. Those with red pennants are checkpoints at which riders must stop to get their cards signed by the checker and the time entered. Winner is the rider who covers the course in the fastest time. This cycle chase in sand, though slower, demands considerably more skill than racing on dirt.

CAT AND LYNX   Among the experts on animal character and behavior are the Bushmen of South Africa, who live in widely scattered groups through the central Kalahari Desert and in districts about the Ovambo River north of Damaraland. From their study of animals, they have learned to appreciate all their characteristics and personalities. They are proud of their ability to act out animals.

In this chase game for two, the Cat and the Lynx, and the spectators, all the players have a chance to express what they feel and know about the two animals.

Lynx, the fastest runner in the forest,* is always It chasing Cat, the quickest of wit but the most boastful of creatures.

Any large area indoors or out is suitable for the chase. Line out a rectangle twenty-five feet wide and fifty feet or more long. Place haphazardly within the space six or seven large cartons. Players divide into two teams; one team stands at one side of the rectangle, the other team at the other. A player from each side draws straws to see which team is to be Cats and which Lynxes. Then the first player in the Lynx team confronts the first player in the Cat, and they exchange disparaging remarks in Bushmen fashion, rather like this:

> Lynx: Good morning, stupid Cat.
> Cat: *You* call *me* stupid? Ha, ha, ha. I'm the most cunning animal in the forest and you know it.
> Lynx: You're not as cunning as you think, and you can't run as fast as I can.
> Cat: Oh, you're the one who runs fast. Ha, ha, ha. But if you don't think I'm cunning, try to catch me.

No matter what dialogue the two players make up, the key words for the start of the chase are "try to catch me." As soon as he says them, Cat darts off and Lynx gives chase, weaving in and out among, round

---

* The cheetah, an East African big cat, is the fastest of the land mammals, and has been clocked at 55 miles an hour for up to half a mile or so. It is long-legged, lanky, and sway-backed. Indian princes once used the cheetah for hunting. The lynx is the fastest cat the Bushmen know.

and about the cartons. They must not move the obstacles or even touch them so as to jostle them; players must walk and run in as catlike a manner as possible. Lynx must not reach over a carton to try to tag Cat, but must tag his back while running after him.

Players on both teams, watching the chase, clap and count, "One and, two and, three and, four and," on up to "twenty and." If by that time, Lynx has not caught Cat, he returns to his team and Cat to his; second Lynx goes and challenges second Cat, and the game continues in the same way. If, however, Lynx catches Cat, the latter must join the Lynxes.

If, after all the Lynxes have chased Cats, some Cats have been caught, then the Lynxes have won the game. But if all Cats have managed to escape, the Cats have won. When all the Lynxes have chased Cats and all the Cats have been chased, the Cats turn into Lynxes and the Lynxes into Cats.

LYNX AND SNOWSHOE RABBIT Western lynx range mostly in Alaska and Canada, where the snowshoe rabbit abounds. The lynx has long, sturdy legs, broad feet, and hindquarters so well developed that when it walks on level ground it appears to be walking downhill. The rabbit that developed snowshoes on its hind feet—hence its name, snowshoe rabbit—is the only rabbit that is as speedy as the lynx.

Eskimos, old and young, enjoy play in imitation of animals, and this is a chase-game in which they wear snowshoes and try to catch one another as lynxes and rabbits.

Small or large groups of children can participate indoors or outdoors in this adaptation. It also makes a good party game for any age.

Supplies needed are grocery bags (one for each player and extras for replacement), lengths of stout string, and a whistle, rattle or other sound-maker.

Players are divided into Lynxes and Rabbits. Lynxes put the right foot in a bag and tie it on about the ankle with string. Rabbits tie a bag on the left foot. Lynxes and Rabbits then stand alternately about two feet apart in a circle. Upon signal, they start to run, each runner trying to tag the runner ahead. When tagged, a runner stops, takes a step to the left and stands still. Players continue to run around the outside of the circle formed by the tagged runners until four or five runners remain. Then one of the tagged players is given a whistle, which he blows at intervals. Remaining runners must change direction whenever he whistles. Chase continues until one runner remains.

FOLLOW THE REINDEER As the Indians of the western plains of

North America followed the buffalo upon whom they depended for food, clothing, and shelter, various native peoples of the Arctic tundra, such as the Eskimos and Lapps, followed and depended upon the reindeer, or caribou, as the Eskimos called them. Among the Lapps who are scattered on the northern fringes of Norway, Sweden, Finland, and Siberia in the U.S.S.R., some still cling to the old customs of the reindeer nomads. Siberian Lapps may at times be following their herds only jet minutes away from Eskimos tending their herds of native caribou or imported reindeer in Alaska and Canada.

Follow the Reindeer is a walking team race for boys and girls, all ages, playing either indoors or out. It is more fun outdoors, however, for players have a better chance to improvise. The game is imitative, patterned by children at times after the meandering movements of reindeer foraging for moss and lichens in the frozen subsoil, and at other times after a dancer's pantomime of a great migration to summer or winter pasture.

Players divide into Reindeer and Herders, one Reindeer pairing off with one Herder, and scatter over the playing area. The deer should wear some sort of head gear to distinguish them from Herders.

Upon signal Reindeer begin to move around, walking and stopping as though grazing. Herders move when Reindeer move, stop when they stop. It is to be noted that reindeer herd the herder rather than the other way round.

Objective of the walking race is the catching of as many Reindeer as possible within a time limit set before the start. Limit is usually from five to ten minutes.

Reindeer may be caught *only when in motion*. Fast walking, but absolutely no running, is allowed. Variations in pace, quick stops and starts, and changes of direction afford much more fun for everyone than just fast walking. Herders must catch half or more of the Reindeer within the time limit for their side to win. When they win, Herders put on Reindeer's headdress and become Reindeer for the next race.

DEER-BONES' STRING CATCH   This is a game of skill and pass-the-time known in many variations throughout the cold northern deserts of unbroken daylight in summer and darkness in winter. It is designed for limited space and limitless time. It is most often played during the winter nights by children of reindeer peoples—Finns, Lapps, the Chukchis, and others of Siberia; the northern Koryaks and Lamuts, and the southern fishing, hunting, dog-sledding Kamchadales of the Kamchatka Peninsula between the Sea of Okhotsk and the Bering Sea.

To make the deer-bones' string, boys and girls gathered the dry, small bones (usually the ankle bones of deer) and strung eight to ten of them, small end of the bone down, loosely on a thong. At one end they added a tassel of pebbles in a little leather pouch. At the other or broad end of the deer-bones' string, they fastened the long bone of a bird's wing, such as that from a gyrfalcon or other great northern falcon, hawk, or sea eagle.

Sides were chosen and the first player (selected by counting out or some other method) held the wing-bone end in one hand and the tassel end in the other. Then, with an upward swinging motion, the player tossed the deer-bones' string into the air, catching the first bone of the string with the fingers of one hand, as it fell. The player continued catching the first bone as many times as there were bones on the string until he missed, when the string was passed on to the first player on the opposing side. When he missed, the string passed to the second player on the opposite side, and so on. A side could not pass on to the next bone until one of its players had succeeded in catching one bone the requisite number of times.

Winner of the game was the side that first caught all the bones the proper number of times. Ultimate triumph was winding up the game by catching the tassel eight or ten times.

The game is still played in the old way with deer's bones and bird's wing in isolated places, and with a string of bottlecaps, stout cord, a bag of pebbles, and a piece of wire for the bird's wing by children in modern northland towns and villages. The number of times each bone must be caught is reduced to 2 or 3, which may count 8 or 10 points, with game 80 or 100 points.

BONE HORSES   This game was similar to Deer-Bones' String Catch, but it was played by children of the People of the Buffalo, roving the grasslands of North America—Sioux, Crow, Cheyenne, and other tribes —with the small bones, 3-4 inches long, which they gathered at places where buffalo, caribou, elk, moose, and cattle had been killed. According to the shape of the bones, they were horses, bulls, cows, calves, or whatever the players wished to name them. A player, his "herd" gathered in his hand, tossed it up in the air, calling out as he did so what animal or animals he was going to catch. If he succeeded, he continued to play until he missed. Greatly skilled players could name three or more animals and catch as many at one time. Pebbles of different colors and sizes or little seashells serve today's child equally well anywhere.

Games Inspired
By Herding of Livestock

IN TEMPERATE LATITUDES, such as the Mediterranean region, northwest and southwest North America, and various other mountainous regions on the continents and islands, live pastoral peoples who move herds of cattle and flocks of sheep and goats with the seasons. The reason for this is the fact that lowland pastures which are available only in the winter are close to highland pastures which are available only in summer. Thus, in those places, people learned from nature to round up their stock seasonally and drive the animals to new pastures—a practice known as transhumance. Games connected with roundup and driving cattle are worldwide.

Sisteron in the highlands of Provence in the south of France, is one of the great centers of transhumance. The seasonal migration of sheep covers the roads like a living woolen blanket.

In the Valais, the French-speaking canton of Switzerland, a cowfight determines *la reine des vaches* (the queen of the cows) who will lead the herds from alp to alp, i.e., from one mountain pasture to another, and on the long tramp back to the lowland at the end of summer. The queen becomes queen by defeating all who challenge her in a battle of horns. When she has subdued her rivals, the whole herd accepts her as its leader and follows her obediently.

Transhumance is less and less observed throughout the world as the availability of conveniently packed feeds for traditional transhumants becomes more widespread.

SHEPHERD, SHEEP DOG, AND SHEEP   This is basically the same kind of hide-and-seek in the British Isles, New Zealand, and Switzerland. A Shepherd and a Sheep Dog are chosen by counting out or other method. The other players are Sheep who stand in a line. The Shepherd counts them by days of the week (Sunday, Monday, etc.) or months of the year (January, February, etc.). Then Shepherd says to Dog, "I have to go look for some sticks to build a fire to cook my supper. You watch the sheep and don't let any get away while I'm gone."

Dog barks and says, "I won't, Master."

Shepherd leaves and Dog lies down and pretends to go to sleep, whereupon Sunday (or January) tries to run and hide before Dog wakes up and catches her. If she succeeds, the Shepherd returns, counts the sheep, scolds and pretends to hit Dog for not taking better care of the Sheep. The Shepherd goes off again and the performance is repeated until all the Sheep have escaped and hidden. Then Shepherd and Dog go together to find them.

Whenever the Dog succeeds in catching a Sheep that is trying to run away, the Shepherd returns, praises him, then leaves.

ROUNDUP TAG   Boys take part in rounding up cattle and horses on ranches in North and South America, in the Camargue of southern France, and in Australia and Finland.

The Rhone delta begins at Arles, France, where the river splits into two streams, between which is a vast marshland called the Camargue. On the reclaimed salt-drenched land in the northern parts of the delta, where the sweeter grasses afford fodder, herds of half-wild cattle roam as in the days of the Old West in North America. The French can well claim that the cattle's *gardians* are the ancestors of cowboys, for the *gardians* in broad-brimmed hats, carrying rope and trident, round up the cattle for the yearly *ferrade,* or branding. It's holiday, with people from all around coming for the branding and the rodeo, which has changed very little since ancient days.

Roundups at some livestock stations in Australia include getting in the domesticated water buffalo. In Finland, Lapp boys and girls help with driving reindeer into corrals and roping them at roundup, when the deers' ears are given special notches. These earmarks are registered with the Lapland Reindeer Raisers Association, just as cattle brands are registered in the United States.

Roundup Tag is a game for boys and girls of all ages. One player is chosen to be Cowboy or Cowgirl and is given a stocking, stuffed with wads of paper, or some sheets of loosely rolled newspaper for a "lasso." To begin, Cowboy quickly lassos a player by swatting him and thus obtaining a Jackaroo (Australian for apprentice cattleman).

Jackaroo then chases another player. When he succeeds in catching a player, he calls for Cowboy to come lasso him. Jackaroo must hold the player until Cowboy can rush over and swat the player three times to acquire a second Jackaroo who must, in turn, chase and catch another player. Game ends when all players but Cowboy are Jackaroos.

WRINGING THE CHEESE DRY   Little girls played this simple game in Cornwall, England, east from the Severn Sea. There, among hills purple with heather or yellow with gorse, and the gigantic rocks, clusters of shepherds' cottages dotted the moorland. One great mass of flat rocks, in particular, was piled one rock upon the other with the smallest on the bottom, like one of the old presses in which Cornish housewives used to "wring" out the whey from their cheese. And they called it the Cheesewring.

The same kind of game is known in certain pastoral regions of most countries noted for their cheeses, notably Switzerland, Germany, Denmark, France, and Italy.

To play, girls stand in two rows and step forward and backward several times. Then they sing out:

> Turn, cheeses, turn,
> Press the whey from the curd.
> Turn, cheeses, turn,

Upon the last words, "Turn, cheeses, turn," the girls change to the opposite side, whirl about and sit down quickly. They repeat these actions and words three or four times, then all join hands and skip around in a circle.

The game can be used effectively in a program for some special occasion by providing background music and having the girls wear colorful wide skirts which fan out as the girls turn and spread out in a circle when they sit down.

Games Played
By the Waterside

THE SEA NOT only provides food for those who dwell on its shores, but also opportunities for trade with many different peoples, and for far-reaching communication. Because of these important opportunities, the seashore is an environment some geographers speak of as having an educative influence upon people. The tide, animal life of sea and shore, salt marshes, sand dunes, beaches of shingle or pebble, rocks and cliffs afford infinite variety for nature study and diversity for play, games, and contests such as sand castle building and digging "wells."

To archeologists, geographers, biologists, and others concerned with relations of living things to different conditions in different parts of the earth, it appears appropriate that civilizations began at lakesides and in river valleys. Here people could master conditions. They learned, for example, to deal with flood and drought, and to utilize what the lands offered in plants and animals. The waters afforded fishing and convenient transportation for pooling inventions and experience, and exchanging products with neighboring villagers. Among the inventions, games were not the least.

HERQR RELAY RACE   This game comes from the custom of the Danes and other Norsemen of sending an arrow (*herqr*) of iron or wood to announce the arrival of enemy forces and summon all men to take up arms. Each farmer was responsible for seeing to it that the arrow went on to the next farm.

This is a race against time, say, five or so minutes, so a timekeeper with a watch is needed. Lacking a watch, use a 3-minute egg sandglass and turn it at 3-minute intervals.

Before the start of the relay race, draw a goal line and two circles two feet in diameter with circumferences touching the goal line. Circles should be about four feet apart.

Fifteen to twenty feet in front of the goal line, draw a starting line. As many sticks (representing arrows) as there are players on a team are placed within the team's circle. Players divide into two teams with their Chiefs, and each team lines up back of its Chief behind the starting line.

At a signal, each Chief races to his team's circle behind the goal line, picks up a stick, returns and hands it to the next player in line, who dashes toward the goal line, drops the stick in the opposing team's circle, picks a stick from his own and races back to the line, and hands the stick to the next player, who repeats the performance. Opposing players should avoid physical contact, even so much as touching one another.

Winner is the team with fewest arrows in its circle at the end of the time set. This is a race that frequently ends in a tie the first few times, and thus makes a good lead-in to definite win-or-lose competitions.

FOUR-DOOR WIND TAG   There are almost as many different names and variations for this game as there are shores, such as the "windy coast" of western Africa from around Gambia to Cape Negro, and windy islands, such as Tristan, which lies past the Cape of Good Hope on the way to Australia. There the lobster-fisher families weigh down their roofs with anchor chains. Four-Door Wind Tag is a Baltic Sea version from the many islands with fishermen's cottages, all of which have doors on all four sides, for the winds blow so hard that the cottagers always leave on the leeward, or side opposite to the direction from which the wind blows.

For a group of 9-15 players, prepare four placards or directional posts—North, South, East, West—and set them up in the four directions. One player is selected to be Wind; the rest divide into four groups (not necessarily of equal number) and stand in lines 10 or so feet apart, each group facing in one direction, i.e., north, south, east, or west.

Wind runs around outside the groups, then suddenly calls out, say, "East." At once, the groups facing east and west must run around and change places. Wind must try to occupy a place facing west before East players fill them. A player without a place becomes Wind. There are going to be scrambles in the beginning until players catch on to what is the leeward or opposite direction, but the mixups add to the fun.

HOOK THE DRIFTWOOD STICK   This favorite of Greek children can be played on any soft, sandy shore. Fasten a long piece of cord to the handle from a broken cup, mug, or vase. Draw a line in the sand and put a stick of driftwood a foot back of it. From a toeline 4-5 feet away, players take turns trying to toss the hook-and-line, catch the stick, and draw it over the first line. Note: the sand must be soft in order for the hook to get under the stick when the line is thrown. When only a sandbox is available, children can play, standing around outside the box and hooking a stick or pencil to the side of the box. Players make up their own rules and points required for individual or team winners, if they wish.

CORACLE RACE   Coracle racing is common at sea-, lake-, and riverside. The light, portable, oval-shaped fishing boat of hide—or, later, canvas—stretched over a meshlike framework was made by many different peoples. It was used, and often still is, by people all over the world, including the Welsh in Great Britain, American Indians of the Atlantic seaboard, the Indonesians of Guam and other isles of the Marianas, the inhabitants of the Balearic Islands and those of the Caribbean, and fishermen of southern Spain.

By substituting tubs, large plastic washpans, inflated inner tubes of auto tires (sit on them), any group near any swim-safe water can hold a race very nearly like a race in coracles. As Jim Hawkins of Robert Louis Stevenson's *Treasure Island* said of Ben Gunn's coracle, "Turning round and round was the maneuver she was best at."

Two or more contestants, each seated in a "coracle," race to a goal a short distance away, paddling with their hands.

Partners compete in a coracle-fishing race. Each partner, seated in his coracle, holds one hand of his partner and paddles goalward with the other hand. First pair to pass the goal wins.

FISHERMEN AND GHOSTLY CHILDREN   An old custom and a tourist attraction of Japan's "iron coast," where the red cliffs are pierced by caves and there's much fishing and swimming, is the origin of this game. The big cave at Kukedo is called "the cave of the children's ghosts," and tourists entering the cave must pass among the little piles of stones without causing any to fall. The ghostly children, they are told, pile up the stones each night, and a stone accidentally knocked down by a visitor must be at once replaced.

A related game is known as far away as the Ryukyu Islands, of which Okinawa is the main island of the chain, stretching between Japan and Taiwan. Most dwellers of the Ryukyus say they have the feeling of being Japanese.

To play, children divide into two teams, Fishermen and Ghosts, with each team having a supply of stones, shells, or any suitable objects, which are then marked with the team's color.

Teams separate and run to their "caves" to hide the objects. Within a set time they return, and each team describes to the other the "cave" where the objects are hidden. Each team then goes off to find the other's hidden stones and bring them back to the meeting place. Winner is the first team to succeed in doing so. Players are not permitted to cover the objects; one must be able to see them.

In another version, only the Ghostly Children have objects and there is only one "cave." Ghostly Children, each with a stone, go hide and the Fishermen hunt for them. Ghosts try to slip past Fishermen and put stones in the cave, then remain to guard against a Fisherman coming to the cave and taking them. A Fisherman may chase and try to tag a Ghost, but a Ghost cannot tag a Fisherman. When a Fisherman tags a Ghost, he either removes the Ghost's stones from the cave or prevents him from placing one there, and the captured Ghost must join the Fishermen in hunting for Ghosts to tag them.

FISH TRAP   Riverine peoples, among them Nigerian farmers in the Niger and Benue river areas and the Congolese of Africa, originated this game. Indians around the James and Columbia rivers of North America and fishermen in Scotland also made fish traps that were really pens of stakes or stones into which they drove the fish. Lakeside people in Italy also trapped fish. Seashore traps were made so fish were pushed in by the tide and couldn't get out.

The game is for swimmers in lake, stream, or pool. One player is chosen to be Fisherman; the rest are Fish. Fisherman swims out a way from the water's edge and treads water, while Fish stand along the side. When Fisherman shouts, "Jump in!", Fish dive into the water and try to get past him without being tagged. In a pool or narrow stream, Fish must reach the opposite side to be safe; otherwise a rope stretched between two stakes at a distance from the bank or shore serves as a goal line.

Those tagged by Fisherman stand beside him and help to trap the others as they swim back and forth. When four Fish have been caught, they join hands with Fisherman, two Fish with hands clasping on each side. Only those at the ends are permitted to tag, the others forming the trap to prevent Fish (who may dive under, leap over, or use any ruse) from getting to the other side. Last Fish caught becomes the Fisherman for the next game.

Children in forest places where vines hang from trees beside the streams add a special fillip to the game by swinging across from side to side on vines, trying to avoid tagging from below by drawing their feet up as they skim past the trap.

BAT'S TOUCH   In places along the western tributaries of the Amazon and Orinoco rivers in Colombia, bats of very strange nature come in at night at windows and doors which are always open. While people sleep, bats flit about the rooms unless strings of leaves are hung round the beds. When the bats fly past, causing a breeze, the leaves rustle and the bats are frightened off.

The tag of Bat's Touch makes a good game for a party or for Hallowe'en as well as any time after dark at camp or outings, or in a dimly lighted, shadowy room. There is little danger of players being hurt in running, for the secret of avoiding being tagged is creeping about.

In preparation for playing the game, hang many strings of leaves, rattles, bells, or anything noisy from high wires running across the room or from branches of trees in the open air. For outdoor play, the boundaries of the Bat area must be clearly defined in advance.

One player is chosen Bat Catcher; the rest are Bats. The Catcher tiptoes about, trying to avoid making the strings rattle and giving away where he is. Bats move around constantly as quietly as they can among the strings of noisemakers and try to avoid getting caught. Bat Catcher whispers in the ear of the Bat caught and takes him off to Bat Cave (out of the room or anywhere outside the Bat area). Game continues until all are in the Bat Cave. First one caught is the next Bat Catcher.

CATCH THE BUTTERFLIES   This is a noncompetitive game of Tchikao Indian children of the upper Xingu River in Brazil, where they actually play at chasing the white butterflies that come in great clouds at times.

It can be simulated with groups of six to eight small children, each one of whom has a cork with a tissue-paper butterfly stuck on it. Children stand in a circle and bat the butterflies back and forth, trying to keep them in the air like a white cloud of real butterflies. Any player may pick up a butterfly if it falls, but he must not move from his place, and, when he picks it up, he must call out the name of the player to whom he is batting it. A butterfly that is out of reach is considered to have flown away.

Game continues until only one butterfly remains and a player fails to catch it when it is batted to him. Children then pick up their butterflies and go on playing as before. If the children want to see how long they can keep all the butterflies in the air someone can act as timekeeper.

LOOP THE SHUTTLECOCK   A competitive team game similar to Catch the Butterflies, this is played in Ghana and the Ivory Coast, situated just under the bulge of western Africa. Here myths of the river gods of the Tano and Bia are told, timber rides the four main streams, and coffee, cacao, and bananas grow.

Even numbers of eight or more can play, divided into two teams; Throwers and Loopers. Needed are a shuttlecock and long sticks with a loop of stiff grass rope. Africans make the shuttlecock of a corncob with a tuft of pieces of banana leaves, palm fronds, or feathers. A substitute for the stiff grass rope is a loop of wire.

Draw two toelines, 10-12 feet apart, on the ground or on the floor of an inside play area. One team, the Throwers, is given the shuttlecock; the other has the sticks with loops at the end. Teams line up side by side behind their toelines. First player on the Throwers' side throws the shuttlecock as high and far as he can toward the Loopers' side. The player who thinks he can pass the loop over the shuttlecock while it's in the air, calls out, "It's mine" and tries to do so.

If the shuttlecock falls short of the opposing team's toeline, the second player takes his turn throwing it.

If the Loopers miss looping the shuttlecock three times in succession, they lose the game. If they succeed in looping it three times in ten good throws, they win. Throwers lose after three failures to throw the shuttlecock over the opposing team's toeline; they win if the other side fails to loop it within ten tries. Loopers and Throwers change sides after each game, Loopers becoming Throwers and Throwers, Loopers.

AMAZON MAIL CARRIERS' RACE   In former days on the upper Amazon River in South America, an Indian mail carrier with down-river mail wrapped the letters carefully in a large cotton cloth which he wore as a turban. Then, floating on his back, he let himself drift downstream to the river town or village where he had mail to deliver. Whole families who lived on the banks often traveled afloat on their backs, carried down to town by the current.

Even beginning swimmers can imitate those mail carriers of the

Amazon in a floating-on-the-back race. Each contestant attaches a matchbox (the size for kitchen matches) to his forehead with adhesive tape. Then, arms held close to sides and without moving feet or legs, he propels himself by paddling with his hands. First to cross the previously agreed upon goal line with his matchbox still dry wins the race. The Amazon carriers never let the mail get wet.

WHO CROSSES THE RIVER FIRST?   This is a kind of chess-with-dice connected with the Yellow River of China. (Chinese, Indians, and Persians all had their own kind of chess played with dice.)

Near the old city of Ch'ang-an was a crossing used by merchants with their caravans and armed escorts. Robber bands often attacked the rich caravans at the crossing. This game is related to the fighting between merchants and robbers from opposite sides of the river. It was popular with ox-drivers and rivermen, old and young.

It appeals today to those who like a combination of skill and chance, something that demands a little more thought before each move than checkers and far less than chess and can be played lightly.

Prepare a playing board by drawing the "river" across the middle of a piece of cardboard or other suitable material 20 inches square. Line off each half of the board with eight squares across and four squares up as in the sketch. Make heavy lines, for play is on the lines, not the squares.

Needed for the 32 playing pieces are 16 red and 16 black checkers of wood or other substance into which a pin can be firmly stuck. The red pieces represent a merchant prince and his escort; the black, a robber chief and his band. Sides consist of the following pieces:

Red	Black
1 merchant prince	1 robber chief
4 outriders	4 robbers
4 camels	4 camels
4 horses	4 horses
3 guns	3 guns

All pieces but the outriders and robbers should bear some identification. Available and inexpensive are flag pins or pins with heads of different colors used to indicate various things on maps. The merchant prince and the robber chief may be distinguished with two flag pins or in some conspicuous way. See the diagram for the setup of pieces at the start of a game.

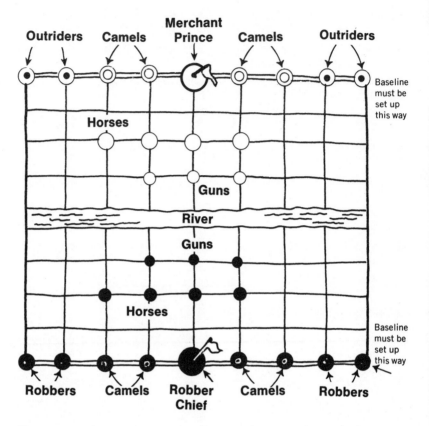

Horses can be set up on any lines so long as they are 2 squares away from base line.

Guns can be placed on any lines, 1 square away from river

The objective of the game is to block the robber chief or merchant prince so that it is impossible for him to move. The robber chief or merchant prince is often hemmed in by his own pieces, which, in turn, are kept from moving by his opponent's pieces.

Movement is on the lines from one point to another, back and forth, and diagonally in some instances. The various pieces can move as follows:

Outriders and robbers: Must always move in a forward direction. Cannot cross river.

Camels: Can move squares diagonally, but cannot jump over an intervening piece. Can cross river.

Horses: Can move two squares back and forth, jump over intervening piece. Can cross river.

Guns: Can move forward, backward, or diagonally, but in order to move, must jump a piece. Can cross river.

Merchant prince or robber chief: Can move forward, backward, or diagonally, one or two squares; can cross river. It cannot jump another piece, and is the *only* piece which cannot be jumped, but must be prevented from making any move at all.

Moves are made on the throw of the dice as follows:

Turn up 5: Robber chief, merchant prince, robber, outrider can move.
Turn up 4: Camel can move.
Turn up 3: Horse can move.
Turn up 2: Gun can move.

First player to throw 5 at start makes first move in game.

Only one absolute rule for game: touch a piece, move it. After a while, players who enjoy the game usually invent rules of their own.

CARRYING MILLET TO THE MOON This Dogon myth-related game of chance can be carried on any place where sand or mud is handy, including a sandbox.

The Dogons, whose sculpture has had great influence on modern European art, live in the African Republic of Mali which lies astride the Bandiagara cliffs at the bend of the Niger River. Their mud houses and granaries, some square with rounded corners and flat roofs, others round with conical straw hats, sit close together on rocks on clifftops and cliffside and on the fallen rocks below on the plain. They prize their granaries, for in them is stored enough food for their families not only during the dry season, but also the surplus millet, sorghum, and rice which insures them against hunger in times of crop failure. To them the universe is like a granary—its base the sun, its top the sky with the moon.

In order to play Carrying Millet to the Moon, four children must first cooperate in making a granary of sand or mud. If sand is used, it must be kept wet. The granary should be about 20 inches or so square with corners rounded, flat on top, and about 18 inches high. In each of the four sides, gouge out 5 steps, beginning about 3 inches from the bottom.

Needed are a little block of wood, sides numbered 1 to 6; a small piece of bright cloth tied to the end of a stick for a banner; and 6 shells, stones, or mud pellets (the millet) for each of the four players.

First player tosses up the block of wood. If the 1 turns up in two tosses, he puts one shell or mud pellet on the first step on his side of the granary, and tosses the block again, trying for 2. If he fails, he passes the block to the player on his left. It's only on the first toss that a player gets two chances. Game continues with players trying to get their grains of millet up the steps to the top. First to get all six to the top wins the game and plants the banner.

It is not necessary to get one pellet to the top in order to start another going up the steps. But all must be started at the first step and proceed upward step by step. Only one pellet at a time can occupy a step.

DRIVE THE SPARROWS FROM THE PEAS   A kind of hide-and-seek known on the banks of the Don River that flows through the western U.S.S.R. to the Black Sea, this game is basically the same as the game Gypsy played in the region of the Don River that flows eastward through southern Aberdeenshire, Scotland, to the North Sea.

In the Russian game, Grandmother (sometimes Grandfather) sets the children to driving the sparrows away from the pea field, then leaves them. In the Scottish game, it's Mother who cautions the children to watch the house while she's away. As the children run about frightening the sparrows off the peas, a Giant comes and one by one takes the children away with him. In Scotland, it's Gypsy who comes to the house and entices the youngsters, one by one, away from the house. Each child is hidden. When all are hidden, Grandmother or Mother goes seeking them to bring them home. Each one she finds must join her in seeking the others. The Giant or Gypsy, when all children are found, becomes the Grandmother or Mother for the next game.

Part V

GAMES OF TRAVEL
AND TRAVELERS
ON THE GREAT ROADS

Games Played on the Silk Road
From China to the West

HODOLOGY, THE STUDY of roads (from the Greek word *hodos* for road), reveals the effect of roads upon peoples and their games. To the hodologist, the scientist who makes a study of roads, the roadway is like a brand burned into the soil by man, for it marks where the seeds of man's life—houses, settlements, and towns—grow and prosper.

Roads spread knowledge and, as a result, have always been linked with learning. Even the verb "to learn" goes back to the original root which meant "to follow a track."

Since the time man made footpaths of animal trails, roads have brought about diffusion and assimilation of cultures, in particular, games and customs. Certain world-famous roads had a deep and lasting influence upon the minds and imaginations of many different peoples.

For centuries the difficult road by which silk made its way westward to Greece, Rome, and all around the Mediterranean provided the only link between China and the West. The road affected the cultures in all the lands through which it passed.

Sericulture (silk culture, which includes methods of raising silkworms and making silk) was one of the best kept secrets of all time. Chinese Princess Lei-tsu is supposed to have invented sericulture in some remote past in Shantung, and, without question, it was begun and carried on entirely by women and girls and remained for centuries a home industry.

China traded in the silk which was the chief source of her wealth and glory for almost 2,000 years, without disclosing how it was made.

From Ch'ang-an, the silk capital of Old China, skeins of silk yarn and rolls of material traveled by the caravan route from the Jade Gate at the west end of the Great Wall of China across desert and mountains to the Stone Tower on the headwaters of the Yarkand in present-day Soviet Central Asia.

It was usually a seven-month journey. Along the way were garrisons and frontier stations which served as halts for caravans and centers for news and trade. There, travelers, waiting for the next caravan or for the hour of theirs to depart, whiled away the time playing favorite games.

CHUCK STONE   The Chinese disliked going beyond the Great Wall. To them, China was both home and the world. Travelers west, upon leaving the outpost at Jade Gate for the frozen marshes and sandy wastes beyond, turned and threw a stone against the outside of the Wall. If the stone bounced off it, that meant the traveler would have a good journey and return safe and sound. If the stone fell straight down, the traveler left with a heavy heart, for that meant the journey would be long and fraught with danger.

Behind the safety of the Great Wall's outpost of Yu-men Kuan, children played at Chuck Stone. It's a game for few or many and for any age able to throw a stone with some accuracy.

Three or more piles of small stones are placed in a row about a foot or so apart. Players, each with his own chucking stone, line up and take turns casting.

A player calls out the pile and the stone he is aiming for as he throws. If he hits it, he keeps it, and continues playing. Any stones dislodged from a pile in a cast are left where they fall and used as targets in subsequent casts.

Player having the most stones after all stones have been hit and claimed is the winner.

KANG TILES   The games of Kang Tiles, Double Sixes, and Pitch Pot were all played at Lop Nor. This was not just another Chinese garrison, standing guard over the Silk Road from its small stronghold of huts clustered about a tower, but an important crossroads center. It could accommodate the big caravans with as many as a thousand camels in a single caravan-pool, in its caravanserai (literally, caravan-serai or caravan-house).

Chinese soldier-farmers, stationed at Lop Nor with wives and children, raised crops on the red clay terraces.

Persians from Iran and merchants from northern India and Central Asia halted to pasture their skinny, footsore camels; tend to the raw backs of their horses, donkeys, and mules, and repair harness, check merchandise, and patch clothes.

During the halt, they carried on trade in spices, cosmetics, glassware, and dyed textiles from the Phoenician coast and the Mediterranean, silk fabrics from India, and a host of other products.

Families, moving from one place to another, always traveled with the caravans, which traveled in convoy with companies of archers for protection against roving bands of robbers. Caravans had to go absolutely on schedule like a train, bus, or plane, for there was always the danger of water running out and, at certain times and seasons, rivers were in flood and snowstorms frequent and terrible.

Kang Tiles was a kind of "while-away" dominoes that the children played in cold or rainy weather, sitting indoors on the warm *kang,* the big platform-bed made of clay or mud which was heated from underneath.

Two, four, or six may play with an ordinary set of dominoes consisting of 56 pieces, or "tiles," by removing the blanks and any ten other pieces, so that out of the 54 only 44 pieces contain duplicates. (Children often make their own tiles today from heavy cardboard or linoleum, substituting flowers, animals, or other objects for dots, making sure that eight or ten tiles are unmatchable.)

Tiles are turned face down in front of the players and well stirred about. In turn, players take a tile and turn it face up. They continue, with the objective of getting as many duplicates as possible. Players may exchange tiles in order to obtain duplicates. Winner is player with most at end. Or, different values may be given the various duplicates and player with highest score wins.

DOUBLE SIXES   In some ways similar to backgammon, this game is enjoyed mostly by 8- to 12-year-olds. Chinese girls especially liked this game for two, although four may play as two pairs.

Needed are 32 checkers for "horses," half one color, half another. On a large piece of craft paper, on the floor or ground, draw horizontal and vertical lines to make 8 squares across and 28 up.

On slips of paper are written these directions: place horse in field (4 slips); turn to right (2 slips); turn to left (2 slips); ride forward (6 slips); jump the one in front (4 slips); gallop 6 squares (2 slips); move backward (2 slips); back to left (2 slips); back to right (2 slips); stand still (2 slips); move one horse to opponent's base and take over a square "66," which means move a horse to opponent's field and leave it on a square (2 slips). If an opponent's horse happens to be there, it must be removed and opponent must wait to draw a place-horse-in-field slip to put it back in his field. Slips are well mixed and put in a bowl from which players draw them. After each slip is drawn, it is put back in the bowl. Slips may be remixed from time to time.

Players sit at the narrow ends of the playing board and place 8 of their 16 horses on the first line of squares in their field. Two lines of squares make up a player's field. The 8 horses remaining to each player must be placed upon the field upon drawing the direction, "place horse in field," from the bowl.

Player's objective is occupying opponent's field first with his horses.

PITCH POT   This is a game of chance which grownups and children— whether Indian, Syrian, Afghan, Arabic, Persian, or Chinese—played during the halts of caravans at Lop-Nor on the Silk Road. Men played for stakes, often their camels or horses. Children sometimes played for "cash"; these were small, round copper coins with rectangular holes, *tsien*, which travelers carried by the hundreds and thousands on a string run through the hole so as to be able to count them more easily. When in Cochin China, the Japanese also made a practice of carrying strings of cash.

A variety of Pitch Pot consists of throwing arrows (use chopsticks) into any container with a narrow mouth. Any number can play.

One player may hold the container or it may be placed on the floor, with players throwing from an agreed-upon distance.

A tally-keeper is provided with a quantity of strips of scrap paper, about the size of bookmarks, for tallies, which are numbered 10, 15, 20.

Each player is given 10 throws. The first successful throw into the container counts 10 points, and each successful throw thereafter up to 5 throws, 15 points each; the next 5, beginning with the sixth throw, count 20 points each.

The tally-keeper at the end of each player's turn gives the player the proper tallies. Players must throw quickly, or the tally-keeper will call time on them. Highest scorer after all have taken turns, wins.

LAU IP TSIN   Lau Ip Tsin (also known as Five Bamboo Arrows), Meisir, Mei-ir, Hole Ball, Five Stones, and Guard Hole were played at the Stone Tower, near present-day Tash-Kurghan in Central Asia.

The Stone Tower was the last Chinese outpost on the Silk Road. Few Chinese wanted to live that far from home, so it was manned in part by Roman mercenaries whose while-away games were mostly some kind of finger changing or those played upon a diagram of one sort or another with pieces moved according to the throw of the dice. (For finger changing games, see Part I.)

As a center for East-West commerce, the shops of the bazaar were filled with goods from Mediterranean lands, the Middle East, Asia, and even the North Atlantic and Baltic Sea regions.

There was a market place for horses, camels, donkeys, mules, and even the lumbering yaks that could pick their way with heavy packs through the high, narrow, snowy mountain passes of the Pamirs. Merchants bargained hotly for the famous Fergana horses, an Afghanistan breed from around Samarkand and Bokhara.

In the open market places and the inns, travelers played games of chance while they waited for the passage of a caravan. Chinese, Persians, Afghans, Arabs, Indians, Uzbeks, and others from what is today's U.S.S.R. liked games with dice and various kinds of chess.

Lau Ip Tsin was Chinese. The arrows were given the names of different colors or different grains, such as rice, millet, barley, etc. They were given values, and players bet on drawing the arrow with the highest value. It was also much used as a means of drawing lots.

MEISIR   This game was enjoyed by the Arabs and was played with seven arrows, labeled North, South, East, West, Upper (above the earth), Lower (lower depths), and Middle (of the earth). They were shaken one by one from a quiver after the players had guessed North, South, etc. The player whose guess first proved right got to start whatever game was to be played next.

MEI-IR   This Arabic game was usually played with five marked arrows which were shaken from a holder; players, sitting around in the winter time, used to bet their camels on their guesses as to which arrow would be shaken out first, or which combination would fall first.

HOLE BALL   To play, dig as many holes in the sand or in soft ground or snow as there are players. Place the holes in a straight line about three feet apart. A small ball, stone, shell, or piece of wood is needed with which to play.

Number the holes and the players, and set a score for game, say, 25 or 30.

The first player takes his stand some eight or ten feet from the first hole and tosses the ball into one of the holes. If he succeeds in getting it into Number Five, that counts 5 for him and the fifth player has his turn next, and so on. Each player keeps his own score by writing his

name on the ground with a stick and placing a stroke for each point up to 5 and a slash across for 5, as in the diagram.

FIVE STONES   The name of the game comes from the Greek word *pentalitha* and is a game played by Greeks and others old and young at the Stone Tower, the western terminal of China's Silk Road. It was a special favorite of men who played for stakes and of girls who played for fun.

The "stones" were knucklebones, the little, knobby tarsal bones from the feet of sheep, goats, or calfs. Modern jackstones are man-made imitations.

The Chinese sometimes called the game Chance Bone and the Romans, Chios or Dogs.

To play, five (or six if desired) modern jackstones are needed for every two or three players, who take turns at the various throws. The first to complete successfully a prescribed series of throws is the winner.

First player scatters the jackstones, tosses up one stone (the Jack) and picks up one or more from the ground or table while the Jack is in the air, and so on until all stones have been picked up.

As soon as one player fails, the next begins. Before the start, players make a rule either to repeat or not repeat successful throws on successive rounds and continue from the point at which they failed.

The ancient Greeks marked the knucklebones with consonants and vowels and used them for alphabetic divination. Today's young players mark the jackstones with letters of the alphabet and in successive throws try to pick up words. For example, jackstones having the letters B, R, U, S, H or S, P, R, A, T have possibilities. Using six jackstones, the possibilities are even more for word-forming. Winner is player who forms most real words in an agreed number of pick-ups.

KAAB   This is the Arab version of Five Stones. It was and still is played by boys in the cities of Mecca and Riyadh and elsewhere in Saudi Arabia, and in many Asian countries. The boys saved the little knucklebones from the hind legs of lambs and colored them so that each boy could identify his own knucklebones. They boiled the outside skins of red or yellow onions, sometimes the leaves of henna, for coloring.

To play the game, the boys draw a throwing line on the ground, then about sixteen feet from that draw a goal line. Each player puts one of his bones on the goal line; then boys take turns throwing a bone at the ones on the ground. They spin the bone between their thumbs and first fingers as they throw it. A player hitting one of the bones on the line picks it up and keeps it. If he misses, he leaves his bone on the ground for the other players to throw at, and he loses his turn. The game continues until all the bones are hit and picked up. The winner is the player who has hit the most bones.

GUARD HOLE   This game was brought to the Stone Tower in Central Asia by Greeks, Romans, and Arabs who had gone adventuring north on the amber routes to the Baltic Sea region. Giant pine forests had died there thirty or more million years ago and left the resin that became amber, worth its weight in gold when made into figurines by Etruscan amber workers. It was considered a magical stone and was also used for jewelry. Both the Arabs and Romans used the Arabic word *ambar,* but the Greeks named it *elektron* because of its electrostatic properties. Like many later gold-seekers, these amber-seekers often returned without any hoard of the thing they sought, but with a store of information about people, their work, and their games.

Guard Hole is played by any number, usually outdoors. It is not a game for dawdlers, for speed makes it exciting. Each player has his "hoard of amber" (ten or more pebbles or pieces of wood). He makes a small pocket in the sand or soft earth and stands beside it. A light, soft rubber ball is a modern substitute for the round stone needed for rolling and throwing by the players. The holes should be either in a row or a circle, about three feet from one another.

One player starts the game by stepping back and rolling the ball into one of the holes. The player into whose hole the ball rolls takes it out quickly and tries to hit the other player. If he succeeds, the hit player puts a pebble in his pocket in the earth. If the thrower fails, he puts a pebble in his own hole.

As soon as a player has five pebbles in his hole, he is out. A large group can be divided into teams. The winning team is that with players left guarding their holes.

COUSIN JACKS   This is a version of Five Stones found in Cornwall, England. Cornish tin miners called themselves "Cousin Jacks." To Cornwall went the Greeks, then the Romans, for tin to make brass armor, cookware, and innumerable other things. Sailing out of Marseilles, once the Greco-Roman port Massilia, in what is now France, the sea merchants coasted northward with pottery, salt, and brass utensils which they bartered for large blocks of tin cast in the form of knucklebones. Returning traders often crossed the Channel to France and, with a pack train of the big tin knucklebones of Cornwall, went by the overland Tin Road down the Rhone River valley.

To play Cousin Jacks, five modern jackstones (really six-knobbed metal knucklebones) are needed. The game consists of tossing up first one stone, then two, then three, and so on, and catching them on the back of the hand.

Different throws have names: "One, pick up Jack"; "One, two, Nuggies and Buccas or Boccies"; "One, two, three, Mackerel and Scads"; "One, two, three, four, Donkeys Trotting on the Road"; "One, two, three, four, five, Horses in the Stable."

Small children find the game fun for them when they can toss a ball in the air and pick up stones on the first bounce.

CANTILLOS   Five Stones was known as Cantillos in Ecuador, Mexico, and other Latin American countries, where it was brought by the Spanish via the Romans, who played it on the Silk Road with the Chinese. And, after the Conquest of Mexico, Chinese were brought by the Spanish to Acapulco to work in the mines and textile mills. In free time, when they had any, they played knucklebone games that had been played centuries before at way stations on the Silk Road.

The Latin American version of Five Stones is played with a grass ball (substitute a soft rubber ball) and marbles or stones.

Drop twelve marbles or stones on the ground. The ball may be tossed in the air and caught before it touches the ground, or it may be tossed and allowed to bounce before being caught. Meanwhile the marbles are picked up in various ways: (1) Pick up one marble with each toss of the ball until all are picked up. Then pick up two with each toss, then three, and so on. If a player misses, another player has a turn. (2) Toss the ball and put down one marble at a time until all are down, then two, then three, and so on. (3) Toss ball and catch it on back of hand, meanwhile picking up the marbles, one, two, three, and so on. (4) Cup the hand on the ground and while the ball is in the air, push one marble into the cupped hand; on the next round push two, then three, and so on. A player may go through all the ways of picking up and putting down the marbles while catching the ball in midair, then go through the procedure again, letting the ball bounce before picking up. The game is long-lasting, so players should play at a lively rate once they've acquired skill.

In Haiti, the girls were fond of playing Cantillos, but they played it with little stones, and without any kind of ball. Since stones don't bounce, one jackstone was thrown in the air while the other jacks were scooped up.

Games Played
On the Great North Road,
Built by the Romans
In Britain

WHEN BRITAIN WAS a Roman province, the Romans built the Great North Road as part of their tricontinental road system. This network covered the whole of Europe from Scotland to the African Sahara, and from western Spain to the Euphrates River in western Asia.

The Great North Road today, as in Roman times, runs from London north through the middle of the country to Edinburgh, Scotland, some four hundred miles away. During four hundred years of occupation, Romans worked laying or repairing it. The flat, paved road was fine for games like Hopscotch and Bokelers.

HOPSCOTCH This game on the Great North Road, the way the children of Britain played it, used many different diagrams, but the accompanying one still is among the most popular.

Usually 8- to 12-year-olds play in groups of two to eight on a single diagram, although in parks, playgrounds, and on sidewalks, there may be as many as a dozen games going on at one time. It is a girls' game and few boys take any interest in it.

Here is one method of play: Carrying the puck on the back of the right hand, players in turn hop on one foot to 5, jump with left foot in 6 and right in 7, hop into 8, 9, 10, 11, 12, and jump with both feet into London. They return, hopping and jumping, to Home.

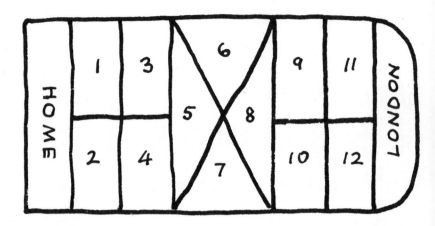

Then the puck is thrown to London from Home, and the player hops and jumps to retrieve it, and back again. The player continues to toss the puck into the squares—12, 11, 10, and so on—until she misses, steps on a line, or, while standing on one foot, fails to pick up the puck from its square and return without missing a proper hop or jump. After the first throw to London, hoppers go only so far as the square into which the puck is tossed, then return.

A variation in play is that of pushing or sliding the puck with the hopping foot, in certain squares or triangles. Another is leaping over squares, hopping on one foot, and kicking the puck into the next square or triangle with the other foot at certain points.

The Scots had a variation of Hopscotch called Hap the Beds. In the latter a flat stone was slid along from square to square by the foot on which one hopped. There were eight beds or squares one after the other, making an oblong, which were numbered except for one at each end, called "Kail-pot."

In Scottish Hickety-Hackety a pebble was used for a puck and was sometimes called the "frog." When Hopscotch reached the United States, the puck was often called the "scottie."

In Argentina, Hopscotch had the name Rayuela, which was also a name given to the game of Pitching Pennies.

Pico, Hopscotch Vietnamese style, calls for players to hop in pairs, arms across shoulders, from square to square, after tossing the pebble-puck.

HOP-ROUND   The Romans brought this version of Hopscotch from

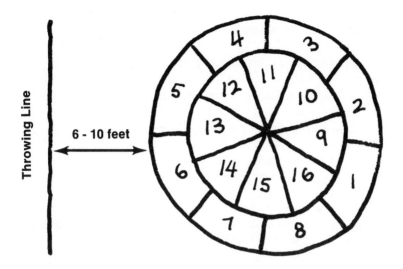

home and showed Britain's boys and girls how to play it on the Great North Road. See the diagram.

Two or more may play, with each player having five pebbles. The first player tosses the pebbles, one at a time or all at once, from the throwing line, with the objective of obtaining as high a score as possible; a pebble that stops on 1 counts as 1, another on 15 counts 15, and so on. In order, however, to secure the score, the player must hop into every sector in which a stone rests and pick it up, without stepping on a line or putting the other foot to the ground. He may claim then any sector of the rim or pie wedges, and the next player must hop over the sector, although he must not omit picking up any stone of his which has fallen or which he has cast into it.

The winner is the player with the highest score after all have had their turns, or whoever reaches a certain score first. Objective of the game is claiming as many sectors as possible.

Modern hopscotchers make their own diagrams on oilcloth or some plastic material, put on a nonskid back, and keep them rolled up until wanted indoors or outside on the ground or sidewalk.

HINKELBAAN   This game, whose name means literally "limp" or "hop-path" or "court," was the Dutch version of Hopscotch that came with the Roman soldiers, marching up the Roman roads to Britain. Its diagram contained five squares, one after the other, then two squares across, and a large square at the end. In the two squares, players must *"springen met de deide beene,"* that is, leap with both legs. Players tossed a stone into the successive squares, but they hopped on one leg only as far as the square into which the stone was tossed, picked it up, then returned.

When a player had completed the diagram, he stood with his back to it and tossed a stone over his shoulder, trying to place it in a square. If he succeeded, the square became his *huis,* or "house," and he could stand with both feet in it upon his return. Other players had to hop over it. Winner was the player to gain the most houses.

German children called the game Hinkspiel and played it the same way as Hinkelbaan. Sometimes when children had two houses, or squares, joining each other, they would permit another player to rest in one of them.

BOKELERS   This was a Roman game which the British children played on the Great North Road. Needed are five-foot poles, like billiard cues, and wooden disks about one inch thick and three inches in diameter. On the pavement draw five concentric circles, the innermost circle having a radius of about six inches. Each succeeding circle has a radius six inches larger than the preceding. Spaces between the lines of circumference are numbered, beginning at the outermost circle, 1 to 5, with the 5 a bull's-eye at the center.

Appearance of the circles should be that of an archery target lying on the pavement.

From a starting line twenty or so feet away, players prod the disks toward the target. Objective of the game is getting the disks as close as possible to the bull's-eye or on it, and knocking opponents' disks away.

Two to eight may play; usually four to eight divide into sides. Twelve disks are sufficient for four players, giving each player three shots. For eight players sixteen disks are minimum.

After all disks have been played, individuals or teams are given the sum of the numbers on the spaces in which their disks rest.

WE ARE THE ROMAN SOLDIERS   This combative game no doubt reflected the attitude of Britain's grown-ups rather than that of the young ones, who lived along Roman roads. Adults resented the Roman soldiers who cut through forest lands, building roads to make the work of the Roman governor and the tax gatherer easier and more efficient. To children, the legionaries were a source of infinite curiosity.

To play the running, scrambling tag, We Are the Roman Soldiers, divide participants into two equal sides, Romans and English. Distinguish one side from the other by bands of colored crepe paper tied about heads.

In a large open space, line off a no-man's-land about twenty-five feet wide and as long as needed for the number of players, who stand on each side and back of the no-man's-land's boundary lines.

At the start, the following dialogue takes place:

> Romans: Have you any bread and wine,
>   For we are the Romans?
>   Have you any bread and wine?
>   We are the Roman soldiers!
> English: Yes, we have some bread and wine,
>   For we are the English!
>   Yes, we have some bread and wine.
>   We are the English soldiers!
> Romans: Will you give us some of it, etc.
> English: No, we'll give you none of it, etc.
> Romans: We'll tell our magistrates, etc.
> English: We don't care for your magistrates, etc.
> Romans: Then are you ready for a fight, etc.
> English: Yes, we're ready for a fight, etc.

Everyone yells and rushes onto the no-man's-land, trying to tag opponents. A player must be tagged by two opponents simultaneously before he is captured and can be held prisoner behind the lines. A prisoner may be released by two teammates getting into opponents' territory and taking him across into their own. They cannot be tagged while going through the no-man's-land.

Winning side has most prisoners at the end of some time period, say, fifteen minutes.

This game in a way became a record of historical events, for the dialogue varied with successive invaders, beginning with the Romans. Methods of play ranged from dangerous throwing of sticks and stones to gentle, chanting circle-tags. Red Rover, Red Rover, Come Over, Come Over (the red, originally *rede,* referred to "red gold" of ancient times and Red Rover was a rover, usually a sea-rover or plunderer, with fair or reddish hair) and We Are the Rovers harked back to Vikings, Danes, and other Norsemen. These as well as Prisoners' Base and others with many different names are all forms of invader-defender games such as We Are the Roman Soldiers, and are adaptable for play in winter and in snow when snowballs are used in invading or defending territory.

KING CAESAR   This game is a reminder of Roman roads and the occupation of Britain. Details of Roman soldiers, laying a section of highway or repairing a road, attracted like magnets the local children who hung around, watching them work. From his seat on a pile of rubble, the work director seemed a Caesar in his own small way, for when he told a soldier, *"Vade"* (go), *"Veni"* (come), *"Fac hoc"* (do this or that), the soldier obeyed at once. In imitation of the work director and his work details, the British children played a game.

Any number of children of various ages can play this tag, provided there is large space available either indoors or out.

A player becomes King Caesar (It) by drawing lots or by being chosen. Players break up into groups of two or three and select sanctuaries such as trees, bushes, and the like outdoors, which they mark in some way. If indoors in a large recreation area, set up some kind of sign posts.

To start, King Caesar stands in the middle and shouts, "I say come out!" whereupon all players must run and try to exchange sanctuaries before being tagged by King Caesar. Any tagged must help him catch the others.

Taggers must say, "I've caught you" and count to five before the tagged player is properly captured. King Caesar and his men can take anyone at any time who is not actually touching a sanctuary. Players should dare King Caesar and his captives by venturing away from sanctuary before and after his command of "come out," when all are required to exchange places.

Game is ended when all are captured.

COUNT OF THE SAXON SHORE   There are echoes of Saxon and Viking encounters in this competitive tag game which large groups of young boys enjoy playing outdoors at the shore or in a park or wooded area.

Divide boys into two sides: the Count and his Shore Patrol, and Captain and Smugglers. One of the Smugglers, whose identity is kept secret from opponents, is given a little bag of salt, a piece of bright wool, silk, or anything on which the children have declared a duty or customs tax. The Smuggler with the Goods hides it somewhere on himself. The objective of the Smugglers is getting the smuggled item ashore to their *halke,* or hiding place (a certain tree or spot), without losing it to the Shore Patrol.

At the start, the Count and his Shore Patrol conceal themselves within their own territory. The Smugglers take up places all around the edges of it. When the Count says he and his patrol are ready, the Smugglers come ashore and the patrol men try to capture them. In order to capture a Smuggler, a Shore Patrolman tags him, then searches him for the Goods. He is allowed only to the count of ten, thus: "one and, two and, three and," etc. If he finds the Goods on the Smuggler, the game ends.

If the Shore Patrolman fails to find the Goods, he orders the Smuggler to raise his hands and puts him offshore again. If the Smuggler who holds the Goods reaches the Smugglers' *halke* within the previously agreed-upon time limit of 10-12 minutes, his side wins. If the Smuggler fails to reach it with the Goods, but is free on shore, the game is a tie. Smugglers who do not have the Goods should try to draw attention of Shore Patrolmen to themselves and away from the one with the Goods.

Sides can be changed after one or two games.

Foot Races Derived from
The Runners on Inca Roads

THE EMPIRE OF the Incas was a narrow strip along the Pacific Coast, stretching from Quito in Ecuador to Talca, about 120 miles south of Santiago, the present capital of Chile. Two main roads, the coast and the mountain, ran almost parallel the length of the country and were connected by numerous crossroads. All roads connected to Cuzco, the capital. About a fifth of the present Peruvian system consists of repaired original Inca roads.

Running messengers called *chasqui* (chas-kee) were assigned to relay stations called *tampus*. These were small day-rest shelters 2-2½ miles apart for two or four runners, and larger overnight houses about 4 miles apart for groups, along all the post roads. At every station a *chasqui* in brightly colored, big-checkered tunic and cloth helmet was always on watch for another brightly dressed *chasqui* coming down the road from either direction.

As soon as the watcher saw a runner, he dashed out and ran beside him while the runner gave him oral instructions and handed him a *quipu* (kee-poo), or "talking string." The watcher was now the new runner and began to race toward the next station two miles away, leaving the previous runner behind at the *tampu*.

Typical *chasqui* schedules were: Lima to Quito (over 3,000-foot altitudes in places), 3 days; Lima to Cuzco (1,230 miles), 5-7 days;

Cuzco to far end of Lake Titicaca, 3 days; Chalca, a fishing village on the sea, to Cuzco, 2 days. Modern runners testing times and distances found they had to be in excellent condition and become accustomed to the high altitudes in order to equal the *chasqui.*

Quipus, or talking strings, were usually made up of a main cord about a meter (39.37 inches) long, to which were attached separate clusters of different colored cords with knots. For instance, red meant soldiers, yellow was for gold, white for silver, green for Indian corn (maize), and so on. Various color combinations also had meanings.

Single-loop knots represented the decimal system, thus: a single knot was 10; 2 single knots, 20, etc; a double knot, 100; triple knot, 300, etc. "Long" knots (those having more than one loop) were used for the numbers 1 through 9.

Children of noble families had to study and learn to read *quipus.* Complicated official messages were read by an especially appointed group, the *quipucamayo-cuna* (kee-poo-ca-ma-yo-coo-na), or Keepers of the Knots.

CHASQUI RELAY   This game can be played as a relay race by boys and girls almost as the actual relay was carried on by the Inca running messengers long ago. Those of about eight to twelve years old especially enjoy making their own *quipus* of lengths of yarn in various colors (the Incas used alpaca, or llama wool) and knotting them in the Inca way. This relay race is a good social activity indoors or out for groups of various ages.

In preparation for Chasqui Relay, players gather to make *quipus,* basing the messages upon colors to which they assign meanings. For instance, green is for leaves, white for snowflakes, orange for parrots, etc. Knots are assigned numbers as in the Inca *quipus.* Each *quipu* should have its own mixture of several colors and knots. When ten to twelve *quipus* are ready, place them in a small basket.

Mark off a starting line and a goal line 30-35 feet away. Two players are appointed Keepers of the Knots.

Players divide into two or more teams, depending upon size of group, each team with its Captain, and form lines behind the starting line.

Keepers of the Knots call the Captains aside and whisper the same message to each of them. The message is composed by the Keepers and should consist of 8-10 words in an awkward sentence whose subject is unclear. For example, "They heard about it, but who can tell?" Or, "Take ship at sea or ship of desert, depending."

Keepers whisper slowly and distinctly. Each Captain repeats the message verbatim in whispers to a Keeper in order to make sure it was heard correctly. The Keeper hands him a *quipu* from the basket and the Captain returns to the head of his team.

Upon the signal "Go!" each Captain with his First Messenger runs toward the goal. While they run, the Captain whispers the message to him and hands over the *quipu*. The Captain remains at the goal line and the First Messenger goes back to starting line for the Second Messenger, to whom he whispers the message while accompanying him to the goal line. First Messenger remains at goal line with Captain, and Second Messenger goes to starting line for Third Messenger, and so on.

As soon as the Last Messenger on each team receives the message and the team's *quipu,* he runs and stands beside the Keepers. When all Last Messengers are with the Keepers, each Last Messenger in turn repeats the message whispered to him and reads the *quipu* of his team. Then he tries to make a sentence with them.

The messages will be unrecognizable and reading the *quipus* only adds to the confusion and to the general amusement. After the Last Messengers have finished, all players on each team have a chance to say what they thought the message was.

Suggested method for scoring teams' efforts:

1 point for each correct word in message.
2 points for finishing relay first.
8 points for reading of *quipu* and using it in sentence containing whispered message.

Highest possible score, 20 (if whispered message contains 10 words).

APURÍMAC BRIDGE OBSTACLE RACE   The Incas of South America had wheels, but they put them on playthings. They used no wheeled vehicles because their land was highly unfavorable to wheels, and they lacked draft animals. The llama, like the camel, to whose family it belongs, was useful only as a pack carrier. Nonetheless, Inca engineers built some of the world's most amazing bridges and roads, cutting stone staircases in cliffsides, tunnels in solid rock, and constructing stone steps (*patapata*) on steep hills and stairways to mountaintops in the sky.

Pedestrians, litters, and llamas with their loads traveled the roads and "the little brothers of the road," as the Incas called their equally amazing bridges. They were of two principal kinds: the reed *balsas* (boats) or floating pontoon bridges as crossings for streams in treeless country, and the suspension spans across gorges. The latter were an invention of the Incas.

The awe-inspiring suspension bridge over the Apurímac River struck terror to the hearts of Spanish gold-bearers as they stepped upon it, swinging in the afternoon winds like a hammock 118 feet above the torrent. Noted North American author Thornton Wilder made the bridge known to the world with his novel, *The Bridge of San Luis Rey,* which was translated into many languages and made into movies.

The approach to this famous bridge, as to most Inca bridges, was like an obstacle course. In modern Peru, the road can actually be taken by fit and healthy climbers who want to see where the longest continuously used bridge in the Americas—crossed by millions in its 600 years—spanned the gorge above the thunderous Apurímac, the Quechua word for "the great speaker" or "thunderer."

Large or small groups of children of various ages can pretend to climb the Inca road by having fun in this obstacle race.

Construct a course in a large open or inside space, using the following items: (1) wooden boxes or children's building blocks of various sizes to make stairs, steps, and narrow squeeze-through passages, (2) automobile tires or plastic hoops or tubes for laying on the ground in zigzags, (3) a barrel, big paperboard drum, building blocks, corrugated cartons, or anything else available that can be adapted as a "crawl-through."

The course should be intricate, requiring agility and skill, but not physical strength. Children make signs with numbers and names for the obstacles, as follows:

No. 1. Start. A zigzag of tires or hoops into each of which players must either hop or step with one foot only.

No. 2. Steps. Three boxes or blocks about a foot or so apart. Players must step on each box as though going up steps.

No. 3. Narrow passage. Blocks placed close together, leaving just enough room to squeeze through.

No. 4. Tunnel. Blocks or barrels give just enough room to crawl through.

No. 5. Stairways. Two or three series of building blocks with a step up to a board laid across to another block and a step down.

No. 6. To the bridge. Several blocks staggered in a line. Those in race must weave in and out before reaching the bridge.

No. 7. The bridge. This is the end of the course.

With a large group, players may lose interest, waiting their turn to run the course. In that case, a player with a pastel crayon (different color for each station) can be stationed at each obstacle and mark the palm of each runner as he completes the obstacle. Older and younger players can enjoy competing if older players are given a handicap, such as a little bag of sand or pebbles to carry in one hand.

APACHETAS   *Apachetas,* or "burden depositories," are as much a part of Inca roads as their *topus,* or distance markers. (Modern English-speaking peoples mark roads with signs called milestones as did the Romans. In countries using the metric system, signs give the number of kilometers.)

As soon as an Indian starts up a steep hill or mountain road, he picks up a stone to take with him. At the highest point, he drops it on the heap of stones that's there. Then down the other side he goes, feeling lighter and less tired. To him it seems he has cast off some of his fatigue with the stone. Mountain passes and high points of roads all have these small stone heaps.

Apachetas adapt very well to a lively game for parties, outings, and social gatherings. Players draw lots for Leaders, or *Curacas,* as the Indians call them, who choose sides.

Mark off two lines, one at each end of the play space. The sides line up back of the lines, one side opposite the other.

A pile of mixed nuts or peanuts in the shell are placed on the floor at the left of each Leader, and an empty wooden bowl on the floor at his right.

Upon the signal *"Vaya!"* ("Go!") each Leader, without using his right hand, slides onto the back of his left hand as many nuts as possible. He carries them across and puts them in the empty bowl on the opposite side. Players follow in turn their Leaders until their piles of nuts are gone, and the nuts are in the bowls. Winning side is first to exhaust its pile of nuts. Dropped nuts must be picked up and replaced in the team's pile.

APACHETAS RELAY RACE   This is a good social game in which players divide into teams and line up behind a starting line as in an ordinary relay race. At some distance away, on a goal line, boxes, stools, or anything of the sort available are set up opposite the teams. On each of them is placed an empty bowl.

First player on each team is given a small wooden spatula; the second player is handed a bowl of peanuts in the shell.

At the starting signal, first player on each side lifts a peanut from the bowl with the spatula and, balancing the peanut on the spatula, crosses to the empty bowl opposite and drops it in. He returns and hands the spatula to second player, who hands the bowl of peanuts to third player. Second player then repeats performance of first player, and so on until the bowl is empty. First team to finish is the winner. Any peanuts dropped must be lifted up by the spatula—no fingers allowed.

Games Suggested
By Famous Roads
Of the New World

"BY THE North Sea [Atlantic Ocean] comes every year from Spain a fleet of near 20 ships with best commodities not only of Spain but of most parts of Christendom," wrote an old Mexico City chronicler. There was another fleet just as big which touched South American ports. The fleets wintered in the Americas; then both returned to Spain with enormous quantities of gold and silver from American mines, and tropical luxuries such as sugar and cacao beans for cocoa and chocolate.

Along all the *caminos reales,* or royal roads, some of them merely mule and donkey tracks, flowed the riches of the Spanish Empire in the New World to ports all around the Gulf of Mexico and the Caribbean. It is little wonder that pirates lay off the sea lanes, waiting for the gold ships; that bandits ambushed rich pack trains on lonely trails; or that tales of lost mines and of buried treasure flourished throughout the web of *caminos reales.*

EL CAMINO REAL TREASURE HUNT   Treasure hunts have long been popular at children's parties, at outings, and on gift-giving occasions such as Christmas among Christians, and Hanukkah (Festival of Lights) and New Year's (Rosh ha-Shannah) among Jews. This is a hunt, however, for large or small groups anytime and almost any place.

Much of the fun of the hunt is having mysterious rhymes and codes

168

which point the way to the treasure. They should contain some Spanish and French words along with the English to be just right for hunting treasure on *el camino real*, especially the one that went northward from Mexico City to the Rio Grande, then to San Antonio, and on to New Orleans—a trilingual route.

Although codes should be kept simple, they should be brain teasers. The group hunts in pairs and proceeds from clue to clue until the treasure is reached. Objective is reaching it first, but not at the expense of trying to interpret the clue correctly.

One rhyme might be:

> It is an *arbol, arbre,* tree.
> It's the nearest one you see.
> Stand there, look north, you cannot fail
> To see a *boîte aux lettres, buzon,* or box for mail.
> On it there's really nothing new,
> But near it arrow points to next *piste, pista,* clue.

TREASURE MAP GAME FOR CAMINOS REALES   Two teams are chosen for this hide-and-seek. Pretending to go off with the treasure to bury it, one team hides, then sends its captain back to the other team. The captain (who should be imaginative and a good talker) draws a map on the ground with a stick, showing where his team is and the treasure is buried. He makes the map as complicated as possible with such old treasure map instructions as these:

Start where you see wrought-iron spike in oak tree (park tree protected by stakes); trail winds down a hill (any slope), crosses a ravine (any long depression in ground), turns north from fort (any building), passes mound of stones (any masonry), goes around haunted lake (wading pool), continues to right of geyser (drinking fountain), etc.

The players try to find the hidden team from the clues on the map. When they do, both teams race back to the starting place. The first to arrive with most members is the winner.

COMANCHE BALL AND DARTS ON EL CAMINO ANCHO   It is said that the name of the Comanche, a North American Indian, was abbreviated from the Spanish *El Camino Ancho*, the Broad Road or Broad Way into Mexico. Every September when the prickly pears were ripe on the cactus, Comanches rode south in land which had once been their hunting grounds but was now occupied by ranchers. They went beyond the Rio Bravo del Norte (Rio Grande), down into Mexico, making raids upon cattle and horses.

Ranchers had reason to fear the time of the Comanche moon, for, in a fight, the Indians were equal to the best in horsemanship and the use of bow and arrow.

To play Comanche Ball and Darts use a fiber ball or any ball made of soft material (for instance, yarn wound over wire frame) which can be easily pierced. It should be somewhat smaller than a volleyball. Darts can be made of large corks, two simulated feathers, and a toothpick at one end for a point. (Have a supply on hand for replacements.) Since all throwing of darts is directed downward, it is not hazardous to use a point of some kind.

A fairly steep incline on hard ground, a concrete ramp, or the small children's slide (when everyone is tired of sliding) is the place to roll the ball. A player is stationed at the top to set the ball in motion, and another at the bottom of the incline to throw it back. Players with their darts line up on each side and throw their darts at the ball as it rolls down. To hit the moving target counts ten points. If a thrower hits the ball in such a way that it can no longer roll, he's entitled to high score (twenty points), although each of the other players may toss a dart in an attempt to hit the ball for one point. Game is fifty points.

FOLLOW THE SIGNALS   This game is suggested by the Pan American Highway. The Mexican portion opened in 1950 stretches from Ciudad Juárez, which is opposite El Paso, Texas, to Ciudad Cuauhtemoc, Chiapas, on the border of Guatemala.

In South America the coastal Pan American Highway runs for miles alongside the ancient Inca road and in some places is actually laid over it. In Huncayo in the Andes, the road was first the royal road of the Indians, then the King's Highway, and now part of the modern highway.

Follow the Signals is a game for two of almost any age. It is played with a made-up road map and four miniature (matchbox) cars.

On a large sheet of paper draw a map (see suggested map) with some big squares for towns, small circles for signals, and connecting lines for roads. Write in the names of towns and Latin American traffic signals,* repeating them as many times as needed to fill the circles. Suggested signals are:

---

* A universal custom that needed no traffic signal was driving on the left-hand side of the road. This was the rule of the Roman roads which influenced traffic customs on all inherited Roman roads. The left-hand custom, however, was changed at the time of the French Revolution. England, despite the change on the Continent, held to the old left-hand side of the road.

One player places cars in these towns

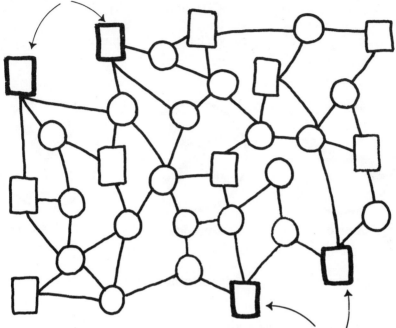

Other player places cars in these towns

No hay paso (No thoroughfare)
Cuidado con el ganado (Look out for the cattle)
Peatones obedezcan las señales (Pedestrians obey signals)
Escuela (School)
Transito (One way)
No se estacione (No parking)
Alto (Stop)
No voltear en U (No U turn)

Each player places a car in each of the two towns at his side of the map. He moves from town or signal to a connecting town or signal in turn, with the objective of overtaking his opponent and avoiding being overtaken himself. The player whose car is overtaken on a signal must remove it. A car is safe in a town and may not be overtaken there, but may not stay there longer than one move. All moves are forward, or to left and right, but not backward. Winner is the player who overtakes both his opponent's cars.

If players wish they may use symbols instead of language signals. As a matter of fact, people at the United Nations Educational, Scientific and Cultural Organization (UNESCO) have been especially interested in developing universal symbols for marking roads because of the almost impossible task of developing alphabets for hundreds of languages spoken by peoples who have not created a method of writing. See the

Curve   Crossing   Fork Ahead

picture showing several samples of symbols internationally understood. There are many more.

HUNT FOR THE LOST MINE   This is a variation of Paper Chase that used to be played on horseback in England and Scotland. Famous British author Robert Louis Stevenson played it when he lived on the West Coast of the U.S.A. and in Hawaii and taught it to his Hawaiian friends.

This version of Hunt for the Lost Mine is appropriate to the Pan American Highway, which runs through lands in North America where an expedition led by Francisco Coronado and the Black Moor scout, Ésteban, searched for the Seven Golden Cities of Cibola. And in South America, the road runs where Spanish, Portuguese, Dutch, French, and English hunted for El Dorado, the Gilded Man who, newly painted each day with gold dust, washed the gold off each night, and everywhere lost gold and silver mines abounded, according to all accounts.

The hunting game can be played with a large group of boys and girls of various ages in a large park, in woods, at beach, or at camp.

Needed are a pouch containing hand-size stones painted yellow for gold nuggets and a quantity of bamboo garden stakes (or any kind of stout sticks) to which slips of colored paper are affixed for trail markers.

Print *Más Allá* (Farther On) on all the slips except one, and on that print *Está Aquí* (Here It Is).

Three players are chosen to be Miners, the rest are Seekers. Give the Miners several minutes to start laying a meandering trail of stakes and stones. When all stones are gone, they drop the empty pouch. Within a short distance from the empty pouch, they set up the last stake, which is lettered, *Está Aquí*. The Miners then scatter and hide within a range of 60 to 70 feet.

The Seekers follow the trail and when they find the empty pouch, they look for the last marker. Upon finding it, they race off in different directions to catch the Miners, who must not move while the search is on.

Group decides before the hunt starts upon the number of points to be given for finding: (1) a trail marker, (2) each nugget, and (3) each Miner.

STICK COUNTING   Along the Alaskan-Canadian, or Alcan, route built up the northwest coast of North America to Alaska, small children on farms and in villages and towns play this old Indian game.

Throw small sticks, all about the same size, onto a pile. Players in turn run past the pile and snatch up some, with the objective of snatching as few as possible. The number of sticks picked up by each player is counted and a score kept. The sticks are put back every time so that all have the same size pile to snatch from. The one who has picked up the fewest odd number of sticks wins. Number of times players must snatch sticks for game is set before the start.

Games Spread
By Wayfarers
And Peddlers

GAMES PLAYED BY men, women, and children who passed up and down the earth's famous roads and highways reflected not only peoples' diverse heritages, but also the common experiences of all travelers.

The English-speaking peoples say, "A rolling stone gathers no moss." But the Chinese say, "A stone that rolls shines. People, like separate stones, need to rub against one another to become polished and to shine. And to travel a lot is to be polished by many different kinds of stones."

What land was without its road, what road without its peddler? A famous Chinese painting called "Five Hundred Articles" shows one of China's many knickknack peddlers with his tall bamboo baskets, their tiers of trays loaded, swaying at the ends of a long pole over his shoulder. Among the 500 articles are house and garden wares, masks, butterfly nets, and, of course, toys, for what peddler was without toys when at each farm he would be surrounded by children as soon as he stepped into the dooryard?

There would be rattles, shinny sticks, battledores and shuttlecocks, and all kinds of tops: peg tops, conch-shell tops, whipping tops, humming tops (a hollow body caused the hum), whirligigs, teetotums, and even more.

"Mercachifles" (peddlers of trifles) the Spanish called these mer-

chants of the road with toys and tops. In Britain, the merchant with his pack on his back—"a trunk with many kinds of things"—was prohibited from taking shortcuts across fields and had to keep to the roads when selling his goods, among them toys, which was synonymous with tops.

Following are some games suggested by travel or spread by itinerant peddlers.

BAGHDAD JOURNEY   A jingle recalls the time when Baghdad was "a city with no peer throughout the whole world" and a Caliph's wealth was measured in perfume instead of petroleum:

> King Charlemagne back from Baghdad came
> With many gifts from the Caliph—
> A clock and a horse for the polo game,
> And an elephant for his bailiff.

It is not known that the King of the Franks who visited the Caliph and came back with those fine gifts actually rode the horse in the Arabic game of Polo when he returned to Aix-la-Chapelle, but he did ride the horse. Whatever use to which he put the elephant, he did not give it to the sheriff for the pursuit of thieves on elephant-back.

For an indoors social event, a game of Baghdad Journey can be fun for all, including the Traveler, who is chosen by lot. The journey is supposed to take place in the days when post and parcel messengers, afoot and on horseback, could be afforded only by the rich; the poor waited until a friend or relative was going on a journey and entrusted the traveler with letters and packages. Seldom did anyone begin or return from a trip without gifts and extra bundles.

Members of the company are seeing the Traveler off on the long journey to Baghdad. As the Traveler comes around to say good-bye, each individual gives him a gift and asks him to take a package to a friend, relative, or business acquaintance. Everyone gives something to the Traveler and the more unwieldy it is, the better, The Traveler must try to carry in one load as many packages as possible, to a designated spot in the room, for he must repeat trips until no package remains. Then he chooses the next Traveler.

Winning Traveler is the one who makes fewest trips.

GULLY   This was a game of tops as universal as the pothole or gully in a road, from which it derived its name. For play, choose the whipping top, which has a hard point and a peg around which to wind the string. To keep it spinning, a stick with several leather or cord thongs is needed with which to whip or flick the top. The place to play is hard ground or pavement with a gully or a shallow gutter.

First player sets his top spinning a foot or so from the gully and steps back. Then each player in turn sets his top going at least two hand-spans away from the spinning top. He flicks it with the thongs on the stick to keep it reeling toward the first player's top in an effort to knock it into the gully before it stops whirling. If he fails, he must spin his top and let the other players take turns trying to force his over the edge. Ten points for each top sent into the gully. Game is 30 points.

TOWN TOPS   These were actually tops that belonged to towns or villages in England, and were used in the yearly top-racing contests. Skilled spinners practiced throughout the year for the event. Then they sent their town's tops whipping and flying up and down the roads, "driving them giddy until they fell asleep," that is, stopped spinning and toppled over. Once the event was over, the tops were put away until the following year. (Spinners practiced with their own tops.) So "to sleep like a town top" or "like a top" meant to sleep well.

Spinners had rhyming "spells" which they said over the tops at the start of the race:

> Top go up, top go down,
> Top go all around the town.
>
> Whir, whir, swing the top round
> Spin the wheel, spin it round.

Then, each spinner made a twist of the twine, and, as he hurled his twister, the twine coiled out and the top touched the ground and began to spin. But unless the spinner urged it on with his "whip" (stick with thongs on its end), it simply went round. And they had a rhyme about this among the town-top spinners:

> A town top whirling round on the road
> Was asked by a fast-hopping toad,
> "How is it that you hobble and bobble
> But you never go forward unless you are prod?"

During the race, the spinners flicked their tops and made them do all sorts of tricks. In this they were like the professional top-spinners to the Japanese emperor, who could put on marvelous performances with tops. And Indian children of the Zuñi, Hopi, Navajo, and other tribes of

Southwest North America not only called the top *"Nimitchi,"* meaning "the dancer," but also could make their tops dance by flicking them with buckskin thongs.

Top-racing contests are full of fun and excitement, provided participants have gained skill in top-spinning by practicing for them. It is to be noted, however, that skilled spinners of eight or nine can compete on an equal basis with those much older. Skill in top-spinning is not geared to the age of the spinner. It makes an excellent activity for groups of mixed ages and boys and girls. A race course can be laid out in almost any recreation area.

TURBO   The name of the game is Latin for "spinning top," and boys of Rome scratched a design on the pavement for a game with these tops.

Draw a circle with ten unequal segments; number the largest I, next largest II, next III, and so on in Roman numerals on to the smallest, X. Using any kind of spinning tops, players set two or more whirling at a time within the circle. The number on which a top stops or falls over when hit, is the number of points its owner gains for the round.

Players themselves set points for game.

MOTECA   This is the word for "tops" in the Dominican Republic on the island of Hispaniola in the Caribbean Sea. It is played with tops and buttons. Buttons are placed on flat stones inside a circle which is drawn on the ground. Players may not step inside this circle. A player spins his top, then scoops it into his hand without causing the top to quit spinning. Then he throws the top so that, if he is successful, it knocks a button from a stone and across a goal line, drawn a little distance from the circle on the side opposite the shooting side. Player keeps the button. If he fails, the button is replaced and another player tries to dislodge it.

The winner is the player with the most buttons when the game ends.

COMMERCIAL TRAVELER   This paper-and-pencil game for one or two, or for four playing as partners, is enjoyed by young and old who like puzzlers.

On a sheet of 8½ x 11-inch paper indicate North, South, East, West. Then draw 8 squares across the sheet and 8 squares down, 64 in all. Each square represents a town, a crossroads shopping center, or a city suburb. The commercial traveler must pass through all 64 of them *just once* on his sales trip.

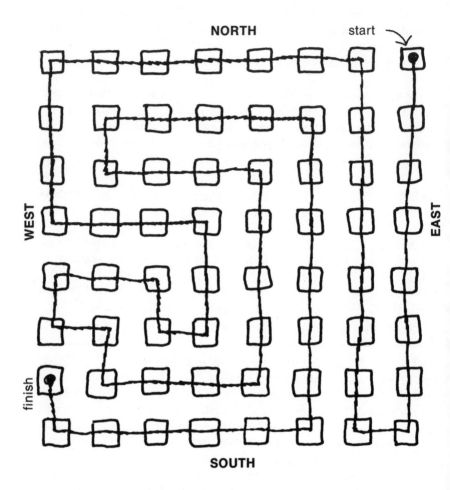

To play, start the trip at the square in the northeast corner, as in the diagram. Draw connecting roads (lines) between the towns, centers, and suburbs, completing the entire sales trip in fewest straight (i.e., no diagonals) journeys as possible. One solution is shown in the diagram.

Commercial traveler does not have to return to the starting point, but may end the game anywhere just so he has gone through all 64 squares just once. *Don't* draw line in space directly at left of starting square.

Sometimes children pretend to be foreign tourist guides on a. many-countries tour and give the squares names of different towns, countries, and historic places. Or they may pretend to be on a tour of sports spots—skiing, mountain climbing, surfing, and Olympic Games sites.

WARDERERE   A world-famous merchant of the road was the New England, or Yankee, peddler, who was usually both tinker and peddler. With a pack on his back, he bought, sold, swapped, and mended his way all over North America, through Mexico and Central America, and as far as the Andes in South America.

When he wore a pack, he rank a bell to announce his approach to a farmhouse. Later, when he had a horse and wagon, he did not need a bell. The banging and clattering of tinware hanging from strings like fringe round his wagon's top could be heard a mile away.

From tin pans, plates, and pots beyond the tinker's mending developed the game of Warderere! or The Tin Watchman, a kind of hide-and-seek that is still liked by children from seven to eleven in small or large groups outdoors.

To start the game, the player chosen for Watchman throws a tin pan or pot lid (or anything unbreakable that size) as far as he can, then begins to walk toward it, looking straight ahead. While the Watchman's back is turned, the other players run and hide. The Watchman must try to locate hiders and, at the same time, keep any hiders from running and touching the tin. Those who succeed are free to hide again as soon as the Watchman turns his back.

Watchman does not have to tag hider; all he has to do is see who and where the hider is, go back to the tin, and call out the name and hiding place. For example, "Joan, you're behind the sandpile."

A hider who reaches the tin safely calls out, "Warderere!"

Next Watchman is the first hider discovered.

While-away
Games

THE WHILE-AWAY game was always popular with travelers during short stays at inns and for tiresome stops waiting for transportation. Drovers, muleteers, and drivers of camel caravans and pack trains used it for passing the time at halts in journeys. Oxdrivers with wagon loads of timber traveling North China roads stopped regularly at certain inns at nightfall. After their evening meal, they often enjoyed a game of chance, such as Teetotum, also known as Whirligig.

TEETOTUM   Children make their own teetotums from small blocks of wood, with a peg, pointed at one end, through the center. Number four sides with the numerals 0, 1, 2, 3.

The game is played by twirling the teetotum by the peg with the fingers and guessing which side will come up when it falls over. It can be used instead of dice in many different games of chance. If desired, letters or designs may be placed on the sides instead of numbers.

SPIN-IT-OUT   This game with teetotum in which letters are substituted for numbers, is enjoyed by small children.

Three sides are lettered, say, with C, A, T, or H, O, E and the fourth side with a question mark. Objective of the game is to spell out the word "cat" by spinning until all the letters needed come up, or, if the question mark comes up, substituting any letter that will make a word. For example, if a player has A and T and the question mark comes up, player can say "B" or "M" or, if he has O and E, he can say "T" and have the word "toe."

Players take turns spinning and before each spin announce the letters they already have, thus, "I have C and A and I'm looking for a T." Letters do not have to come in proper sequence.

GOOSE GAME   A favorite at French inns and stopovers after travelers brought it back from journeys to Greece and lands around the eastern Mediterranean is this game of chance for two or four players. It has appeal for a wide age range. For youngest players, simplify by eliminating Toll Gate and Bridge.

On a large piece of paper or cardboard draw a scroll and make a

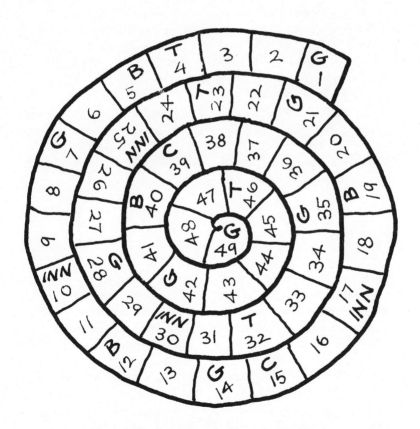

Goose Garden

"jardin de l'oie" (goose garden) by dividing it into 49 squares, numbering all as well as labeling some of them. Squares 1 and 49 and every seventh square between label "Goose." Squares 10, 17, 25, and 30 label "Inn." Squares 4, 23, 32, and 46 label "Toll Gate." Squares 5, 12, 19, and 40 label "Bridge." Squares 15 and 39 label "Cricket."

Needed to play are a button or counter of some kind and a numbered teetotum (such as is described above) or two dice. The counter is moved the number of spaces indicated on the spin of the teetotum or the throw of the dice. Special rules apply when a player's counter stops on a penalty or advantage square. Penalty squares are those marked "Inn," "Toll Gate," and "Cricket." A player whose counter stops on a square marked "Inn" must wait there, losing one turn at play. If the counter stops on "Toll Gate," he must back up one square. When a counter stops on "Cricket," the player must start all over again from the first square. The advantage squares are labeled "Goose" and "Bridge." A player whose counter lands on "Goose" may fly over the next two squares if the counter does not alight on a penalty square, in which case he may fly over that also. If a player's counter lands on "Bridge," he may cross the bridge to the square on the other side.

The first player to move through the Goose Garden and fly out at square 49 is the winner.

Played with a scroll of 63 squares and different penalties and names for squares, the game was known as Jeu de la Revolution Française (Game of the French Revolution). Players with some knowledge of the American Revolution can turn the 49-square Goose Game into Game of the American Revolution.

TIC-TAC-TOE   This is a familiar while-away for two which can be played anywhere and has been. It was scratched on the earth, pavements, and walls around the world long before there was general agreement that the world was a sphere that could be gone around.

Draw a big crosshatch. First player starts by marking 0 in one of the spaces and the second follows with an X in another space. Players continue in turn until one player (winner) succeeds in getting three 0's or three X's in a row—horizontal, vertical, or diagonal—or the spaces are filled without any rows of three, and a new crosshatch must be drawn.

FORKS AND CROSSROADS   Here is a traveler's paper-and-pen game, playable anywhere, for from two to four or more.

On a 6-inch by 9-inch card or piece of cardboard, four players take turns making 0's for farms and crosshatches, as in Tic-Tac-Toe, for towns, until they are well scattered about the page and there are about seventy-five of each. Taking turns, players then drive cars (their pens or pencils) quickly without looking, up or down the page, across, or diagonally. Each farm passed through counts one point; each town, three. The players initial each farm and town they pass through. Game continues until one player has forty points and wins the game.

Games with Links
To the Crusades
And to Pilgrimages

TRACES OF THOSE foreign wars of Christendom called Crusades survive in games whose origin lay in roadways from Britain through Europe to *Outremer* (Across the Sea)—the Holy Land of Jews, Christians, and Moslems.

HENCHMEN AND RAIDERS   During Norman times and later, pages in noble households in England were called "henchmen" because, when out on horseback with the lord of the castle, they rode on each side of his "haunch." Before they were out of their teens, many of these young knights-in-training would be off with a company bound for Jerusalem. In the meantime, they helped guard the lord and his castle. Here's a game that grew out of it. As many boys and girls as want to can play, for space outdoors is required.

A round space is marked off to represent the castle. The lord is out with a foraging party and has left henchmen behind to look after it. While he is gone, the castle is attacked by raiders.

Divide players into Henchmen and Raiders. To start, Henchmen stand on the alert as Raiders go off a distance. Upon signal, they return and try to get into the castle by crawling or sneaking past defenders.

As soon as a Raider manages to make his way inside without being seized and held by one or more defenders, he shouts, "The Hole's won!" And the Henchmen surrender.

The donjon, or keep, was the last inner defense of the castle, particularly if it were Norman. It was commonly referred to as "the Hole" and if it was won, the castle usually was won.

A Henchman seizing a Raider cries, "One for the Castle!" and the Raider must stay and help defend the castle.

GOING TO JERUSALEM   Often called Musical Chairs or The Chair Game, this game is a reminder of Crusaders' journeys and has been played by generations of children of English, German, French, Bulgarian, Czech, Polish, and no telling how many other nationalities.

Needed are a large room and chairs. Players sit on chairs, back to back. As soon as the music starts, players get up, one chair is removed, and they march round the chairs, to music. The music stops suddenly and they scramble quickly for seats. Of course, one player finds none vacant and becomes a spectator. Another chair is removed, and the game continues until only one or two players remain.

A piano, guitar, tin whistle, mouth organ, or any other musical instrument, including a drum, that anyone wants to play can provide background for marching. In the absence of such instruments, clappers, rattles, or anything to beat out a rhythm make the game just as much fun to play.

HOW MANY MILES TO BABYLON?   An English Mother Goose rhyme introduces children of nursery school age to Crusaders, Christian kings and knights who launched military campaigns in order to claim the Holy Land from the Moslems during the eleventh, twelfth, and thirteenth centuries. The game employs a dialogue which apparently tells of a knight stopping at a castle to ask directions to the nearest city, which is Babylon (modern Hilla in Iraq). The dialogue is as follows:

Knight:	King and Queen of Cantelon,
	How many miles to Babylon?
Residents of castle:	Eight and eight, another eight.
Knight:	Can I get there by candlelight?
Residents of castle:	If your horse be sound and your spurs be bright.
	How many are there with ye?
Knight:	More than ever ye dare come see.

To go via Babylon seems a round-about route for a knight from Britain to take if he's going to Jerusalem. But a Crusader was often a wandering knight who "rides from land to land and sails from sea to sea" and sometimes never got to Jerusalem at all. The number of men he implies he has with him is no doubt pure bluff.

Younger boys and girls enjoy playing this tag game out of doors. On a wide play street, mark Safety Towers at two corners across the street from each other. In an open place, estimate distance between Towers according to abilities of the children.

Two of the best runners take their stations between the Safety Towers; the other players gather around one of the Towers. The two runners go up to the Tower and ask, "How many miles to Babylon?" The others reply, "Eight, eight, and another eight" or "Three score and ten." Runners ask, "Can we get there by candlelight?" Players reply, "Yes, and back again."

With that players quickly scatter and head for the other Tower. Runners try to tag as many as they can. Those caught fold their arms and are out of the game until all are caught by the runners, or until time runs out. If within, say, 10-12 minutes the runners have not caught all players, that game is called and two new runners are chosen for the start of a new game.

HILL DILL   In this variation of How Many Miles to Babylon? the players are arranged on two opposite lines, facing the center. One player, chosen It by lot, takes his place in the center. He then calls, "Hill Dill, come over the hill, / Or I'll catch you standing still."

He claps his hands three times, at which the players run across to the other side. While they are crossing, they may be tagged. Those tagged must then help in catching others until all have been tagged. The last one tagged begins the game again.

SALADIN AT ZION'S GATE   In medieval times, Christian knights of many nationalities built fortresses on hill- and mountaintops of the Holy Land, then a part of the Byzantine Empire. Moslems laid siege to the various citadels from time to time, but with intervals of peace between sieges so long-lasting that Christians and Moslems began to feel at home and neighborly. People invited one another to camp entertainments and their children played together in mock battles.

Two major figures in legend and story of both Islam and Christendom were Saladin, the great sultan and hero of Islam, and the Christian king of England, Richard the Lionhearted, who exchanged friendly presents during a Crusade.

It is only in much later times that "Zion" came to mean the country of Zion. The word, it is believed, was derived from a general Arabic term, and a Hebrew word as well, applying to an elevation in the land or something set up on a height, thus a citadel. The "Zion" in the game is a citadel, such as Saladin's Fortress at Latakia, Syria, a popular present-day tourist attraction.

Boys and girls are divided into two groups for this gentle circle game of Saladin at Zion's Gate. Those in the first group, the Christian Knights, join hands and stand in a circle, representing the fortress called Zion. Saladin and his Moslems form a ring around the fortress. Objective of the game for those in the outer circle is to get inside Zion. Only one at a time may attempt to break through, then only when two of the Christian Knights lift their hands to form a gate or portcullis. The Christian Knights, of course, try to form the gate when Saladin's men are off guard. Both circles keep in motion and those inside sing:

> Come you early,
> Come you late,
> If you'd get in,
> Find the gate.

When all of Saladin's men have got into the fortress, groups change places and the game starts over.

EVERY WORD TRUE   Travelers on business, pleasure, or pilgrimage always encounter many diverting and strange adventures. Not the least of them is listening to accounts of highly improbable happenings and tall tales of fellow travelers.

Children of about ten and older find this game of telling implausible stories interesting for just-sitting-around fun. Before the game starts, prepare twenty or twenty-five 3 x 5-inch file cards on each of which is stated a problem that had to be solved, a fantastic situation encountered, a test of courage met, etc. For example:

Ten of us were out there in the desert with only one camel. What could we do?

We heard a dreadful noise, then flames shot out from the cave. And somebody shouted, "Dragon! It's the Dragon!"

And there right before us was a glass mountain. No way at all to get around it. Absolutely no way.

We were in just about the middle of the river in a terrible storm when the ferryboat struck something and started to sink immediately.

To start the game, distribute slips of paper and ask players to write leads into exotic, unusual, or fantastic travel stories. For example:

We were on our way to Canterbury—people from all over England were making the pilgrimage that year—when . . .

I met him in Rome on the way to the Forum. He told me that . . .

Oh, yes, I was finally able to get to Mecca. You see, what happened was . . .

I make regular business trips through Greece, buying honey, cheese, goods like that. One day I was on my way to Thessaly and . . .

In India after we visited the Deer Park near Benares where Buddha preached his first sermon, we decided to take a side tour and lost our way and . . .

As soon as a player finishes writing, he places his slip in a "journey" bag. Some players probably just can't think of anything; so at the end of five minutes, call time, for there will be sufficient journeys.

Players divide up into teams of three or four individuals. Each team draws a card from the pack of travel problems and a slip from the bag of journeys. Teammates are allowed several minutes to consult; then they take turns telling their stories in three minutes or less, beginning with the lead-in, then stating the problem, and going on into an explanation—the more elaborate and implausible the better—of how they solved the problem, met the fantastic situation, or faced the test with courage and brilliance.

All players vote for the team with the best story. Most points should be given to the most improbable. In other words, the taller the tale, the higher it's rated. Incidentally, voting for one's own team will get one nowhere.

CANTERBURY TALES   Among the most famous travelers' tales are *The Canterbury Tales* of the early English poet, Geoffrey Chaucer, who died over five and a half centuries ago. The stories (mostly in verse) are imagined as being told by pilgrims about themselves and their experiences. The pilgrims included a knight, miller, monk, cook, lawyer, housewife, merchant, parson, clerk, doctor, sailor, prioress of a convent, nuns, and so on.

The pilgrims started for Canterbury to the shrine of Thomas à Becket, the martyr, from Tabard Inn, Southwark, on the south side of the Thames River, on a warm April morning. They took the Pilgrims' Way as it was then called, the road that was followed by pilgrims from the west of England or by foreigners from abroad landing at Southampton, to reach Canterbury by way of Winchester.

To start the "storytelling game," which was what the Canterbury pilgrims called their own storytelling, players sit in a circle and, if they wish, imagine themselves on the Dover Road, which follows in part the old Pilgrims' Way, or the road to Rio, Rome, Jerusalem, or any other road.

Slips of paper and a pencil are passed round and each player writes the name of a business, occupation, or profession on the slip. The slips are gathered up, mixed thoroughly, and each player draws one.

Then start by having players draw lots, just as Chaucer's pilgrims did, to see who is to tell the first story. Beginning with the first tale-teller, go round to the left, with each relating in a few sentences an incident or account of something which contains three hints as to his assigned business, occupation, or profession. For example:

"You must believe that I am not a thief although I do take cases. It all started when the first person came to see me with a case and I simply took it. And, then, after a long argument, he paid me for taking it. What's my profession?"

The other storytellers are allowed three guesses or a few seconds to answer. Obviously, the profession in this instance is "lawyer," although it could have been "doctor" down to the last sentence, in which the hint is "argument." Thus, it is sometimes a good idea to dole out the sentences and let the other storytellers begin to guess after the first hint is given.

If a more complicated quiz-type game is wanted, storytellers divide into teams and allow so many points for near guesses and so many for correct guesses. Team with most points after all have told tales is the winner.

WOULD YOU BELIEVE THAT?   This variation on *Canterbury Tales* calls for quick thinking. It is a game for anyone who likes question-and-answer fun. In preparation for it, make up a quantity of 3 x 5-inch file cards with words that sound or are spelled alike but have different meanings: bare, bear; deer, dear; lark (a bird, and a jollification); tear (I shed a tear, I'm going to tear it up); bark (a dog's bark, and bark, a ship); road, rode; aisle, isle; band (music), band (around the head); bank (river), bank (to put money in); be (to be or not to be), bee (can sting you); bluff (they called his) and bluff (high, steep bank by river or sea), etc. Only one word is on each card, but if the words are spelled differently, there must be a card for each spelling; thus, there will be a card for "bear" and another for "bare."

The cards are passed round and the first who thinks he can use the word on his card in a sentence beginning, "Would you believe that . . ." volunteers to start the game.

For example, the player with the card on which "bear" is written asks, "Would you believe that I caught with my hands a bear cat?"

Players are given a moment to think and consult with one another; then someone volunteers to answer, for instance:

"No, I'd believe you if you said you caught a cat with your bare hands."

Or, for example, this:

"Would you believe that I saw a mouse tear a lion?"

"No, I'd rather believe you saw a mouse cry a lion-size tear."

Or for example this:

"Would you believe that a bark frightens me, but I love dogs?"

"Yes, all you're saying is that you're afraid of sailing in a bark."

TELL A TATAR TALE   This is a variant of Would You Believe That? in which words are not important, but what is left out of the account—the missing fact—is all-important. For example, here is an old Tatar telling about his braggard son:

"I never knew my son could brag so much. He's like the hunter in that old Tatar story we heard as children. The hunter told how one time he saw a huge wild animal at the top of a mountain. It was way out at the edge of a rocky ledge. The hunter climbed higher and higher until he reached the ledge; then he slowly crept up to what he saw now was an enormous bear. And he cut his claws right off."

"Cut off his claws?"

"Yes, clipped them as neat as you please. You see, a previous hunter had already cut off the bear's head and taken it with him. My son is just like that Tatar hunter. He's never been out hunting in his life, but he can tell you everything about a hunt."

Tell a Tatar Tale is best enjoyed by teams of two or three players each, who together make up tales about bragging, each with the most important fact missing. If sources for stories are needed, they are readily available from the daily newspaper, the weekly news magazine, or the newscasts over radio and television.

DICEN QUE   This game was played by twenty-two boys, the youngest four and the oldest ten, from an orphanage in Coruna, Spain, on a medical expedition to the Americas, organized in 1803 by order of King Charles IV of Spain, who was determined to wipe out smallpox not only in Spain, but in all Spanish possessions with a saturation program. This was the world's first immunization expedition.

The boys carried smallpox vaccine encased in limpid blisters on their arms.* Shortly after arrival in the New World, the first carriers were joined by twenty-six nonimmune little boys of New Spain who were one by one inoculated with the virus from the first carriers.

The boy vaccine carriers traveled with the doctors who vaccinated and set up inoculation stations as they went along. They traveled throughout the islands of the Caribbean. They went to towns, cities, and Indian villages of South, Central, and North America. They visited schools, army posts, *estancias*, and cow camps, giving training programs and recruiting local people to staff disease-prevention centers.

On the long, wearying rides on the backs of donkeys strung out on mountain roads and jungle trails, the boys played Dicen Que (They Say That), a game children still play and enjoy with few or many players. It is especially recommended for use while going somewhere in the family car, by bus, train, plane, or just hiking along. The game is sometimes called Los Embustes, meaning, as the Americans might say, "telling whoppers."

The idea is that the first person who thinks of a whopper announces that he has a *"dicen que"*; then everyone must be alert to think of the reply. As soon as the player has said his *"dicen que,"* another must try to top it with a rhyming reply.

Actually, it is a back-and-forth, gossip kind of game that can go on endlessly or until the players have thoroughly worn it and themselves out for the time being. There are frequent intervals between parts of the dialogue, and there are bursts of imagination that cause rhymes to come spinning out. A *"dicen que"* can be picked up at any time, dropped, and picked up again as soon as the mind stirs.

Here are the Spanish phrases used in Dicen Que, together with their English translations:

---

* As soon as the blister healed, it could no longer produce the needed virus for inoculation; the boy was immune to the disease, and the doctors arranged for him to be placed with a foster family or in a boarding school or orphanage.

Spanish	English
Dicen que (dee-sen kay)	They say that
¿Es verdad?	Is that true?
Que sí (kay see).	Oh, yes.
Que no.	Oh, no.
Que sí, así dicen.	Oh, yes, so they say.

Here are some samples of *"dicen que"* as the vaccine carriers introduced the pattern for it, though the gossip (the "they say that") is modernized in a combination of Spanish and English.

First player:* *Dicen que* rabbits grow as big as bears in Cordova.
Everyone else: *¿Es verdad?*
First player: *Que sí.*
Second player: And they make their lairs on stairs in Cordova.
Everyone else: *Que no.*
First and second players: *Que sí, así dicen.*
First player: *Dicen que* chickens catch and eat the foxes in Tarragona.
Everyone else: *¿Es verdad?*
First player: *Que sí.*
Second player: And they fatten them in boxes in Tarragona.
Everyone else: *Que no.*
First and second players: *Que sí, así dicen.*
First player: *Dicen que* all the fountains flow with honey in Andalusia.
Everyone else: *¿Es verdad?*
First player: *Que sí.*
Second player: And the bees fill hives with money in Andalusia.
Everyone else: *Que no.*
First and second players: *Que sí, así dicen.*
First player: *Dicen que* boys never have fights in Madrid.
Second player (after intervening Spanish dialogue): They're always flying kites instead in Madrid.
First player (after intervening Spanish dialogue): *Dicen que* all the trees are made of cork in Cadiz.
Second player (after intervening Spanish dialogue): From the trees they build the fires that roast the pork in Cadiz.

---

* The first player in each instance is the player who introduces the particular *"dicen que"*; the second player is the one who first thinks up a responding rhyme. The Spanish dialogue fills in the intervals when players think up rhymes. This is much better than the usual method in many present-day dialogue games of allowing a certain number of seconds of silence in which to think.

Tricks and Stunts
In Imitation of
Artists of the Road

WAYFARERS WHOSE BUSINESS it was to startle and amuse walked from fair to fair. There were minstrels, tumblers, jugglers, acrobats, magicians, professional storytellers, and strolling players. And there were gypsy musicians, dancers, and tellers of fortunes on roads in Hungary, Spain, Ireland, England, and most everywhere else.

You could have your portrait done in wood or the carver would put it in a nutshell. Singers commented on current events. Like living newspapers, Spanish, Haitian, Caribbean, North and South American singers recited and commented on the day's happenings, the social or political scene, to their own musical accompaniment.

Some of the tricks and stunts of these artists of the road are fun as games for social affairs, carnivals, and fairs for the young and, perhaps, not so young.

THE GREAT KHALAT OF BUKHARA, LONDON, NEW YORK, AND NAIROBI, CLAIRVOYANT IN MANY LANGUAGES The Great Khalat declares that while he is out of the room, his assistant will point to someone, and he will name the person. He leaves and stands behind a closed door.

Assistant says, "I'm pointing to someone. Who it is?"

After a moment, the Great Khalat answers, "I believe I have the name . . . yes, oh, yes . . . now it's coming clear . . . There's a "c" in the name. . . . Let's see . . . there's an "r." Ah! You're pointing at Marcia."

The trick is that the clairvoyant and his assistant arranged between them for the assistant to point to the last person who spoke before the clairvoyant left the room. Any other arrangement between them that's feasible may be used.

The Great Khalat now says that he is able to repeat any letter of the alphabet that the audience may name while he is out of the room, and he leaves.

The audience, without the assistant saying anything, agree upon a letter, say, H. Upon the Khalat's return, the assistant says, "What would you buy if you went to La Maison Française?"

"Ah, ah, I see a trick in this," says the Khalat to his assistant. He pauses, then says slowly, "I want to buy a house and you're trying to send me to the store for it. I say the letter is H, in spite of being misled."

The Khalat has translated the French *maison* to English *house*. The Spanish and Italian *casa* could be used for house as well. Players need to know but a very limited number of words in two or more languages in order to be able to play. By making ground rules about naming something in the room or immediate area, it affords a fine trick-game for bilingual, trilingual, or multilingual groups. Also the name of the thing may be used just as well as a letter of the alphabet.

MADAME MATILDE JE-NE-SAIS-QUOI READS MINDS Madame asks players to write the name of something on a slip of paper. Slips are all folded and dropped in a box, including Madame's own slip. Closing her eyes, Madame draws a slip from the box and, holding it against her forehead, concentrates for a moment. Then she names what is supposedly written on the slip, opens it, reads and nods as if in confirmation. This first time she simply names what she has written on her own slip.

She quickly draws another slip and proceeds as before, except this time she gives the name of the object on the first slip, which one of the players, of course, had written. She continues until someone catches on to the trick, or all the slips are read, including the last, which the mind reader has taken care to see is her own. Naturally, Madame must fold her own slip somewhat differently, tear a corner off it, or otherwise make sure that it can be identified by touch.

LADY MOLLY POURQUOI CAN TELL YOU YOUR THOUGHTS She can if she has an assistant unknown to the others, who is to write a particular word. Lady Molly begins by asking for four volunteers from the group. Her unknown assistant volunteers, of course. Then she asks each to write the name of something he or she is thinking of at the moment. Her assistant writes the word agreed upon before, for instance, flowers, swimming, or Portugal.

When the volunteers have folded their papers, the thought-reader places them between the fingers of her left hand, making sure to place her assistant's next to the little finger. Starting with the paper between thumb and index finger, Lady Molly rubs it between fingers and thumb of her right hand. Closing her eyes in thought as she does so, she says very slowly, "I see an O." She repeats this and uses other thought gestures as she apparently struggles to get a letter or several letters. Then she slowly puts them in sequence to spell the word. Finally, she announces in triumph, "Flowers!" or whatever the word is. "Am I right, did anyone write flowers?"

And, naturally, the assistant admits to writing the word.

After glancing at the paper, as though to reassure herself, Lady Molly puts it away. She continues the thought-reading performance with the next slip, announcing the word that was written on the first paper, and so on until all the slips have been spelled out.

BALANCING ACT   The group all get a chance to see how well they can balance a box and a small book or notebook. Two players place the objects on their heads, and the second player chases the first. The one whose objects fall first is out and chooses a replacement. Objective is staying in the game longest. All may play at the same time if there are objects available. They march round and round, dropping out as their objects fall off their heads. The last one to drop out is the winner.

DARING ARTISTES OF THE HIGH WIRE   Young children like to try to walk a chalk line blindfolded. At parties, those who succeed find cookies or lollipops at the end of the wire.

Older players may be given a spoon with a pingpong ball in it and asked to walk the chalk line blindfolded. Or a player may be asked to keep a balloon bouncing on his hand while walking the chalk line blindfolded.

AT PIEPOUDRE COURT   *Piepoudre* means "Dustyfoot," from *pied,* the French word for foot, and *poudre,* meaning powder or dust. This was a summary court set up at every fair or market to administer justice there. And many a "dustyfoot"—peddler, tinker, merchant of the road, wayfarer, strolling player, or singer with lute or guitar—was hauled before the court, for they were the first to be suspected when something was discovered missing.*

In this game one boy plays the Justice sitting on the bench, and the other children play the accused standing before him. A suggested dialogue follows:

> Justice: Did you take the gentleman's pet monkey?
> Accused: No, Your Honor, I did not take his monkey.
> Justice: Did you see the gentleman, carrying his pet monkey in his sleeve?
> Accused: No, Your Honor, I did not see him or his monkey. Until now, I haven't laid eyes on the gentleman.
> Justice: Do you have the gentleman's pet monkey up your sleeve?
> Accused: No, Your Honor, I do not have it up my sleeve. I'll show you. [*Shows he has nothing up his sleeve.*]
> Justice: Then the monkey must be hidden someplace. Where did you hide it?
> Accused: No, Your Honor, I did not hide the monkey.
> Justice: You did, I say; so you are fined two buttons [*or anything that he thinks the accused may have that is of no particular value.*] Pay the clerk.

The game continues with one accused "dustyfoot" after the other until someone catches on to the trick: the Justice closes one eye every time he puts a question, and the accused must also close one eye every time he replies. Case is dismissed as soon as an accused does close an eye in replying to one or two questions. Justice can continue until most of the group knows the trick.

Justice may use any other gesture, as subtle as he can devise, instead of the blink of an eye.

Those who have paid fines may redeem them in a forfeit game, such as Animal, Vegetable, or Mineral, in which the fines or forfeits are covered up. In order to redeem his own forfeit, a player must guess by asking questions, what the forfeit is that is held up while he is blindfolded. The other players who can see what is being held up, of

---

* This is what happened to Anne and Nick, the heroine and hero of *The Innocent Wayfaring* by Marchette Chute. New York: Scribner's, 1943.

course, reply to his questions. If he succeeds in guessing what the forfeit is, he receives his own back.

The game is also played with pictures of objects pasted on cards for forfeits which are passed out to all the players.

First Justice is drawn by lot. If game continues, the first to catch on to the trick becomes the next Justice to hold Piepoudre Court and must devise a new trick.

Part VI

GAMES AS MAGIC AND SYMBOL

Magic Instruments
And Games
For Securing Food
And Hastening Crops

THERE IS AN expression, "*Modes de vie, modes de jeu*" (ways of liveli-hood, ways of play), that has always been true of mankind since women first grew food crops about the dwelling place, men armed with stick or sharp stone stalked prey in imitation of other predators, and children observed and imitated everything, and participated in many things with their elders as well as with their peers.

Among early and primitive peoples games were a part of adult society and were sacred and magic-working for the most part. And, as one would expect, they had much to do with the insurance of a food supply for the community. Food in plenty was an expression of individual and group wealth as well as a status symbol.

People of Zambia, Africa, say that the god sent grain for man's food and told mankind to take care of it. Malagasy tell stories of the origin of rice. Sierra Leone and Guinea have little ancient soapstone or steatite figures called "rice gods." Yoruba of Nigeria say the earth gods came down from the sky on spiders' webs (cats' cradles) to see to growing things.

Dinka of eastern Sudan say farmers have to be careful in hoeing the ground, for they must not hurt the earth god. Indians in North Amer-ica, after the coming of the Spaniards, took off the shoes of their horses to keep from hurting Mother Earth. Respect for the earth and the earth's creatures was expressed in poetic legend, mythology, and magic-working games. Hence, in most cultures, no matter how sophisticated, a great number of games preserved by the young were—and perhaps still are—closely connected with the work of obtaining food and with religion and magic.

CAT'S CRADLE No sooner does a scientist state that in a certain part of the world the game of Cat's Cradle is unknown than another scientist proves the first wrong by finding a new artifact, a remnant of vanishing Old Stone Age people, or a group of modern folk who are making cats' cradles.

Makers of cats' cradles are creating simple or highly intricate forms, each of which has a name, by looping, crossing, and crisscrossing a big loop of string with their fingers until a figure appears between the hands. To people of the Stone Age, there is magic in the making. To the sophisticated, the magical meaning has long been lost, and the string figures are merely a game of great fascination and artistic skill.

The string figures are known by as many different names as there are languages and dialects throughout the world. Here are some examples of one name given certain figures: in Germany—*Hexenspiel* (Witch's Game); India—Scissors; Hawaii—*Hei* (Net); Ulungu of Tanganyika—*Umuzwa* (Wooden Spoon); England, Australia, U.S.A.—String Puzzle, Picking Up and Taking Off, Taking Off; Cherokee Indians of North America—Crows' Feet; China—Sawing Wood. In Japan and Korea, they like to make animals and things; in New Zealand the Maori, and in the Hawaiian Islands the Polynesians, devise scenes representing their mythology, such as Maui fishing up the enormous island. (See Part II for Maui's sun-snare game.)

To many Papuans of New Guinea in the South Pacific the magic of cats' cradles remains. From the time they select a plot of ground and clear it by burning, to the time they harvest their crops, they try to influence, aid, and urge on the growth of their vegetables with various practices, among the most important of which are their magical games.

After planting yams, a chief crop, children and grown-ups make cats' cradles so that the leafy parts of the yams may grow plentiful, big, and green. When the young, tender shoots appear, sticks are placed in the ground to support the winding tendrils, and the new stems are tied to the sticks with pieces of string used in playing Cat's Cradle.

In the Gazelle Peninsula of New Pomerania, the time to play Cat's Cradle is when the breadfruit trees begin to form their fruit. Here's a cradle that the youngest player can make in a few swift motions:

Take a piece of ordinary string about three feet long; tie the ends together neatly, to make a big loop. Number the fingernails on each hand with paint or ink, beginning with the thumb—1, 2, 3, 4, 5. Place the loop around fingers 1 and 5 on each hand, as in the diagram.

Now, put R2 under L palm string and L2 under R palm string.

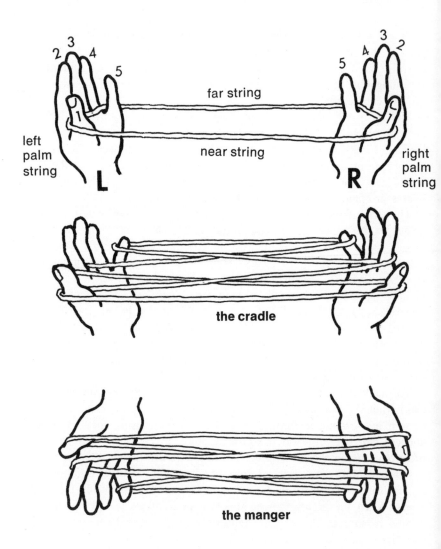

far string

near string

left palm string

right palm string

L   R

the cradle

the manger

Draw string back as far as it will go. The result is a string cradle (see diagram). To make the cradle rock, move the hands forward and backward with the fingers up. To transform this figure into a manger, simply hold the fingers pointing downward with the hands stiff.

On the island of Crete in the old days, just such a cradle, big and made of stout rope, was used to capture and entrap a bull or other animal.

Until just recently in Poland, Austria, Germany, Hungary, Czechoslovakia, and several other countries in other parts of the world where there was a Roman Catholic majority, such as the Philippines, the cradle-manger figure was a game for the Christmas season.

I HAVE A YAM   The Papuans and other peoples of Oceania, that is, inhabitants of the many, many small islands scattered like stars over the Pacific Ocean, often make trick cats' cradles and play the trick on others. This is a trick cat's cradle that anyone can make and have fun with.

Arrange string loop as in the beginning for the cat's cradle illustrated above. Then continue with these steps (see diagram on p. 204).

Step 1. Pick up from outside Far String with L2 and R2. Draw hands apart, holding fingers up.

Step 2. Put L1 and R1 under Far String and pick up on nail side of L1 and R1, the Near 2 String.

Step 3. Bring L1 and R1 back under Near 1 String. Hold hands with fingers up.

Step 4. Bring L5 and R5 over Far 2 String.

Step 5. Pick up on nail side of L5 and R5 the Near String (one nearest you, going across from L1 to R1).

Step 6. Return L5 and R5 to upright position.

Step 7. Pick up on nail side of L1 and R1 the Near String (one nearest you).

Step 8. Hold L1 upright.

Step 9. Take L2 out of loop and hold loop between L1 and L2. This is the "yam."

Then say, "I have a yam. Who will have it?"

When someone comes for it, offer the loop and at the same time pull the strings with the right hand, and the "yam" turns into straight string again.

Then exclaim in astonishment, "Oh, it disappeared!"

The steps given represent only one method of doing the same cat's-cradle trick. It is not only fun to experiment with different ways of doing this particular figure, but also with "picking up and taking off" to create string figures. Or for those who discover a real liking for making

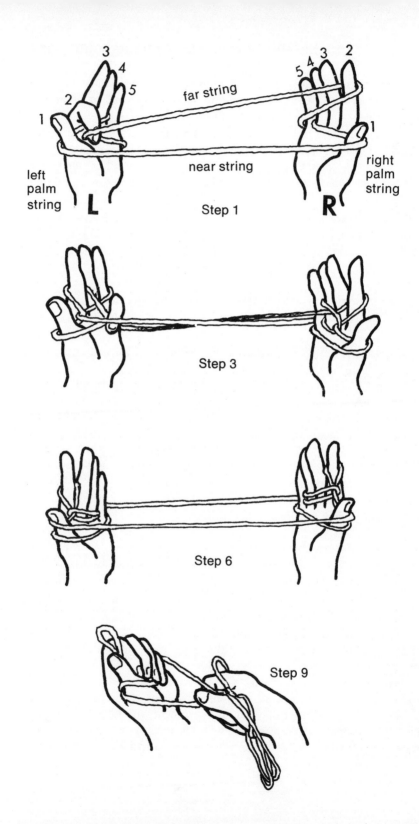

far string

near string

left palm string

right palm string

3 4 5 2 1

5 4 3 2 1

L

R

Step 1

Step 3

Step 6

Step 9

figures, there are books* available on the subject, which illustrate Cat's Cradle for one, two, three, or even four players who use one loop. Alternately taking the strings off one another's hands, two or more players can make beautiful figures that flow one into the other rather like a time-lapse film of the unfolding of petals or leaves. Many designs from string figures are to be found in the art and wood carving of peoples in Africa, Asia, Europe, the Americas, and the islands of the seas and oceans.

SQUASH BLOSSOMS   The Pueblo Indians of the North American Southwest hurried up the crops with "squash blossoms." The Huichal Indians of Yucatan called them "gods' eyes," but they were almost identical. To make "squash blossoms" and "gods' eyes," the Indians strung yarn over crossed sticks in spider-web fashion. They made them

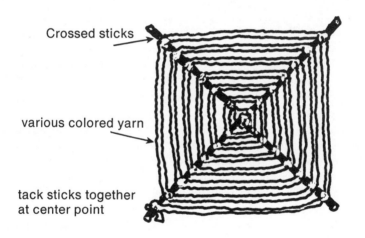

Crossed sticks

various colored yarn

tack sticks together
at center point

during the sowing-growing season and played games with them, one of which consisted of throwing them up in the air and catching them. A group of children with three or four squash blossoms stood scattered about a play space, tossing them toward one another. Each player caught whatever came within his reach without his moving from his position. When all the squash blossoms had fallen to earth, they were gathered up and the game was begun again.

String Figures and How to Make Them, A Study of Cat's Cradle in Many Lands, by Caroline Furness Jayne. New York: Dover Publications Reprint, 1962. *String Games for Beginners,* by Kathleen Haddon. Cambridge, England: W. Heffer & Sons, 1967.

SWING, SING, ROUNDABOUT, SWING   The most modern agricultural methods, equipment, and scientific magic—improved seeds and strains, fertilizers, pest and disease controls, and all the rest—cannot guarantee a bumper crop. Farming is still a chancy thing, but certainly far less chancy than it used to be when farmers depended solely upon custom and tradition, charms and magic-working swinging games.

Before planting corn and beans in his *milpa*, the burned-over clearing, the old farmer of Guatemala and Mexico invoked the blessing of the sun, the rain, and the wind gods upon his cornfield, and added:

Grant that thieves don't steal the maize (corn) before it can be
    gathered,
That the raccoon and skunk won't find it,
That the frost won't nip the maize while it's in the silk,
That the four-eyed devil won't sow borers in my field to eat the ears
    and stalks of my maize,
But that the kernels will grow clean and close on the ears like the
    teeth of a little girl.

From invocations people went into swinging-singing games. Surviving from long ago in Crete is the hastening of the ripening of grapes by women and girls who swing and sing for days on end until they go to the vineyards to harvest the fruit.

In the King William Cape area of New Guinea in the South Seas, men, women, and children start to swing and sing as soon as the yams are planted. In preparation for the swing-sing, they fix Malacca canes to tree branches everywhere about their gardens.

As they work and as they go to and from the gardens, they sing swing songs, often a single word over and over, such as names for the countless varieties of yam; or they repeat an exclamation of delight over digging up a fine, big yam.

To play the work-play game of Swing, Sing, Roundabout, Swing a woody place is needed so that sturdy wooden canes can be fixed to stout tree branches. High exercise bars may be substituted for tree branches and lengths of rope with a knot in them for canes, if the game is played in a gym.

Four or five "garden rows" 15-20 feet long are marked off, the rows having a tree branch (or bar) with a cane (or rope) hanging from it at ends of alternate rows, as in the diagram.

Players are divided into two groups, each with a leader. One group starts at A and must pass up and down the garden rows, progressing toward the right; the other group starts at B and goes up and down the

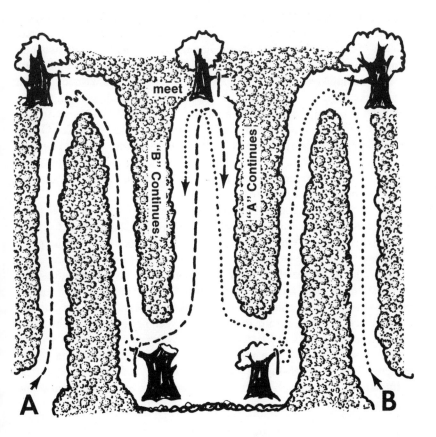

rows toward the left. Pace must be kept to an even, quiet walk; there must be no pushing or shoving and, when swinging, the cane is grabbed, swinger steps back, swings and lands on both feet, then goes on, all in rhythmic motion.

Each player swings on the cane at the end of the row. Each group chants a refrain, such as, "Round about the garden patch, up and down the garden rows we go. Up and down the row, the row, and swing around the yams, the yams." Reciting nonsense words or sounds is just as good.

First group to reach the end of the rows of the garden patch is the winner. Players must return and stand as a group at the place where they started.

The game is not as simple as it appears, for direction, chanting (or singing), pace, and the rhythm of the swing on the cane must be coordinated.

THE MANY HAMMOCKS OF GUAYAQUIL   Back in the days of Queen Victoria, an English traveler to Guayaquil, Ecuador, remarked on the great number of immense hammocks "made of a network of strong grass, dyed various colors," which hung from the high roofs of the verandas of the houses. At the first house he visited, all the hammocks were occupied by ladies who sat or reclined, swinging ceaselessly while one of them plucked a guitar.

Later, when he saw Indians playing *Chuke* (see Part II under Games to Accompany the Growing and the Hunting Seasons) and swinging to bring success to their bananas, rice, corn, beans, potatoes, or other crops, he was reminded of the ladies of Guayaquil, swinging in their great hammocks to keep themselves cool.

An adaptation of the Latin-American swinging magic-game requires a playground with a row of swings for children six and older. Children divide into Swingers, who sit in the swings, and Starters who do the pushing. Each Swinger has a Starter who pushes until all Swingers have their swings going together. They go as high as is considered safe. Then Starters run off and hide. Swingers must "let the old cat die," that is, permit the swings to come to a stop by themselves, then jump out and try to catch Starters before the latter can get back to the swings and occupy them. Successful Starters become Swingers. Those who are not caught in, say, six or seven minutes and who are still hiding, must run back to the swings. Swingers give chase and try to catch any Starters before they can reach the swings. All caught act as Starters again and game continues.

BATTLE OF GIANT TOPS   A surprising number of different peoples spin tops at sowing or harvest time. The Kai of New Guinea use a kind of wild fig for a top and spin it after the taro, a starchy, tuberous root vegetable that is a staple of diet in the tropics, is planted in order to assure that it will grow round and fat in the earth. Some tribes belonging to the Dayaks of Borneo open the sowing season by putting on magical masks and spinning tops. They also usher in the rice harvest by pelting one another with their pea-shooters. The Kayans spin enormous tops. The spinning represents the endless agricultural cycle of the successive steps: planting, tending, and harvesting the crop; thus, one top spins, stops, another takes its place spinning, stops, yet another replaces it, and so on.

Each player in Battle of Giant Tops needs a big oval-shaped, shiny top weighing 1-2 pounds. (Kayan men use tops weighing between 4 and 5 pounds.) Make the tops of big hollow balls, either rubber or plastic. Fill them with gravel or plaster of Paris and put a long dowel, ½-⅝-

inch thick and pointed at one end, through the ball and glue in place. Pointed end should protrude no more than 2 inches. (If balls are not available, large fruit juice cans will do.)

Players stand in a circle and draw lots for first to spin his top. In turn, then, they squat and spin the tops by rolling the dowel back and forth rapidly between the palms and dropping them into the circle with the objective of causing another's top to stop spinning while one's own continues to revolve. Tops that cease to spin or are stopped by another's are picked up immediately by their owners. The top that continues to spin longest is winner. Game starts again as soon as only one spinning top is left.

For other games with tops, see Part V.

ANDAMOS A CAZA DE   The name of the game means "we're going hunting for." The game is akin to the typical turkey shoot of pioneer days in Appalachia and later of settlers in the West in the U.S.A. The turkey shoot is still held in county and country fairs today and is a standard event for a community carnival or fun-fest. Contestants shoot at a turkey cutout at these affairs and prizes are given for best shots. Bow and arrow (blunted tip) or darts are used, of course, instead of the pioneer's gun. Practice target shooting by the young is a game, but it was a meaningful show of skill in a society that depended upon hunting for meat.

In Andamos a Caza de, children of Central and South America hunt with a whirlibob, which they usually call *cometa*, comet, for it seems to resemble one as it goes streaking toward the target. Their whirlibob is a little leather pouch, weighted with small stones or packed with earth, to which are attached leather strings for throwing. (Put sand in the middle of a man's handkerchief, tie it round with string to make a little pouch, and use the corners for whirling and throwing.)

The game is played while walking to or from some place, or just walking around, one player at a time naming a target. All players must carry a supply of pebbles, beans, bottle caps, or the like. The player who gets first chance to select and throw at a target is chosen by some method of counting out or drawing straws.

As the group walks along, first player sees a tree with a big knothole he thinks he can hit, for example, so he says, "We're going hunting for warthogs." (Any animal at all may be named, although players seem to want to name unusual, exotic, or even fantastic creatures from stories and tales.)

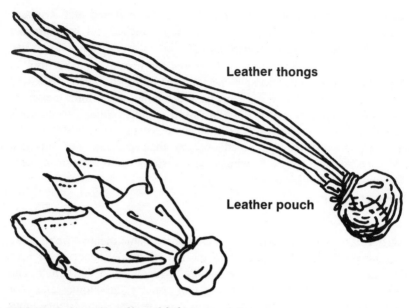

Whirlibob from handkerchief

"I'm hitting the first one," first player continues and, swinging his whirlibob by the strings, lets it fly at the target. If he fails to hit it, he just waits until the others in turn have tried, then gives each one who hit it a pebble, bean, or whatever. If first player succeeds in hitting the target, he receives pebbles from those who failed. Whether he wins or loses, he names the next target selector, who repeats the performance. Winner is the one with the most pebbles at the end of the "game walk."

SHOOTING THE PAPAGAI   This is the name of a kind of turkey shoot, or We're Going Hunting For, played in Louisiana. Darts or whirlibobs are thrown at a target cut in the shape of a cow. Shooter calls out the cut he wants and attempts to hit that part of the cow—beefsteak, rib roast, etc. French-speaking children try for *flanchet, filet, romsteck,* etc., on a *boeuf,* that is, a beef or steer. They often make their whirlibobs of a small rubber ball to which a strong rubber band, which has been cut in two, is attached.

THE MONSTER SWALLOWED THEM   A bullroarer or monster— the words are the same in many tongues—is a noisemaker of great antiquity used in connection with various ceremonies and dramatic games up to the present time in a good many places. The bullroarer is said to have been invented by women in ancient times. It is usually made of a wooden slat tied to the end of a thong or piece of strong twine, which sometimes, in turn, is tied to a stick. When it is rotated, it gives a buzzing sound which varies with the shape of the slat and the rapidity of the whirling.

The bullroarer's use was widespread; it was found in all of Europe and Central Asia, Tibet, India, among the Indians of South America, particularly those of Brazil; and among peoples of East Africa, the Polynesians of Oceania, Australian aborigines, Indians of Canada and the North American Northwest, and so on and on. English-speaking peoples call a particular angular figure in geometry rhombus or rhomboid from the Greek word for a particular kind of bullroarer. Eskimos of Alaska made the roarer of bone in the form of a fish with serrated edges and whirled it in fishing ceremonies. Some peoples painted or carved symbolic, geometric designs on the roarer. In New Guinea bullroarers resounded all during the taro-growing season, becoming especially pervasive just before harvest.

See the sketches of three bullroarers, any of which shapes or all of them may be used in the game of The Monster Swallowed Them. Each shape makes a slightly different sound when whirled fast.

In this dramatic game, the Monster comes while the Villagers are working in the fields. He wakes the sleeping Children by walking round and round them, whirling his bullroarer, his "thunder" as he calls it. They wake up very slowly, for they are very tired. In the course of waking and luring them away, the Monster puts down his "thunder" and forgets to take it when he goes with them to his secret place.

The Villagers return, find the Children gone, and, seeing the bullroarer, say, "The Monster (Giant, Whale) came and swallowed them while we were away."

One of the Villagers picks up the bullroarer and whirls it, whereupon the Monster comes running.

"Give me back my thunder," he shouts.

"Give us back our Children," the Villagers shout back.

"You'll have to pay a forfeit," says the Monster.

"And what's the forfeit?" they ask.

"A bag of barley and a basket of yams," replies the Monster.

"We haven't any barley, and we haven't any yams," declare the Villagers.

"Then I'll swallow you instead," threatens the Monster, pointing to the Villager with the bullroarer.

"You'll have to catch me first," the Villager says, and runs off quickly, whirling the bullroarer, with all the other Villagers following. They pass the bullroarer from one to another in an effort to keep the Monster

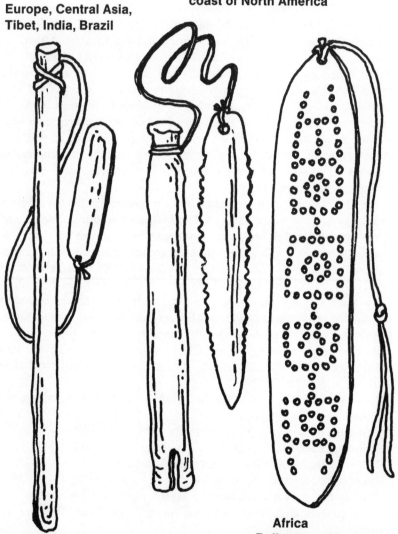

Europe, Central Asia, Tibet, India, Brazil

Eskimos of Alaska, Canada, Indians of Canada and Northwest coast of North America

Whirl round by thong or hand. Buzzing sound varies according to shape and rapidity of motion.

Africa
Bullroarer with geometric designs also typical of Polynesia

from catching anyone with it, until all the Children have reached the village and are safe. The Children must start to run back to the village as soon as they hear the buzzing sound. If the Monster succeeds in catching someone with his "thunder" before all the Children are in the village, the one caught becomes the Monster, the Children become Villagers, and the Villagers, Children. In the event he fails, he must continue to be Monster, but Children and Villagers change roles.

Winding and Circle Games Performed to Wake the Earth In Spring

THE GREAT SEVENTEENTH-CENTURY Peruvian poet, Juana Inés de la Cruz, in a play she wrote when she was yet in her teens, had the Old Indian Faith say, "Still my task is to protect / Ancient rights, and still I can. / Here I stand for all the manners, / Speak for all the ancient ways / Of these lands and of these peoples."

The same may be said of children who "speak for all the ancient ways" by retaining the archaic in their games. The Maze Game, Los Zopilotes, Troy Town, Snail Whorl—all these and more are names given a singing or chanting, winding circle game that as a dance once belonged to the cycle of rites of agriculture. For instance, a huge snail is shown in a woodcut of spring in an old shepherds' calendar. Even today peoples of most lands think of winter as a time when the earth sleeps and of spring as a time when the earth awakens in a cycle of annual dying and reviving.

Traditional myths tell of this natural yearly cycle. There is Persephone, goddess of growing things, who lives aboveground with her mother, Demeter, during spring and summer, and returns to her husband, Pluto, in the underworld the rest of the year.

In Egyptian lands the harvest is not in the fall, but in the spring (March, April, May). In November, the Nile is sinking, the north winds begin dying away, the nights are lengthening, and the time to sow near-

214

ing. Farmers about December 22 go searching for Osiris, with lighted lanterns and a small, moon-shaped image, which they robe and ornament to represent Osiris, spirit of the waxing year (Set is the spirit of the waning year). Then in a joyful follow-up ceremony, they discover and resurrect the dead god, who comes to life again in the plants and vegetables. (Various Europeans and Americans on New Year's celebrate the dying of Old Father Time as the Spirit of the Year Past and his coming to life again as a chubby baby, the New Year.)

There are myths which tell of heroes who wander in dark forests to slay monsters, like Gilgamesh of Babylonia, or like Strap Buckner of Texas, who knocked down the black bull with his fist. And there are heroes who kill monsters inhabiting mazes in the bowels of the earth, like Theseus of Attica who went to destroy the monstrous bull, the Minotaur of Crete. Every year, this great bull devoured a tribute of seven youths and seven maidens* from Greece. With the aid of the king's daughter, Ariadne, who gave him a ball of string with which to guide himself safely through the deep, winding passages of the Labyrinth, Theseus did destroy the Minotaur.

THE MAZE GAME   This is derived from the dance said to represent the escape of Theseus from the Labyrinth, that is, the dance that people performed to wake the earth in the spring. (Cranes, storks, and other birds were imitated in dances, since they were harbingers of spring.) It spread westward from the eastern Mediterranean and is known everywhere, in one variation or another, in the Western world.

To play The Maze Game, players form two circles at each end of the playing area. One of the children in Circle One is given a ball of twine.

Players in both circles step forward stiffly and bow, turn around and, facing outward, step forward and bow stiffly again. They make a half-turn, begin to move slowly, lifting feet and legs in an exaggerated and pompous walk, and continue around in a circle, chanting:

> Around we go, stepping so.
> Up and down, to and fro,
> Stepping so, around we go.

---

* According to legend, these Grecian boys and girls were trained as bull-leapers or bull-dancers in Crete. Unlike bullfighting, bull-leaping required no weapons. Released from rope cradles (nets), the bulls were "grappled" by the dancers, who went leaping and somersaulting over the backs of the bulls. Anyone who has seen a modern-day rodeo, with cowboys grappling and throwing steers, probably would not be astonished by the leapers' feats at a bull-grappling contest in the arena of the Palace of Minos.

They walk round in that fashion several times; then the player in Circle One with the ball of twine takes hold of the loose end of the twine and passes the ball to the person behind, who grasps the twine with the left hand, passes the ball on to the one behind, and so on until all of Circle One has hold of the twine with the left hand. Players in both circles continue to chant.

As soon as all in Circle One are holding the twine in the left hand, the last player to grasp the ball (what remains of it) leads the others around the outside of Circle Two, whose players immediately face outward, chanting:

> Up and down
> From the town
> To the grove
> Let us rove
> Two by two,
> Two by two.

When a player of Circle One comes alongside a player of Circle Two, player in Circle Two takes hold of the string with the left hand and walks behind player in Circle One. They all continue to chant until all from both circles are going round with slow, strutting steps in a huge ring.

Player carrying the ball then leads the others out into the area until there is a long line; then this player, who is now the leader, begins a spiral walk, the others following, coiling round and round upon itself, in ever narrowing circles, until the slowly strutting players can no longer walk. Game may end at this point, or the last in the coiled line may become the leader and unwind, in ever widening circles, the spiral. Players turn, face in other direction, and change hand holding twine by passing overhead from left to right hand.

Drums, hollow blocks, bell blocks, clappers, or ratchets can be used to give rhythmic background for the chanting. It may be done with music and song; and it makes a most effective spectacle for a special event or occasion.

LOS ZOPILOTES   This is a kind of maze dance game, such as The Maze Game above, that the Mexican Indians did. They may have got it from the Spaniards who got it from the Romans who, probably, got theirs from the Greeks, and so on.

Los zopilotes means turkey buzzards. These birds like the cranes and peacocks do a high-stepping, stately dance at mating season, and peo-

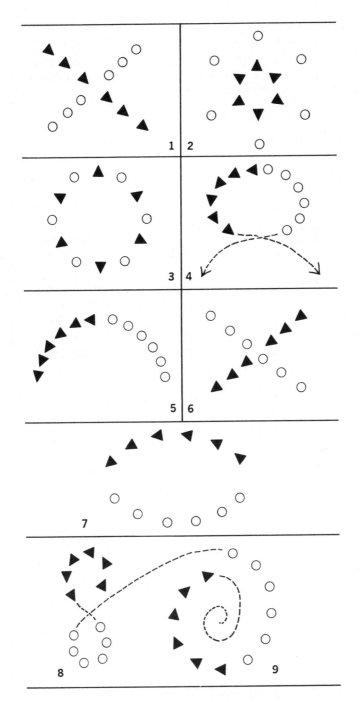

Movement of Players in Los Zopilotes

ples since forgotten times have imitated them. The pavan (pavon, pavane, pavanne, etc., from Latin *pavus,* peacock) is the peacock dance's descendant, its meaning lost, that was a popular Christmas season ballroom dance among British, European, and Russian socialites when crowns and coronets were abundant and meaningful.

The few who have been fortunate enough to see *zopilotes* bowing and stepping, circling and parting, on a Rio Grande sand bar, or whooping cranes making their slow, graceful, formal movements, can readily see how dances and games like Los Zopilotes came to be. Those who have not been so fortunate as to see the live thing can see it on tape or film, then play the game. It adds another dimension to a play experience.

Players for Los Zopilotes are divided into two groups of equal numbers, and there should be at least six in each group for a good game. To distinguish one group from the other, give them different colored crepe paper strings to tie about their heads or loop about their necks.

Following their leaders, the two groups of players move through the following formations, as in the diagram: (1) walk diagonally; (2) walk around in circles, one circle inside the other; (3) form a big circle; (4) split and walk around; (5) form semicircle; (6) form diagonal lines; (7) form one long line and split into two groups again; (8) form circles and walk in figure eight; (9) form line that spirals and winds in upon itself until it is a tight coil, as in The Maze Game.

Players walk slowly, picking their feet up in a showy manner, and their backs held straight. As they walk through the formations, they chant:*

Here we come,
Here we come,
And around we go,
Two by two.

Here we come
And here we go,
One by one,
Just so.

---

* Early folklorists, mainly French and Spanish, made notations of various songs and chants of Quechua-speaking Indians that accompanied a *kaswa,* any of the Indian's mimicry in dance or game form, or dramatic storytelling dances. Quechua was a language common to Indians throughout Latin America. Songs and chants were a mixture of Spanish and Quechua, such as *Playa Huktincito* (Birds of the Beaches) and *Rueday Koson* (We Are Turning Round).

Around we go

And around we go.

And we leave you now

For we can't stay,

But we will come

Another day.

SNAIL WHORL   This is a winding game that requires a wall or fence. Assuming it is on the right, players line up at right angle to it, and clasp hands. The player on the left end of the line is the Leader (L in the diagram). Player next the wall (A in the diagram) forms an arch by putting the left hand against the wall.

Leader, followed by the others, walks hand in hand toward wall and under A's arm. A keeps hand on fence throughout, although she must turn in the other direction when the last player (the one standing next to her) passes under A's arching arm.

Players repeat the same action, only this time the player next to A (designated B in the diagram) does not go through A's arch, but stands beside A, and the others go between B and A. Since all are holding hands, B must cross arms and face in other direction as the girl next to her goes between her and A.

The action is repeated; this time the Leader goes between B and the player next to her (C in the diagram). And, of course, C must cross arms and face in the other direction this time round. Action continues until all are standing with crossed arms facing in the opposite direction. Leader crosses arms as she returns to place.

Then Leader and A sidle round toward each other and lock elbows. Circle is then formed with all players facing outward, arms crossed. They whirl around. Leader and A unlock elbows, and A goes spinning off as she and the player next to her uncross arms and unclasp hands. The rest continue to whirl, and players continue to spin off until all are spinning around, each player alone.

ROUND AND ROUND THE VILLAGE   This was an old singing, winding-in-and-out game in Britain. In the words which follow, the first line of each verse was sung or chanted three times.

Round and round the village,

As we have done before.

Movement of Players in Snail Whorl

In and out the windows,
As we have done before.

Stand and face your lover,
As we have done before.

Now go with her/him to London,
As we have done before.

To play, children clasp hands and stand in a circle, except for one child who skips around the outside, as the others sing. After skipping about several times (Verse 1), the child begins to go in and out the windows—the raised arms of those in the circle (Verse 2). Suddenly (Verse 3) the player stops in front of another, the two bow, clasp hands, leave the circle, and skip around as Verse 1 is repeated.

Then, first child leaves the second and joins the circle while the second child repeats the actions of the first and the circle of children, like a Greek chorus, though a merry one, chants or sings.

The English colonists brought the game to America and it received some new names, among them, Go In and Out the Windows, which was sung in New England much as it was in Old England. In Appalachia it was often played under one of its other English names, Round and Round the Valley. Action remained the same, but the children went round and round the valley three times, then in and out the windows, and the third verse became:

Stand and choose your partner,
As we have done before.

The two did not go to London, but went skipping off to:

Goodby, we hate to leave you,
As we have done before.

Then down along the Mississippi, where levees were constructed to control the flood waters of the great river, children went:

Marching round the levee,
As we have done before.

They went in and out the windows, they stood and chose their partners, and they went skipping off to:

We'll be back to see you,
For we have gained the day.

Who had gained the particular day in the Civil War—whether the North or the South—did not matter to the playing children if they ever thought of it.

TROY TOWN WITH PENCIL AND PAPER   Stone mazes, all of them having much the same pattern, have been found in England, Ireland, Iceland, Sweden, Norway, Denmark, the northeastern U.S.A., and other places. They are all like the labyrinth shown on ancient Cretan coins.

Mazes became fashionable to grow in gardens, particularly those of fragrant boxwood. And the pencil-and-paper game has never been forgotten for hundreds of years. Two and sometimes four play, players

in turn drawing mazes and the others trying in turn to trace a line with pencil that leads to the center, or from the center to outside the maze. No lines must be crossed and dead ends must be abandoned at once if four are playing in order to let the next player have his turn.

THE HORA   *Eretz Yisrael* (The Land of Israel), or simply *Haaretz* (The Land) is the riverbed into which the *sabra*, the youth of Israel, pours its spirit, its work, and its play. One born in Israel is a *sabra*, so called from the name of the prickly pear cactus, thistly on the outside but sweet within.

Everywhere in The Land groups of young and old take part in The Hora, a kind of winding dance game. It is usually started by a half-dozen or so with a chosen leader. With arms across shoulders, they form a line and, singing lustily *"Hava Nagila,"* go weaving, winding among onlookers and around chairs, tables, or other obstacles after their leader. He does traditional dance steps or improvises as he goes, and often makes the line turn in upon itself until it coils up like a spring, then gradually uncoils.

The last one on the line reaches out to draw into the game anyone near. If it continues for some time, those who become tired simply reach out and draw in others to take their places or call out the names of onlookers. Thus, after a while, there may be a completely different group forming the line from that starting it. Dropouts who want to drop in, catch hold of the hand of the last in the line, exchange places or ask for any two in the line to make room. Leaders may change at any time they wish and the activity goes on for as long as participants wish it.

This winding game of The Land is an excellent activity for playground or gymnasium, or any fairly large space anywhere, and a large group of children of the same or various ages. It is also a fine all-age "getting-to-know-you" activity. Those who are too little to reach the shoulders of other participants hold hands instead of putting their arms across shoulders.

Community Games—
Symbolic and Commemorative

Tugs-of-war can be symbolic of the contest between seasons, of the struggles between invaders and defenders of a land, or of the gardener's tug-of-war against the elements and the many natural enemies who can eat his crop before he can harvest it.

PULL FOR A GOOD HARVEST   In Japan in past time, villages insured an abundant harvest by turning out on the fifteenth of the first month for the annual intervillage event, the Rope-Pulling Contest. Old as well as young took part and, in order to make up for their lighter weight, women and girls tucked stones into their clothes. The rope, Kei-tjoul, was like a great ship's cable, made of straw, with its ends fraying out into branches which the small-handed gripped. One village was pitted against another. The winning village guaranteed itself a bounteous crop.

With a line scratched in the ground or drawn with chalk on the floor, and a length of strong rope, two groups can take the names of two Japanese villages, towns, or even districts, and one group tug to pull the other across the line for a good harvest.

In Okinawa *Tsunahiki* (Tug-of-War) marks harvest time in mid-August.

CRICK-CRACK CROCODILE This is a back-and-forth dispute over a crocodile in Gambia, West Africa. Two hunters from different villages claim the animal, each hunter for his own village.

Players of the game divide into three teams—two teams of opposing Villagers, and the third team, the Crocodile.

Two goal posts representing villages are set up about forty feet apart. A line is drawn across the middle of the playing space between the posts.

A long stout pole with ropes securely attached at each end is needed. Players representing the crocodile stand, half on one side and half on the other, grasping the pole. Village teams grasp the ropes and pull. Crocodile must try to keep both sets of Villagers from dragging him to their Village within a certain time limit, say, 10-15 minutes.

In order to win, Villagers must drag Crocodile near enough to their Village to loop the end of the rope around the goal post. Winning Village has earned a holiday feast, which the Villagers share with the losing Village.

CATCH AND BIND This was the chief humorous or game method for collecting the local revenue in medieval England at Hock-tide. Paying taxes in the spring is nothing new. The Oxford English Dictionary describes Hock-day as "an important term-day on which rents and the like were paid." It was the first Tuesday after Easter, and Hock-tide included the first Monday and first Tuesday, and with Michaelmas, which occurred in December, divided "the rural year into its summer and winter halves."

The OED further reports that Hock-day was "signalized by the collection of money for parish purposes by roughly humorous methods." (There never has been a satisfactory explanation or definition of the word "Hock" in Hock-day, although there have been many attempts by scholars to furnish one. The American slang word "hock," meaning "to pawn something," is too late, for it came into usage in 1850. An older meaning for "to hock" was "to hamstring," and taxes have done that often enough.)

Perhaps the present twentieth-century and future twenty-first-century taxpayer might look backward for a moment to a spring tax-day of the Middle Ages in England and Scotland and see how "rents and the like" were collected "by roughly humorous methods."

On the first Monday after Easter, women and girls stretched ropes (or chains) across public roads and highways and waited for men and boys to pass along. As soon as any approached the barrier, women and girls grasped the ends of the rope, pulled the passersby to them, and bound them with the ropes. All who could not escape had to pay toll, which went to the parish, an area that often included several towns. On Tuesday, it was the turn of men and boys to catch and bind and exact toll from the women and girls.

Men and boys may have caught and bound more, but in terms of the amount of tolls collected, the winners were the women and girls in nearly every parish, year after year. (In later years when the day became known as "Kissing Day" because more tolls were collected in kisses than cash, the Establishment first denounced, then renounced the day; yet people continued the practice until well into the nineteenth century.)

This game of the Middle Ages suggests itself as a two-team contest for raising money for any worthy purpose—youth service organizations, schools, community funds, etc.—at any neighborhood or local community outdoor or indoor money-raising event such as a carnival, fair, picnic, or sports-and-hobby show.

SAXON AND DRAGON   At Hock-tide in Old England, it was time to play Saxon versus Viking games. Such games as Saxon and Dragon were common. The dragon refers to the Viking ships with the hull and stern the shape of the body and tail, and the high prow, the head of the mythological beast.

The Viking invasions of Saxon England had left a lasting impression not only upon the people, whose high taxes went to pay tribute to the invaders, but also upon the land itself. There was the Danelaw, those districts in the North and Northeast of England settled by Danes and other Scandinavian invaders during early times. A strip that runs through the middle of Britain, the Danelaw was like a foreign land, for it was divided into Danish "ridings" and "wapentakes," and in the Danish "lawmen" were the glimmerings of a future jury system.

In preparation for the game of Saxon and Dragon, a stake is driven into the ground on a line which divides the play area. The middle of a long rope is secured to the stake with a clove hitch.

Contestants choose up sides—Saxons and Dragons—and grasp the

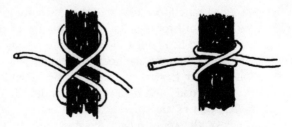

Tying a Clove Hitch

rope tug-of-war fashion. Their objective is pulling up the stake and dragging the opposing side across the line. If the stake is of wood and is broken in the tugging before or after it is pulled out of the ground, that makes no difference and the pull-and-tug should go right on.

Saxon and Dragon is a fine game for a waterside. Place the stake in the shallow water where big and little can play.

After a day engaging in vigorous games, everyone—men, women, and children—in celebration of Hock-day went to see a play, invariably one of the many traditional plays having to do with Danes and Saxons. Perhaps in some such play, Shakespeare found a source for his *Hamlet, Prince of Denmark.*

PROTRACTED COURTHOUSE-YARD GAMES "It was court time and that implies frolicking time," said an 1817 English traveler in the U.S.A. In England there were four terms of three weeks each, the terms corresponding roughly to the seasons of spring, summer, fall, and winter. And they were usually accompanied by sports and games. In the United States, terms were not limited to any fixed period, but held according to the judges available and the number of court cases and time it took for them to be acted upon.

The serious work of meting out fair judgments inside the courthouse was balanced by the fun of Horseshoe Quoits, Tenpins, and wrestling that was going on outside "all the time that could be spared from the court sessions."

Several games of Tenpins and Horseshoe Quoits were played the same way as that described in Part I, except that several different games were kept going with different groups of players. Some had cases coming up or other court business and would have to leave. As soon as one or more players left, others filled their places and played for their group. Thus games could go on all day, continue the next day, and so on until court closed if it pleased the groups. Individual winners were those with highest score at the time one or more players quit the game.

Children like protracted games when they form teams of partners at day camps, and individuals can help roll up big scores for their teams. In the teams of partners, games are carried on continuously by having one or more partners spell one another. For example, a team of a dozen would have four sets of three partners who by taking turns can keep a game of Tenpins, for instance, going on for several days, if they wish. It is a test of a kind of endurance not too unlike that of certain Olympic Games events, such as the races which continue for days, or tournament play in various sports and games. The ability to sustain interest over a lengthy period is a mark of maturity.

Hoop-Rolling Games
And Their Ties
To Magic
And Ritual

IN THE AUTUMN Greek children with their elders sent flaming hoops, called fire-wheels, flying down the hills and slopes, hoping to encourage the sun to stay and to hold back winter.

All during the year hoops were popular. Running or jogging beside one's hoop, jumping over rolling hoops, jumping through them as though they were skipping ropes—all such hoop play, as well as hoop-rolling contests and games with hoops, were recommended as healthful exercise. Hippocrates, the renowned Greek doctor, was an advocate of hoop-rolling as exercise for athletes, who were often shown with big hoops, some reaching almost to the shoulder. The Hippocratic Oath, a code of medical ethics, which Hippocrates is said to have imposed on his disciples, is still in effect in modern times.

No part of the world has been left untouched by play with hoops, although hoops suddenly appear, have a period of almost frenetic popularity (for example, the hoola-hoop), then disappear just as quickly, only to appear again, perhaps, many years later. With some schools and colleges, however, when trees begin to bud and flowers to bloom in the spring, hoop-rolling is a long-established tradition and custom.

Jousts for Hoops make excellent events for a spring games tourney just as in the old days joustings were held at the crownings of kings, weddings of princes and princesses, and at times when work was suspended for a special holiday.

Roman girls rolled a metal hoop, or *trochus*, with a little hooked stick which they called a key. They hooked the key over the rim or under it and sent the hoops rolling up inclines or down them, and went tearing after their hoops to see which went farthest before falling over. They went places with hoops, making them go fast and racing to pick them up, then setting them going again, to see who would be the first to reach their destination.

The Dutch held hoop races with boys and girls, in the streets. Prizes were given for the most skillful. Contestants had to drive their hoops a certain distance, and the one who first reached the goal received a silver coin for a prize. This coin was fastened to the hoop as a trophy, and the more noise a hoop made while rolling over the streets, the greater the honor for the owner. The loud clatter of coins showed that many prizes had been won by the hoopster.

Plastic or wooden hoops are just as good as metal hoops for these joustings.

UNHOOP THE HOOPSTER   This may be played by small or large groups of two teams of players, each of whom has a hoop. Either the hand or a baton (short stick) may be used to roll the hoop, but all players must use the one or the other.

Any large space outdoors will serve for this joust. One team retreats while the other pursues and attempts to unhoop the first by getting close enough to roll hoops against those of opponents and topple them over.

A rope, to which pennants of different colors are attached, is stretched between stakes at a height of about three feet at one end of the playing field. The two teams of hoopsters line up in front of it with their hoops, the Pursuers immediately in front and the Retreaters from six to eight feet in front of them.

Upon signal players on both teams begin rolling their hoops toward the other end of the field. Objective of each Pursuer is overtaking and causing an opponent's hoop to fall even if his own falls at the same time. Objective of a Retreater is running with his rolling hoop to the end of the field and back to the pennant line without having his hoop toppled by a Pursuer. If his hoop falls without interference from a Pursuer, the Retreater may stand it up again and continue. A Retreater must not try to interrupt the rolling of a Pursuer's hoop. When his hoop falls by accident, a Pursuer may pick it up and continue, but if he and a teammate cause each other's hoops to fall, they must leave the tournament field.

As in all tournaments, it is well to have several referees about the playing field to see that the few rules are obeyed and to settle disputes.

The tournament goes to the Retreaters if they reach the pennant line with as many or more players with hoops than the Pursuers; otherwise it's the Pursuers' tourney.

TILT-YARD HOOP JOUSTING   Four hoops and batons for driving them are required. A long area indoors or out is marked out for the tilt-yard, with four lanes, 4-4½ feet wide and with goals at both ends. Players are divided into four teams, each team lined up facing its own lane, at the end of which is the goal line. The leader has hoop and baton ready to roll upon signal. He must drive the hoop down and back in the lane without its falling over, and give hoop and baton to the next player, who repeats the performance.

When a hoop falls, the driver is disqualified and must leave the tilt-yard as soon as a teammate rushes up and takes hoop and baton. Members of teams must not go outside their own lanes and must not interfere with the rolling of an opponent's hoop.

When a driver is disqualified, his team is docked 10 points. A successful drive down and back counts 20 for the team. First team to finish is given a bonus of 20. Winning team is that with most points after all the members of all teams have had a turn at driving their team's hoop.

Teams unskilled in hoop-driving may come up with minus scores. There is a play-off then between the two with the lowest minus scores.

PA-IN-YAN-KA-PI   This Sioux Indian hoop game used to be connected with a ritual of buffalo hunting and was played by men with hoops of ash, about the size of a wagon wheel.

Substitute old automobile tires for the ash hoops of the Indians. On four points of the tire hoop, equal distances apart, make a 2-inch design, two designs on one side and two on the other. Color the designs on one side of the tire red, and on the other side, yellow. Then write the number of points for which each design counts: 10, 20, 30, or 40.

For the two-pronged, forklike long sticks used by the Indians, substitute brooms; two brooms are needed for each two teams.

Players are divided into teams in multiples of two, for two teams play against each other, the winning team going on to play the winning team of another set of twos, losers against losers, and so on.

Each set of two teams draws straws to see which team rolls the tire hoop first. One tire for each two teams is sufficient, although each team may want to have its own.

A player from each team that is to roll first begins rolling the tire hoop, using hand or strong, short stick, as fast as he can. Two players from the opposing team, armed with brooms, rush after the hoopster with the objective of knocking the tire down with a broom as one of them calls out, "Red!" or "Yellow!" The broom-holder who first calls out the color has the try at knocking over the tire, for two may not make the attempt simultaneously. The broom-holder when he cries the color must be in a position to knock the tire over, and not call out at random.

When the tire goes down, all three rush to see if the tire fell on the side with the red or the yellow designs. If the broom-holder called the correct color, his team scores the points marked on that side.

Referees should be scattered about the playing field if there are three or more sets of two teams at play. There should be a score-keeper for every two sets of teams.

The two teams in a set alternate in rolling the tire, until one team reaches 100, which makes it the winner of the game. That team then plays the winner of another set of twos; the losers play the losers. This continues until the two teams with highest scores play each other to determine winner of tournament.

As in all tournament play, games are carried over from one day to another, until the finalists play off each other.

Part VII

MAKING BELIEVE
AND MAKING WORK PLAY

Imitative Games
That Are Part
Of Growing Up
And Learning Adult Skills

THERE ARE GAMES directly related to the ways by which mankind won a livelihood and expressed respect for and joy in earth and sky. Some are allied with work and work habits, particular skills, and occupations of peoples. Consequently, they help one understand different peoples and their environment.

Primitive and early peoples sought a livelihood by hunting, fishing, and food gathering. They, like all other creatures, were completely dependent upon themselves for survival. They domesticated the dog as a hunting partner in the quest for game, and the cat mostly for psychological reasons, although they benefited greatly from the presence of the hunting cats that saved fruits, grains, and edible root plants from birds and small four-footed vegetarians.

Early peoples painted animals and hunting scenes upon stone walls of caves and rock ledges where they dwelt, inviting good luck with the hunt, anticipating the kill in their pictures. They invested their choreography, too, with sympathetic magic, mimicking animals, enacting with gesture and motion the chase and hunt, fishing, climbing trees to rob a honey-bees' hive, and on to the success or defeat at the end of the venture.

The farm child in Ethiopia pretends to milk the family *gamoosa,* or buffalo, then chug-chugs about the yard being a tractor. In the city of Nairobi, East Africa, a Masai or other Kenyan boy races with arms flapping being a bird or with arms widespread as both airplane and pilot. In Swahili, the *lingua franca* of much of Africa, the word for bird and airplane is the same.

Simple "pretends" belong in the game bag as the starting point of dreams that materialize. Cola Pisci (Nicky Fish) of Messina, Sicily, boasts he can swim like a fish and can dive to the ocean floor. And he does when he grows up to be an aquanaut. Young Gascon of Gascony in France shows how he is going to lick the biggest bully in the park. A fraulein of Berlin pops and sputters and with out-thrust stiff arms is both her brother's motorcycle and her brother, as she tears down the sidewalk, dodging pedestrians. She wants to ride a motorcycle just like her brother as soon as possible.

On the Persian Gulf in Kuwait, the little Arab who once upon a time in Kuwait City streets played at peddling water from goatskin bags, now is pretending to be a water-truck driver lined up at a pumping station of the great seawater distillation plant. His sister in that oil-rich country of the Arabian desert, pretends to be cart and mother shopping in the supermarket.

And as soon as desert scrub turns green in the fall, the children of Kuwait will go about pretending to be falconers. One can see at once that is what they are, with their lifted arm and stiff wrist on which perches an imaginary hawk or hunting falcon, and from the peculiar low whistles and odd sounds that they make. Falconry, practiced since ancient times in Asia, Africa, and Europe, is still a popular sport in Kuwait and the neighboring countries of Saudi Arabia, Iraq, and Iran.

"I can chase a wild rabbit and catch it with my hands," a little boy or girl of Norway, Sweden, or Finland tells the mother. An Australian boy plays at driving his father's jumbucks (sheep) just the way the real sheep herder does.

Children are the doctors without license and nurses without certificate in Bathurst, Gambia, as well as in Bathurst, England. In Syria, Turkey, Germany, Poland, the Ukraine, Liberia, or Rhodesia, they are the astronauts, cosmonauts, aquanauts, and the pioneers who perform all manner of things from walking on the bottom of the Earth's seas to walking on the bottom of the Moon's Sea of Tranquility, from journeying to the center of the Earth to journeying to outer space, equipped with nothing but their imaginations. All these daydreams of simple "pretend" are part of growing up. They give children a sense of well-being, of their own worth and personality. They prepare children for skills that assure development of identity and an awareness of human dignity.

Among peoples who live in close association with nature and her creatures, games directly related to hunting, fishing, and food gathering assume an all-important role in the world of children. They afford pleasurable learning experiences in preparation for adult life. Many such games survive in sophisticated cultures, where they are accepted simply as the fanciful escapes and distractions of children, without any awareness of their meaning in the cultural evolution of the world's peoples.

Peoples whose cultures are chiefly technological, however, are discovering the importance of teaching and learning through group activities, such as game-playing, and of therapy based in work, in play, in work-play, and in similar techniques of a nonanalytic and nonpsychiatric nature which are an integral part of so-called primitive societies.

CATCHING A LENDU This is a game which Pygmy children play in imitation of hunters. The life of Pygmy children of the Congo forest seems that of endless mimicry, an expression of the action and reaction constantly going on between man and animal. Children want and are encouraged to imitate the world around them, especially to know the characteristics and habits of all the creatures of earth, water, and sky, and to be able to mimic them. A hunter may have great skill in the use of bow and arrow, throwing stick, spear and net, but he will bring back to camp few fish and little game unless he has learned about creatures and their ways of escaping their enemies.

After the hunting party leaves, the children play at hunting some *nyama* (animal) that they imagine is in their *bopi*, or playground, which is always a few steps away from the principal Pygmy camp. Perhaps the animal is a *lendu*, a forest antelope about the size of a big dog and having very sharp, pointed horns.

The boys stretch a net (discarded as unusable by adult hunters) while the girls take sticks and leafy branches and beat the ground and bushes to try to drive the *lendu*—impersonated by one of their playmates or one of the grandfathers too old for real hunting—toward the boys. They chase the antelope-mime all over the place, as he dodges, twists, turns, wards off attackers with his make-believe sharp horns, and in every way acts as much as possible like an antelope trying to escape from being driven into and entrapped in the net. As soon as they catch it, they wrap it in the net and triumphantly carry it off to camp. If players, however, fail to catch the antelope within a certain time, the animal has escaped and can choose its successor.

Children anywhere can enact the make-believe antelope hunt, for a length of cloth or old tennis or other net can be utilized. Pages of newspaper slashed along one edge make fronds when rolled up, or strips of paper can be made into satisfactory leafy branches. Those who hold the net must not let go at any time. The antelope must be actually enclosed in the net to be captured.

PIGEON OR DOVE NET   Netting games such as this are found in England, the Basque country, France, Austria and Germany, and in many countries of the East. They are children's imitations of their elders' method of catching birds. Pigeon Net is fairly typical of netting games in general.

Players are divided into two equal groups, the Pigeons and the Net, each group standing behind a line drawn at opposite ends of the room or playground. The players of one group join hands to form the Net. The players of the other group represent Pigeons. At a signal both groups advance toward one another. The Pigeons attempt to reach the goal at the opposite end and the Net attempts to prevent this by closing up the ends of the Net. A Pigeon may not break through the Net, but may escape by dodging around the ends. Should the Net break, the Pigeons escape. Any Pigeons caught are out of the game until all are caught. The groups alternate in playing Pigeons and Net.

ROBBING THE BEES   This is a game for small children, which comes from the Congo forest people. In it some pretend they are gatherers, looking for honey trees, and others are bees, defending their hives.

The group divides into Bees and Robbers. They stand in line, Bees at one end and Robbers at the other end of the play area, and each places his right hand on the right shoulder of the person in front. Bees begin to buzz, Robbers to stretch their necks and gaze upward as though looking for bees' nests way up high in the trees. The lines begin to move, slowly weaving and winding toward each other. Robbers listen to the buzzing of the bees, but pretend they can't discover where the sound is coming from. Lines, little by little, weave close enough to touch. At that moment the bees try to "sting" the Robbers by giving them a quick whack on the shoulder and running off. Robbers try to avoid being stung, for any Robber stung by a Bee is out of the game.

Robbers give chase and must capture the Bees before they reach their hive (their end of the play area). Upon being captured, Bees lose their "sting" and turn into Robbers for the next game. All Bees not captured remain Bees. Game continues until none or only a few Bees or a few Robbers are left. Winning side, of course, is that with far the greater number.

CROCODILE RIDES   These are actually taken by children of the Paga people, living near the Upper Volta on the northern border of Ghana in Africa. The crocodiles are raised in their own special ponds and are tame—if any crocodile can ever be said to be tame. Daring children of the Okefenokee Swamp of Georgia and Florida in the United States used to try to catch rides on alligators, but they made pets only of the baby alligators.

In Ghana there is a game of Crocodile Rides, which is very like a game American children usually call Alligator Crawl. Players lie prone and propel themselves forward by elbows and by wriggling on their stomachs in imitation of crocodiles making for their pond in a great hurry. The pond, of course, is represented by some goal mark. Riders are the players who walk beside the Crocodiles, urging them on and watching to see that they use only elbows and stomachs to push and slither themselves along. Winners are the Crocodile and Rider who reach the pond first. Any Rider may challenge any Crocodile who may not be moving in proper Crocodile or Alligator manner.

FAVORITE PETS   "We strictly forbid you all . . . to bring to church your dogs, monkeys, squirrels, rabbits, birds, cats, and such like frivolous things" was an injunction issued often by church authorities in England, Germany, Austria, and France, where people were in the habit of bringing favorite pets with them when they attended service.

But it was useless for bishop or archbishop to order people to leave them at home. People thought up all kinds of excuses and brought them anyway, for they couldn't bear to be parted from their pets and took them everywhere. Village schoolmasters and teachers in town and city schools have made equally ineffective rules about bringing pets into schoolhouse and classroom.

Of course, the sympathies of any boy or girl who has a beloved pet— be it mouse, snake, or salamander—are all against those of the past or the present who forbid pets, so here's a game for them.

Favorite Pets doesn't require any real pets, but calls for good imitations of birds, beasts, and fishes from their imaginary owners.

Players divide into Neighbors and Visitors. Visitors are given several minutes to decide upon some pet to act out when they go to call on their Neighbors. When time is called, Neighbors line up and Visitors approach and face them.

Visitors: Hello, Neighbors, may we come in?
Neighbors: Yes, if you leave your pet outside.
Visitors: But it's snowing outside. [*Any ridiculous excuse will do.*] Our pet is very well behaved.
Neighbors: Show us.

Visitors do a pantomime of a tiger, lion, kangaroo, monkey, parrot, opossum, raccoon, mocking bird, or whatever they have chosen to mimic. Visitors may do the pantomime together or take turns doing various motions, gestures, and a few sounds (as few as possible, usually leaving them to the very last since the focus is on pantomime).

Neighbors must guess what the pet is and if it is a common one such as cat or dog, what kind (for instance, sheep dog, dachshund, Siamese cat, etc.). But Visitors must use their ingenuity and sense memory to make their gestures so precise the Neighbors can follow them easily. Visitors are not to try to trick Neighbors by asking for them to make impossible distinctions, such as gray cat or ginger cat, unless they are very sure they, the Visitors, can really act the difference out.

If Neighbors fail to guess correctly by the count of ten, Visitors give another pantomime with additional clues. If Neighbors fail to guess correctly at the end of three pantomimes, Visitors score 25 points and go off to choose another pet to mimic. For guessing correctly on third pantomime, Neighbors receive 20 points; for correct guess on first pantomime, 30 points; on second, 15. Visitors and Neighbors may change roles on every second or third round if they desire, thus giving both sides chances to guess and to do imitations. Winner of the game is the side which first scores 100.

Though more complex, Shakespeare has the weaver, Nick Bottom, the bellows-mender, Francis Flute, and the others do just such a bit of mummery in the interlude of *A Midsummer Night's Dream*. Snug, the joiner, says to Peter Quince, the director, "Have you the lion's part written? pray you, if it be, give it me, for I am slow of study." And Quince tells him, "You may do it extempore, for it is nothing but roaring." When confronted with the problem of having a wall, Nick Bottom solves it: "Some man or other must present wall: and let him have some plaster or some loam, or some rough-cast about him, to signify wall; or let him hold his fingers thus (fingers held apart), and through that cranny shall Pyramus and Thisby whisper."

Que Faisons-Nous? (What Do We Do?) is a French version of Favorite Pets in which one side may mimic pets or enact a situation or action and the other side must guess what the first side is doing. It is a form of free and simple charade. Suggestions for action are: paddling a big canoe; group of gliders going off hill and then catching wind currents; walking about on the bottom of the sea; walking outside space ship in space.

In Southeast Asia, Vietnamese children play This Is the Way the Elephant Goes, chanting the actions of the elephant as they march round in a ring, with one arm upraised for the animal's trunk and the other wagging behind for the animal's tail. The leader changes the action by naming another animal.

FOLLOW THE LEADER   This game, which is well known throughout the world, has a special miming variation among the Gabon Pygmies. One person at a time gets up before the group and describes in spontaneous song and with gestures fish, birds, monkeys, or other creatures, trying to cause as much amusement as possible by sounding silly and by clowning. By being as ridiculous as he can, the leader hopes to get the others to follow him and to "do as I do."

For example:

A fish does . . . hip! flip!
A bird does . . . viss, viss [flapping arms, elbows bent].
I turn myself to the right. I'm acting a fish. I dart in the water. I leap out of the water. I go flip, flop on the bank. The fish does . . . hip! hip! flip!
The bird goes . . . viss, viss, swoop, whoops!
The monkey goes chitter-chitter, chatter-chatter. The monkey leaps. The monkey runs pitter-pitter, chatter-chatter along the branches. The monkey goes chitter-chitter, chatter-chatter with his wife and his children and his mother and his father and his sisters and his brothers.

As soon as a person in the company wants to join the mime, he does so, following behind the leader and trying to do exactly as he does. One by one as they become interested, those in the company join the line behind the leader, repeating his words and imitating his movements and gestures.

When the leader begins to run out of silly songs and ridiculously exaggerated actions, the company stops mimicking him and stands still. The leader stops too and any who wish volunteer to mimic something. The others vote for the one whose mimicry they think will be most fun.

The above African Follow the Leader quickly becomes Alaskan by using some dramatic action, such as the flight of birds, racing kayaks, polar bears going from ice floe to ice floe, etc. For instance in mimicking the flight of a flock of birds, the mime might describe it in word and action in this way:

I wave my arms in the air. I make my hands flutter.
I wave my arms high and flutter my fingers like birds flying.
I hold my head high; I wave my arms. I flutter my hands. I run through the air like birds flying.
I hold my arms out. I feel the air under them.
The birds stop flying. I stop running. I stand and shrug my shoulders and shake myself. I hold my elbows close to my sides. I sit down. I rest my chin on my chest.

Here are some suggestions for word-and-action:

Angry pussy cat with arched back
Bunny rabbit hopping in garden or eating carrot
Duck waddling to pond
A hoop rolling (do somersaults or cartwheels)
Opossum rolling down slope
Sleeping baby bear
A bouncing ball
Mother taking laundry to laundromat (one child is mother pushing and the other the cart, with legs for the handle)
Tree (do handstands)
Computer being asked questions but giving nothing back but grunts and groans
Spacemen making rendezvous with moon
Dragon and other fantastic creatures from folk and fairy tales
Astronaut doing a moon walk

Hollanders in one of their versions of Follow the Leader used to take long skating trips over ice-clad country streams and canals, with finger-posts to point the way to Gouda, Leyden, and Utrecht, following marked-out tracks. Individuals or teams raced in various contests. There were crossroads and ditches, and the way was dotted with tents, watchers, flags, and *baanvegers* to take care of keeping tracks clean and laying gangways where needed beneath bridges and other places where the ice was bad.

The tents were put up to keep out the wind while skaters stopped for *warme melk en zoete koek* (warm milk and sweet cake). The hot, boiled milk was flavored with aniseed.

SAVEZ-VOUS PLANTER LES CHOUX? This is a French circle and chanting game popular with little children who like making silly motions. Here is a French-English variation that has proved to be fun:

French	English
Savez-vous planter les choux, *À la mode, à la mode?*	Do you know how to plant cabbages, The way they do, the way they do?
Savez-vous planter les choux *À la mode de chez nous?*	Do you know how to plant cabbages The way they do at home?
Oui, nous savons planter les choux *À la mode de chez nous.*	Yes, we know how to plant cabbages The way they do at home.
On les plante avec la main, *Avec la main, avec la main,* *À la mode de chez nous.*	They plant them by hand, By hand, by hand, That's the way they do it at home.

Change *"avec la main"* and "by hand" to the following words accompanied by appropriate actions.

French and English	Actions
Avec les pieds (with the feet)	Stamp gently as though tamping down the soil.
Avec le coude (with the elbow)	Put hands on waist and swing elbows back and forth, shrugging shoulders.
Avec le nez (with the nose)	Make digging motions with nose as pig does with snout.
Avec le genou (with the knee)	Get down on knees and pretend to weed.
Avec la bouche (with the mouth)	Sit back on heels and chew as though eating cabbage.

Portuguese children play Nós Fazemos (We Do) and Que Faz o Gato? (What Does a Cat Do?), which is the same kind of word-and-action game. For *gato* (cat), they change the creature and make the motions of a *pato* (duck), *coelho* (rabbit), or other animal or thing.

LAS RANAS When it starts to rain in Puerto Rico, Mexico, and in lands of Central America, boys and girls put a *capotin* (rain cape) around their shoulders as most children do everywhere. But their *capotin* is a thatch of leaves and the patter of rain on it goes "tin-tin-tin-tin," so the children chant:

Spanish	English
Yo voy con el capotin-tin-tin-tin *Que de hoy a mañana va llover.**	I am going with my rain cape, tin, tin, tin, For it's going to rain any time.
Yo voy con el capotin-tin-tin-tin, *Que va llover.*	I am going with my rain cape, tin, tin, tin, For it's going to rain.
Yo voy con el capotin-tin-tin-tin. *¡Aquí vienen las ranas!*	I am going with my rain cape, tin, tin, tin. Here come the frogs!

And, sure enough, the rain brings the frogs as it does in most places.

When that happens the children gather in a ring, and all squat on their heels, letting their *capotins* fall off their shoulders. They, themselves, resemble nothing so much as a ring of frogs or "hockers"—those little clay figures and sculptures with arms and legs outstretched frog fashion, so typical of early China, Malaysia, Melanesia, Polynesia, Central and South America, and found in lands all around the Pacific Ocean.

After a moment, the children begin to kick out first with one foot then the other. They let their arms swing loosely at their sides, clapping their hands in front, then behind their backs, all clapping and kicking out in rhythm.

Any frog who falls over, picks up his *capotin*, goes to sit in the center of the ring, and covers his head with his rain cape as if he were a frog under a big mushroom. The child who can hop longest without rolling over is the winner.

If leaves and branches from which to make real *capotins* are not available, use sheets of newspaper or pages from large-size magazines.

ONE-CHANCE, ONE-HIT HIGH BALL DART THROW Activities based on fantasy undergo from time to time a metamorphosis, becoming games of skill and of chance, athletic games and contests. This game—as well as the following games of Bat, Trap, and Ball and Hit Moving Target with Grass Ball—is a game of this type.

Giving someone a second chance is a commonly accepted practice

---
* Repeat this verse several times.

among peoples dependent upon technology for their livelihood. They use the tools of work rather than their own efforts to gain a living. But among such nontechnical peoples as Australian aborigines; Eskimos of the Arctic; Indians of Ecuador, British Columbia, and the U.S. Northwest Coast, and the hunting and fishing Nanai of the Soviet North, a second chance is not even thought of. A blowgun's poisoned dart, an arrow, spear, throwing stick, boomerang is aimed at the target—bird or animal—in full expectation of hitting it.

The primitive hunter always thinks of success, never of failure. And those around him think positively, singing songs of success and dancing with movement and gesture symbolic of achievement, as in these dance-song lines of Eskimos addressed to the hunter, which are repeated over and over again: "He constantly bends it; he constantly sends it straight, the big bow. He constantly sends it straight."

When it is a matter of having something to eat or going hungry, the rule is one chance, one hit. The rule lies embedded in a number of games.

One-Chance, One-Hit High Ball Dart Throw is a game of skill for few or many, young and old, in or outdoors. To a pole 8-10 feet tall, affix a 12-inch paper or wooden plate. Set up pole and place a hollow rubber ball in the plate. Players are given rubber-tipped darts. They stand in a circle an average throwing distance from the pole and, in turn, try to hit the ball and knock it off. Nothing is given for a mere hit, but a failure to hit the target costs the player a bottlecap, or other small article which he puts in a central pile or hoard. He puts his initials on the item in order to be able to identify it later. A player who makes a hit after he has lost something to the hoard, may take one item back, and he may continue to do this with successful hits until he has regained all he has lost.

The game goes on as long as the players wish, and any player may leave at any time he wishes. Players also may choose sides and play as teams. The ball is retrieved by someone with a long-handled net (a metal or plastic kitchen sieve attached to a long handle will do), and players take turns at it.

In Hawaii and other islands of Polynesia, the same game is played usually under the name of Hit the Coconut. The coconut is attached to the top of a high pole and players, using bows and arrows, try to hit it, but not to knock it off. Children playing the game with bows and arrows have rubber-tipped arrows for safety.

BAT, TRAP, AND BALL   This is acually a kind of simple Skeet Shooting. It is played with a spring-trap or "trip-stick," ping-pong bat,

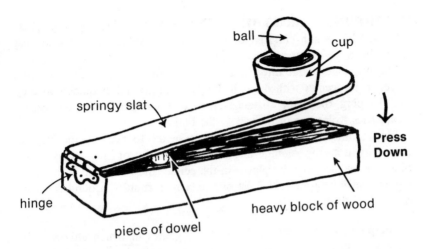

ball → cup

springy slat

↓ **Press Down**

hinge

heavy block of wood

piece of dowel

and ball. Make the trip-stick of a thin piece of springy wood about three feet long and several inches wide. It operates like a springboard when the free end is pressed down, and the ball is flung out of the cup. Diagram shows simple construction.

The trip-stick is placed in the center of a large playfield and markers set up at a distance of 40-50 feet all around.

A player is chosen Trapper; the others are Batters and scatter about the field inside the markers. The Trapper stands at the trip-stick, calls up the first Batter, and gives him the ping-pong paddle. Batter takes up a position ten or so feet in front of the trip-stick and facing the Trapper. When all players are ready, the Trapper puts the ping-pong ball in the cup and presses down the trip-stick so that the ball flies up into the air.

The Batter tries to hit the ball up into the air and, at the same time, give it distance so that it goes beyond the circle of markers, for then it is called a "hit." If the ball cannot be reached by the Batter who is up, and it starts to fall within the markers, any Batter who thinks he can catch the ball, calls out, "It's mine," and runs to get it. If he succeeds, he's next up at bat.

When a Batter makes a hit, he or she names the next Batter up. A fair ball that is not hit by the Batter and falls to the ground without being caught by anyone is a "dead ball." The Batter up loses his turn and the Trapper calls for next Batter up. A "fair ball" is any ball that rises in the air at least shoulder high and within the markers.

A tally of his hits is kept by each player, using a piece of cord and tying a knot in it after each of his hits. All must see player tie the knot.

Winner is the player with most hits after all, including Trapper, have been up at bat.

HIT MOVING TARGET WITH GRASS BALL   For the large grass ball used by Indian children of the Americas, substitute a plastic bag filled with wads of paper. Pack it tight.

Players stand about three feet apart to form a large circle, with one player in the center with the ball. Players run around as quickly as they can, keeping the same distance from one another, while the center player tries to hit one of them with the ball.

Players may dodge, duck, or otherwise try to avoid being hit, but they must not stop running and must not get out of line. As soon as a player is hit, he joins the player in the center and helps him with throwing and retrieving the ball. Last one to remain running around the circle is next ball thrower.

IL PORCELLINO   This is one of the games in which children play the role of little helpers, pretending to assist their parents or older members of the family. Children enjoy being messengers, taking messages from one member of the family to another, or running errands for the mother or the father. They like being little gardeners when others are planting windowboxes, potting plants, or working in the yard or garden.

It makes children feel important to help Dad wash or work on the car, as Dorothy W. Baruch pointed out in her poem, "Automobile Mechanics." Dorothy Brown Thompson in her poem, "I Like Housecleaning," speaks lyrically of the fun children have at spring cleaning, when "strange stored-away things" come to light and "make marvelous playthings." When cupboards, closets, basement, garage, and other storage places are cleared out, what a wonderful chance there is to "go gleaning . . . for new things to play."

Il Porcellino, meaning "The Little Pig," is the way small helpers in Italy make a game of catching the little porker that got loose. They sit in a circle, with one child in the middle. Each of the other children are parts of the pig, including the head, *la testa;* the snout, *il grugno;* the tail, *il codino;* the feet, *le zampe;* ears, *orecchie;* eyes, *occhi;* teeth, *denti.*

When the player in the middle says suddenly, "Get up, head! (*Alzati, testa!*) Sit down, snout! (*Siedi, grugno!*)" those who are head and snout must get up quickly and exchange places before the middle player can get to an empty seat. If the player succeeds, he becomes the part of the pig whose place he has taken, and the seatless player goes to the middle of the circle.

SCARICA BARILI   Boys especially like this vigorous Italian game, whose name means "Unloading Barrels" in English. It is played in pairs, who stand back to back, hooking elbows. One, then the other bends, lifting his partner who kicks his feet up high. They proceed toward a goal a dozen or so feet away, bending and lifting like two men who rise and bend over the handle of a trolley car or handcar as they pump and send the car rolling down a railroad track.

First pair to reach the goal is the winner.

WAS KOSTEN DIE EIER, HERR MEIER?   The English name of this game is "How Much Are the Eggs, Mr. Meier?" The price of eggs is of concern to most families and here is a German game about it.

One child is chosen to be Herr Meier and the others are Kinder (children), who surround him in a circle. The following dialogue takes place:

> Kinder: *Was kosten die Eier, Herr Meier?* (How much are eggs, Mr. Meier?)
> Herr Meier: *Drei Dreier.* (Three pennies.)
> Kinder [*in an astonished tone*]: *Drei Dreier, Herr Meier?* (Three pennies, Mr. Meier?)
> Herr Meier: *Ya, und das finde ich euer.* (Yes, and they've gone higher.)
> Kinder: *Niemand will die Eier.* (Nobody wants eggs.)
> Herr Meier: *So geb ich ein Ei.* (I'll give you an egg.)
> Kinder: *Nein, und gäbst du mir auch zwei.* (No, even if you gave me two.)

As soon as Kinder say the last line, they all dart away and Herr Meier must catch one of them to take his place.

WER KLOPFT?   Children look forward to the time when they are old enough to answer a knock on the door. The first time they can do so by themselves is an event. The knocking and the answering have important psychological implications that are universal and, doubtless, that is one of the reasons Who Knocks? as a game has gone unknown in few places where there are doors to rap on. This is a German variety.

Two children, who are blindfolded, sit back to back in two chairs. The others march around and around the two. Every once in a while one of the marchers will tap a blindfolded child on the shoulder, and the child tapped asks, *"Brüderchen, wer klopft?"* ("Brother, who knocks?") If the tapped child guesses the tapper's name, the tapper is blindfolded and takes the former's seat. Game continues as long as players wish.

EL HERRERITO   This is a dialogue-motion game of Spain that small boys and girls find fun to do. Players sit with drawn-up knees in a semicircle in front of one of them who has been chosen to be El Herrerito (The Little Blacksmith). The latter begins by asking the first player in front of him to his right:

El Herrerito: *¿Es usted un herrerito como yo?* (Are you a black-smith like me?)
Player: *Si, señor.* (Yes, sir.)
El Herrerito: *Pues, mache usted con un macho, como macho yo.* (Then pound with a hammer the way I pound.)

El Herrerito pounds with his right fist on his right knee, and the player copies his action. Then he repeats the question to the next player, who repeats the response to the question and the action. Question, answer, and action are repeated until all those in front of the Little Blacksmith are pounding with their right fists on their right knees.

El Herrerito [*starting over with the first player in front of him to his right*]: *¿Quiere ser un herrerito como yo?* (Do you want to be a black-smith like me?)
Player: *Si, señor.* (Yes, sir.)
El Herrerito: *Pues, mache usted con dos machos, como macho yo.* (Then hammer with two hammers the way I hammer.)

El Herrerito hits left knee with left fist and continues to hit right knee with right fist, alternating right and left. He goes around the semicircle of players as before and when all are doing as he does, he continues with *"tres machos"* (three hammers) and taps his right foot; then *"cuatro machos"* (four hammers) and taps his left foot. All continue in rhythm until El Herrerito begins to eliminate all those who make mistakes. The player who continues longest without any mistakes that El Herrerito can observe is the next Herrerito.

¿CUÁNTAS NARANJAS?   This is a Spanish counting game for a group of small children sitting around in a circle, who are about to go to the market for oranges when the orange seller arrives. The fun of the game is in the fast counting backwards without tripping over words.
A player is chosen to start the game, and begins this way:

First player: *Amigos, vamos a naranjas.* (Friends, let's go for oranges.)
Others: *¿Cuántas vamos a traer?* (How many shall we get?)

First player: *Una para mi y una para usted.* (One for me and one for you.)

Others: *¡Mira! ¡El naranjero está aquí!* (Look! The orange seller is here!) *¿Cuántas naranjas queremos?* (How many oranges do we want?)

First Player: *Una para mi y una para usted.* (One for me and one for you.) *¿Cuántas naranjas hay aquí?* (How many oranges are there here?)

Then first player continues as fast as possible, the others counting with him. Any slip of the tongue and a player must drop out of the game.

First player and the others [*all together, and very fast*]: *De quince, catorce** (from fifteen, fourteen); *de catorce, trece* (from fourteen, thirteen); *de trece, doce* (from thirteen, twelve); *de doce, once* (from twelve, eleven); *de once, diez* (from eleven, ten); *de diez, nueve* (from ten, nine); *de nueve, ocho* (from nine, eight); *de ocho, siete* (from eight, seven); *de siete, seis* (from seven, six); *de seis, cinco* (from six, five); *de cinco, cuatro* (from five, four); *de cuatro, tres* (from four, three); *de tres, dos* (from three, two); *de dos, una* (from two, one); *de una y nada mas* (from one and nothing more).

MEUNIER, TU DORS   This is a rhyme to use for Hide-and-Seek in a version traditionally played by French girls. The player who is It leans against tree or wall and hides face in crook or arm, as she says the rhyme loudly.

The French and English versions follow:

French	English
Meunier, tu dors,	Miller, you're sleeping,
Et ton moulin va trop vite.	And your mill turns too fast.
Meunier, tu dors,	Miller, you're sleeping,
Et ton moulin va trop fort.	And your mill turns too hard.
Meunier! Meunier! Il se réveille!	Miller! Miller! He wakes up!

Players must all be hidden by the time It shouts: *"Il se réveille!"* for anyone she sees she can catch by simply calling out that person's name.

---

* Start the counting backwards with the number of players in the game, for the idea is that there are oranges enough for everyone. In the example above, the number of players is assumed to be fifteen.

Work-play Holidays
And
Their Games

ABOUT TWO HUNDRED years ago, the United States of America was an emerging nation to which the cognoscenti of established nations came to observe and to comment upon in books and through the press. From earliest visitors to New England and to what is now referred to as Appalachia, to later visitors reviewing their "western travels"—all alike commented with surprise on the constant human activity.

"It is well known that they [the Americans] are among the most constantly occupied and busiest people in the world," wrote James Silk Buckingham, one of the many visitors from England.

Busyness but with a difference, they all noted: "Americans seldom do anything without having a frolic. . . . thus they have berrying, husking, haying, reaping, logrolling, barn-raising and house-raising frolics. . . . and they have picking [cotton from seeds], sewing, quilting, preserving, sleighing, . . . frolics."

In other words, Americans everywhere were inclined to have work-play affairs, usually called "bees" or "work-bees," at which special games and competitive sports were played and athletic and nonathletic contests held, such as spelling bees.

And, as the visitors also never failed to note, at these bees there was always plenty to eat and drink, and they usually "concluded with a dance."

STUMP THE LEADER AT A ROLLING FROLIC   It seems likely that the U.S. slang word "stump," meaning to dare or challenge some-one to do something dangerous, might easily have originated with roll-ing frolics. Those were neighborly gatherings to clear woodland for a new settler, or to make a clearing for pasture or field for an old settler. Trees were cut down, then into lengths, and rolled up together; brush was cut and piled up for burning, and sometimes the hardest job of all was tackled—pulling the tree stumps out of the ground by united strength of man and beast (oxen, horses, mules).

At rolling frolics men and boys, especially, liked to challenge one another to feats of skill or strength, each one in turn trying to top the performance of his predecessor. For instance, men juggled a log with their feet as they lay on their backs, hands under the smalls of their backs. The logs got larger and larger as the contest continued. Grown-ups at the frolics as well as the children had the wonderful experience of showing off with full social approval and with acceptance of defeats as well as successes.

Boys and girls can have fun with these suggestions for "stumping the leader." The challenger is in each instance the leader who says, "Watch me, I bet nobody can do this," or words to that effect. The Stumper is the person who accepts the challenge, accomplishes the feat or task, then tops it by making the stunt more difficult in some way. Then the Stumper becomes the leader who challenges anyone to match him. Of course, if the person who accepts the challenge fails, he simply gives way to another who accepts and tries.

The following are some good challenges:

1. Walking a straight line while balancing something on head; while balancing a ruler or long sticks on shoulder or shoulders, or chips (wood) on shoulder; while balancing something on head and on shoulders; while balancing objects, such as paper cups, pebbles, balls, balloons, on back of outstretched hands (balancing objects on hands can also be tried while running).

2. Juggling volleyballs or balloons with feet while lying down with hands under small of back.

3. Running and tumbling a certain distance within a limited time; increasing number of tumbles (somersaults) in the same or less time.

4. Doing cartwheels in a circle; increasing size of circle and number of cartwheels.

LA CONTRADDIZIONE   This Italian game is a Stump the Leader in reverse. A leader, standing before or in the center of a group, makes gestures and motions quickly but precisely so that there is no mistaking them, but makes them suddenly and unexpectedly. For instance, the leader steps forward, jumps up, waves good-by, laughs, stretches out arms, etc., and all the others must do exactly the opposite (hence the name of the game: La Contraddizione, or Contradiction). If the leader jumps up, others sit down; leader steps forward, others step backward.

Those who are too slow or make the wrong motion or gesture are out of game. Leader continues until there is only one left who becomes the next leader.

CLEARING THE FIELD AT A ROLLING FROLIC   Needed for the game is a collection of miscellaneous objects, such as bats, balls, large stones, pans, pots, or anything at hand. The leader or challenger dares anyone to beat his time in carrying first three, then four, then more articles—one at a time—from the field (center of the circle of players) to the brush pile (any designated spot some distance away). Each one who accepts a challenge and succeeds at the feat, increases the kind and number of articles, and, in turn, challenges someone else to beat his time in racing with the articles one by one from brush pile to field or field to brush pile, depending upon where the articles are at the time the challenger makes the challenge.

When the collection of objects becomes so large as to be too tedious for carrying one by one, it is time for someone to say, "I can carry more things and clear the field faster than you."

GRAB AND RUN   This game is somewhat like Clearing the Field above, but is a team form. Three miscellaneous objects—such as a bat, ball, and big stone—are needed. Players divide into four teams; each team chooses a leader, who also keeps score for the team. Each team forms a ring at a corner of a large square play area. Beginning with the leader, who is One, team members count off. All sit down except the four team leaders.

The three articles are placed in the center of the play area. Each leader then calls the number of a member of his team. As soon as the four numbers are called, the four team members whose numbers were called dash to the three articles and try to grab one of them and return to their teams. Since there are only three articles, one team member fails to get anything.

Leaders of successful teams score three points.

Articles are replaced in the center, and the game continues until leaders have called the numbers of all their team members. Team with highest score is winner. In case of a tie, the tied teams use one article in a play-off game.

SORTING CORN   Mark Twain's Tom Sawyer was only one American boy who knew how to turn work into play. People at husking, berrying, haying, reaping, sowing, and cotton-picking frolics built their play right into the work by seeing who could husk the most corn in the shortest time; pick the most pails of strawberries or huckleberries; pitch hay the fastest; swing the scythe and cut the most grain; sew a seam without a stitch showing; and pick cotton fastest, that is, separate the cotton from the seeds by hand.

This last was a frolic for women and girls. Such frolics took place before Eli Whitney, while staying at the Savannah River plantation of Mrs. Nathanael Greene (widow of the American Revolutionary War general), built some "ingenious household contrivances." It was at her suggestion that Whitney worked on a mechanical device for separating cotton from seed and came up with the cotton gin.

Sorting Corn was usually a frolic for the family, including grand-parents, uncles, aunts, and cousins as often as not. In this respect it was like the *esfalhada* (corn husking) and *tosquia* (sheep shearing) in Portugal, which were common tasks.

A game for today can't duplicate the frolic in which the best corn was set aside for seed, the next best went into flour, and after that corn was stored for horses, pigs, chickens, and other barnyard animals and fowls. But a sorting game can be a good contest for a school or neighborhood fun-fair or at a party.

Fill bowls of the same size with a combination of popped and un-popped popcorn, raisins, puffed rice, puffed wheat, and pretzels. (Any combination of three is acceptable.) Contestants sort the contents of the bowls, putting them into their proper jars. Winner is contestant who does this in shortest time. Small prizes are awarded winners and runners-up.

PULLING THE OX (HORSE or MULE) OUT OF THE MUD   This task seemed to be part of most frolics whether the weather was wet or dry. Oxen in particular apparently had a very real talent for blundering into mudholes and becoming so bogged down that they had to be res-cued. Men and boys made the tugging into play and by the time it be-came a game, it was a great deal like Pom Pom Pull Away, Hill Dill, and other kinds of pull-aways and tugs-of-war.

For Pulling the Ox Out of the Mud, the selected It stands in the center of the playfield, with the players lined up 25-30 feet in front of him against a wall or fence. Behind him at the same distance away, should be another wall or fence. Substitute ropes stretched between stakes if walls and fences are lacking.

Sidelines should be drawn, making a narrow passage between them. If there are few players, the passage should be no wider than needed for three to run abreast, but vary width according to number of players.

It shouts:

> Big red ox
> In the mud,
> Old muley cow
> Chewing her cud,
> Pull, pull, pull away,
> Come away or I'll pull you away.

All players must run across to the opposite side. It tags as many players as he can as they dash past him. Those tagged must join him at once in tagging others. Those who step over the sidelines are out of the game. Last one caught is It for the next game.

To vary the game, those caught by any player instead of by It are held while the catcher counts up to ten, in order to be properly tagged. Captive may struggle to get away or not, but this should be ruled upon before the game starts.

AINSI FONT, FONT, FONT DES ZAMI DE PAPA LA CHAISE
This game is played by Haitian children at coumbites, or work-bees. Haitian children can play-make pretty pins of thorns of orange and *amourette* (honey locust), or carry water and hoe the field with grown-ups. Women and girls look after the family, the chickens, pigs, goats, and the *bourique* (little burro), beat the laundry on the rocks in the river, and run the markets, doing all the buying and selling.

On the farm, men and boys plant and cultivate the crops, grind the grain, and, on the coasts, fish. They are expert in the handling of their homemade boats and world champions in the casting of seines.

But when a man or woman has a big job to do, such as clearing a field or raising a *caille* (farmhouse), he or she, like the homesteader in North America, asks for (or is offered) neighborly help.

Neighbors respond by holding a *coumbite*, or work-bee, which concludes with a *bamboche* (party). The response to the call for help is always about three times greater than the need.

Someone sounds the conch shell to start off the work at a *coumbite*, and the work is done in rhythm to the beating of a drum—often only a piece of hollow wood—or to the music made by one who blows the conch shell.

And, as they work, the people sing songs mocking those who shirk. They sing about the man who *tous temps li gagn travaille pour nous* (always has work for us), but when he's needed has something he must do *"nans ville"* (in the city). He's the person who always shows up, though, just about the time the *bamboche* is getting underway, and can eat more barbecued beef, goat, pig, rice and beans, sweet potato pudding, fried bananas, and boiled groundnuts than anybody.

Children imitate the grown-ups, act as helpers and play games, such as this circle tag, *Ainsi Font, Font, Font Des Zami De Papa La Chaise* (say *shez*), which means "Thus Do, Do, Do the Friends of Papa La Chaise" in English.

By counting out, one player is chosen Papa La Chaise, the "tagger"; the others, who are *"des zami"* (friends) of Papa La Chaise, form a circle, with a space of three or so steps between a player and the one behind.

Papa La Chaise walks quickly (*marché donc*) clockwise around the outside of his circle of friends. Then, when it is least expected, he touches a player, who leaves his place and walks quickly (*marché donc*) counterclockwise. When they meet, they bow, shake hands, spin around, shake hands again, and then the friend addresses one of the following verses to Papa La Chaise (or, in the case of the second verse, Momzelle La Chaise):

French	English
Bonsoir, bonsoir,	Good evening, good evening,
Papa La Chaise.	Papa La Chaise.
Comment ou yé?	How are you?
Quand m'a-lé ça ma dit la caille	When I go home shall I say
Comment ou yé?	How are you?
Bonsoir, bonsoir,	Good evening, good evening,
Momzelle La Chaise.	Momzelle La Chaise.
Comment ou yé?	How are you?
Quand m'a-lé, quand m'a-lé ça ma dit	When I go, when I go shall I say
Comment ou yé, Mademoiselle, adieu?	How are you, Mademoiselle, good-by?
Bonsoir, bonsoir,	Good evening, good evening,
Ça ma de Mama e,	What shall I say to Mama,
Comment ou yé?	How are you?
Quand m'a-lé ça ma dit Papa e	When I go shall I say to Papa
Comment ou yé?	How are you?

Bonsoir, bonsoir,	Good evening, good evening,
Quand m'a-lé, et quand m'a-lé ça	When I go and when I go home, do
ma dit la caille	I say
Comment ou yé, Mama, Papa,	How are you, Mama, Papa,
Adieu, adieu, bonsoir, bonsoir?	Good-by, good-by, good evening, good evening?

Once the friend has spoken his words, he and Papa La Chaise (or Momzelle) dart for the empty place in the circle. The one who is left out becomes the next Papa La Chaise. If children wish, they may bow, shake hands, and dart off for the empty place without speaking any lines. Sometimes, Papa La Chaise and his Friend, upon meeting, simply spin around and run for it.

PORTABLE THATCH   Often when a family in Cherrapunji, India, wants to move, the boys—the family's, neighbors' and friends'—remove the portable thatched roof from the house, get under it, and carry it to the place where it is to be erected on the new house. Walking beneath the roof, the boys can see only the feet and legs and the hand gestures of the father or other grown-up, who walks outside, just ahead of the walking roof that resembles a centipede as it goes down the road. The boys follow in the adult's footsteps and are guided one way or the other at a turning, signaled when to stop and start or move to the side of the road, by hand gestures.

Small boys and girls have a moving-day-bee game: each wears some sort of eyeshade so that he or she can't see anything but the feet, legs, and gestures to the right, left, or straight ahead of someone who leads a line of them serpentine fashion up and down, around and about, trying to confuse and lose them from the line. Out of line is out of the game. Last to follow the leader is the next leader.

SHRIMPERS ON HORSEBACK CONTEST   At Coxyde on the dunes west of Nieuport, Belgium, and lying between La Panne and the borders of France, people fish for shrimp on horseback. Mounted on their ponies and carrying baskets and nets fastened to long poles, fisher folk young and old ride into the sea to catch small fish and shrimp. They go about in bands or in pairs, swinging nets and scooping up the seafood and filling their baskets.

This custom of fishing, which has been handed down from parent to child for generations, adapts very well to a contest for swimming or wading pool, for a group of six or even two players. Baskets are placed at two ends of a pool. A large quantity of ping-pong balls are tossed into the water. Each player, armed with a net having a handle, swims or wades about scooping up the balls and putting them in the basket assigned to him or his team. When there are more than two, contestants play as teams.

This game makes a good father-son, mother-daughter event at a swim party at the beach in shallow water when the tide is coming in. Little son or daughter carries the net, rides the shoulders of father or mother, scoops up the fish and shrimp (ping-pong balls), and places them in the team's basket which sits upon the sand at the water's edge. Someone should keep an eye on the basket and move it back from time to time or it will go floating about when the incoming tide catches it.

MANTANTIRULIRULÁ   This game is popular in Uruguay, but it is played everywhere in South America. *"Mantantirulirulá"* is simply a made-up sing-song without meaning, just as English-speaking children have made-up nonsense words, for instance, "ibbity," "bibbity," "casaba."

Five or more may play. One is chosen to be the Employer; the rest are Workers. During the game, as the questions and answers are chanted, Employer and Workers keep walking to and from each other. At the end of all questions and answers, the word *"Mantantirulirulá"* is added.

The Employer says, "I want someone to work for me." The Workers reply, "Which one of us do you want?" The Employer names one of the players, who asks, "What work will I do?"

The Employer names some job, such as gardener, cook, secretary, bookkeeper, or anything else he can think of. The rest of the players ask the Worker if he likes the job the Employer offered him. If the Worker says no and gives some silly reason, such as, "I don't want to be a cook. I'll get too skinny," the other players chant, "He doesn't like that. He'll get skinny."

The Employer suggests another, and another, and still another job until he finally names one the Worker does like. The other players move to and from each throughout the whole time. The Worker who at last says he likes a job, joins the Employer, who chooses another Worker and begins suggesting jobs to him. The last Worker chosen is the Employer for the next game.

Part VIII

CELEBRATING SPECIAL DAYS AND EVENTS

Birthday, Name Day, And Festival Fun Around the World

QUINTILIAN, WHO WROTE twelve books on Roman education in the days of Emperor Vespasian, commended holidays "because relaxation brings greater energy to study, and also to games, because it is the nature of young things to play, and because a boy who is in a continual state of depression is never likely to show alertness of mind in his work."

A part of the celebration of birthdays, the new year, a people's independence, and similar occasions of festivity are games associated with them.

ALLES WAS FEDERN HAT KANN FLIEGEN This is a game especially for a Kinderfest, or children's party, in particular a child's birthday party, in Deutschland from the North Sea to the Alps.

One guest is chosen to be first to call out the names of animals, insects, birds, fowl, fantastic creatures, or things that can or cannot fly (the name of the game means "Whatever Has Feathers Can Fly"). Mostly flying creatures will be named. If Caller is going to name fantastic creatures, he must say so in advance; otherwise it is assumed that the creatures are real. And if the creatures named are fantastic, whether or not they can fly is determined by their ability or inability in legend, story, or tale.

Whenever a flying animal or thing is named, host/hostess and guests raise their arms and pretend to fly, but without moving from their places. Whenever something that doesn't fly is named, all must stand motionless. For instance, if the Caller says, *"Enten fliegen"* (ducks fly), *"Raben fliegen"* (crows fly), or even *"ein Drachen geflogen"* (a dragon flies) then all make flying motions.

But if the Caller says, *"Ein Fuchs geflogen"* (a fox flies), all must remain still, or those who fly are out of the game. Of course, there are animals called "flying foxes" as well as animals called "flying squirrels" but they cannot be said to fly, but rather to glide, and the only "flying horses" remain in ancient legends. Anyone who challenges the Caller as to whether something can fly or not is referred to the host/hostess, who at once calls for a show of hands on it.

Last to remain in the game is the next Caller.

After games, there is the party with a birthday cake, perhaps a *napfkuchen* (butter cake) or *stöllen,* full of fruit and nuts, with lighted candles all around it. The candle-lit birthday cake was taken to North America by the people from Deutschland, and Americans adopted it just as they adopted the German's Christmas tree bright with flickering candles. Now, seldom if ever, is there a birthday party for anyone without a cake aglow with candles for the birthday child to blow out.

BUBBLE-BLOWING CONTESTS   These affairs were once as much a part of the American child's birthday party as Pin the Tail on the Donkey, in which a large outline or picture of a donkey was tacked on the wall or a screen and blindfolded guests in turn tried, to the amusement of the others, to pin the tail where the tail ought to be. The one who came closest to doing it was awarded a prize and everyone else was consoled by going on to the Bubble-Blowing Contests, in which guests competed in pairs to see who in three trials could: (1) blow the biggest bubble, (2) the bubble that lasted longest, (3) the bubble that went farthest through the air, (4) the bubble that went highest, and so on. That continued until the best all-round bubble-blower was found and received an award. However, all contestants were given some remembrance of the birthday since everyone always managed to succeed at something.

Three or four large bowls of soapy water and bubble rings or pipes for all contestants are needed. The number of bowls depends upon the number of different contests. For instance, Bowl 1 may be for biggest bubble, Bowl 2 for longest lasting, etc., and contestants progress from one bowl to another. Each bowl has someone who acts as Official Record Keeper of winners at that bowl.

HIT THE TARGET WITH THOR'S HAMMER This is an ancient game in Scandinavia and in Iceland. The hammer has always been associated with birthdays in Nordic lands, and in very old times a hammer was raised in blessing a newborn child and as a sign of its acceptance into the community.

The birthday hammer of the Viking's god Thor, who gave his name to a day of the week, Thursday or Thor's Day, was a cross with four equal arms. A leather thong or a metal ring was added to one of the arms for greater ease and effectiveness in throwing.

The hammer can be made of two sticks crossed and a leather or twine loop. For the target, set up a large cutout or picture of a mythical beast, such as a sea monster, serpent, or dragon, behind a large hoop a few feet away. Contestants must throw the hammer through the hoop from a toeline and hit the mythical beast on some part of its body. Number of points to be given for each hit is decided before the start of the contest.

Winner is entitled to the first piece of *kringle,* the special birthday cake in the shape of a pretzel with frosting mixed with raisins and almonds.

SPINNING THE YO-YO A yo-yo is probably a birthday child's gift in the Philippines, where yo-yos had their origin long ago. A popular game is spinning the yo-yo and hitting a tin can off a post.

ONE-BASE PALM BALL This is one of the Swedish ball games that are just right for birthdays and name days, for the Swedes celebrate on name days too. The name of the person honored is written in green leaves and flowers down the middle of the table. Ball games and the like are played outdoors unless the weather is really very bad.

Two teams of three or more players each can play on space 35-40 feet long and 25 feet or so wide. A base near one end of it is outlined and 20 feet in front of it is placed a bag to indicate "home." Team up at bat stands along a sideline. Opposing team has one player stationed at the base and the rest scattered about the field. There is no pitcher. The batter stands at home and tosses up a softball, hits it with his hand as far as he can, runs for base, touches it, and runs back home. This counts as a run. Batter may be put out by being touched with the ball, or having the ball caught on the fly by the player at base or a fielder on the opposing team.

PLAYING POSSUM Jumping feats mark the growing up of boys in many places in Africa and in the Australian Outback when there are tribal or village-wide celebrations. High jumping to the sound of drums and singing may go on all day and night.

Although most of the main rituals of a corroboree among the Kurnai of Australia are those of initiation of boys into manhood, there is a game, Playing Possum, in which the boys engage.

The Australian opossum is different from the American, although varieties in both continents belong to the same family—phalanger marsupials. The flying possums have membranes with which to glide like flying squirrels. They are beautiful, wooly animals that race along the high branches, make great leaps, and go flying through the air.

Hunting opposum among the gum trees by moonlight is the hide-and-seek that the boys play, some being the Hunters and others the Flying Possums. It is played as any informal team hide-and-seek game.

KAGE-BOHI-ONIGO   This form of Shadow Tag makes a fine game for a little girl's or boy's birthday in Japan and in Korea on a sunny day outdoors. "It" tries to step on the shadow of players who run about, trying to avoid having their shadows stepped on. Owner of first shadow to be stepped on by It becomes the next It. Players must keep apart so that each player's shadow is clear.

FOUR-AND-TWENTY BLACKBIRDS BAKED UP IN A PIE   This was introduced as a surprise for fun by King Henry VIII of England, as a huge living pie filled with cawing crows and chattering magpies at the feasting during the Twelve Days of Christmas. Consequently, there is truth in the Mother Goose rhyme,

> Sing a song of sixpence,
> A pocket full of rye;
> Four-and-twenty blackbirds
> Baked up in a pie.
>
> When the pie was opened,
> The birds began to sing;
> Was that not a dainty dish
> To set before the king?

The game is played shortly before the arrival of the one for whom the surprise party is given.

Needed are old cotton sheets or blankets (the number depends upon the number of guests). All but one player sit crosslegged on the floor all around the sheet and hold it taut. The player not seated is given a feather which he places in the center of the sheet.

When he calls, "Ready, blow!" players begin to blow the feather back and forth without allowing it to fall on the sheet. The unseated player runs around trying to catch the feather. When he succeeds, he may choose the place of any player, who then must chase the feather. Any time the feather comes to rest, the player nearest to it becomes the feather chaser.

Game continues until the arrival of the honored one is announced by the lookout, when all guests at once hide under the sheet and huddle there as still as possible until "the pie is opened," i.e., the child pulls the sheet off to see what's under it.

ME KAKUSHI   This is a game traditionally played during the Girls' Festival in Japan on March 3. The Japanese Boys' Festival takes place on May 5. They are two great days which have always been important to the Japanese. Since they are centered around dolls, they are *Hina-Matsuri,* or Dolls' Festivals too, and Syok-Kop-Tjil-Ha-Ki (Playing House) is all a part of the celebrations. And, as usual, there is kite-flying. (See Part III for games with kites.)

In many instances, families have sets of *hina-ningyo,* festival dolls, in costumes representative of Japanese history and culture, which they have handed down from generation to generation as heirlooms. The custom of displaying them at the festivals for boys and girls is known to go back at least a thousand years or more.

And, of course, there are the *ukiyo-ningyo,* ordinary dolls that do everyday things.

To play Me Kakushi (Hiding Eyes), one is selected to be blind-folded. That player stands, with outstretched arm and upturned palm, in the center of a ring of players who walk round and round. Now and then a player stops unexpectedly to touch the upturned palm of the one blindfolded, who must try to catch hold of the other's hand. Even catching a finger is considered a capture, and the one caught is blind-folded. She stands beside the first, with arm out and palm up, in the center of the ring.

Game continues until all wear blindfolds.

Whenever the first blindfolded player and later any of the others call out, "Clap hands and say your name," those walking round must do so.

Whenever a blindfolded child says, "Watch out, creep about," the ring of players must quit walking at even pace and go tiptoeing about as cautiously and quietly as possible. They must not cease, however, to touch the palms of the blindfolded to invite capture.

The game is made more difficult by requiring the blindfolded player to give the name of the person caught.

HPOUL-HKOU-TO-RONG-KOING   This is another game for the Japanese Girls' and Boys' Festivals. To play, a good-sized play area and a basketful of big green leaves or long-bladed grass are needed (hence the name of the game, which means "Green Grass Race." Substitute a pailful of sand or sawdust if the greenery is not available.) On the area outline a 20-foot square.

Two players at a time run around the square in opposite directions. Each has a handful of leaves or grass which is exchanged when the two meet. They are given only a second for the exchange and, of course, much grass is lost. None may be picked up. In exchanging each takes offered grass with empty hand.

Race continues until one, the winner, has some left, but the other little or none.

Players may be divided into teams and the team with the most races won, when all have raced, wins the game.

For a really old-fashioned and slower game, Japanese children used to stop to play a game of Ko-No when they met in the race round the square. Two only can play at a time.

KO-NO   To play, four small stones are needed, two colored red and two black. Then scratch a diagram like the one shown.

Player with red stones places them at two corners and player with black stones does the same. Players move alternately along all the lines

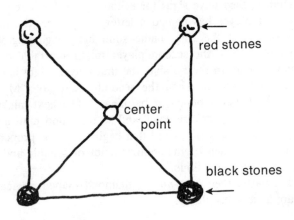

red stones

center point

black stones

and try to block their opponent's stones and prevent their being moved. A player moving diagonally cannot go beyond center point in one move.

MY BRIDE IS GOING TO TAKE WITH HER   As for the way to play Syok-Kop-Tjil-Ha-Ki (Playing House), that is left to the imaginations of girls anywhere who have, or make for themselves, any kind of dolls. But if they would like to play dolls in the old Japanese tradition, they may think of themselves as living long ago and being very rich. Then they can try this dolls'-play game.

In the old days, the Japanese bride when she went to her husband's house took with her such things as a *nagamochi*, a chest full of linens; a *tansu*, a chest of drawers filled with personal things; accessories for the bath such as towel racks and mirrors, and, perhaps, even a fine, ornamented ox-drawn wagon like the wagons imperial and aristocratic families used for traveling. And, in those days, Japanese girls had dolls dressed in traditional costumes, dolls' houses, toy furniture, carts, animals, and all the rest.

But girls today can play the dolls'-play game as of old without any dolls at all. It's like the English and American Alphabet Journey. The players sit around in a circle and one starts by saying, "My bride is going to take with her a T." She may name any letter of the alphabet she wishes, although naming things Japanese gives the game a special flair. And if players who have alphabetic writing systems—Greek, Latin, Hebrew, Arabic, Ethiopic, English, German, French, and so on—want to be even more in the Japanese spirit, they change the name to Syllabary Journey and name words that begin with the same syllable. The Japanese use a syllabary, which consists of 47 basic signs, not an alphabet. That is, they have signs for syllables, not for letters.

After the first player has named a letter or syllable, the players, in turn clockwise round the ring, name something beginning with that letter or syllable. Thus, the second player might say table or tea-tray in the alphabet game. In the syllabic, the first player might have started with, say, the syllable ba. Then the second could say, "My bride is going to take with her a bunch of ba-nanas." The next might say, "a ba-rometer," "ba-zaar," or "ba-zoo," and so on round until a player is reached who cannot think of a word that begins with the proper letter or syllable. That player then begins another letter or syllable and so on as long as players want to continue.

If there's a party, then *kusa-mochi*, diamond-shaped rice cakes, give the party fare a Japanese flavor.

FESTIVAL OF THE TREES   This is a children's holiday in Israel and focuses on children and tree planting, as Arbor Day does in the United States. On the festival day, children are taken usually by bus and the little green trees by trucks through the Judean hills to a site, called The Children's Forest, to the south of Jerusalem. There each child takes a tree and plants it in the field.

Afterwards there are singing and games of all kinds, with ball games especially popular. (See Part III for traditional basic ball games.)

BANOSHA BENDESHESHA?   This game is often played on the double holiday of April 23 in Turkey. It is Grand National Assembly Day, commemorating the opening of Turkey's first parliament in 1923; and it is also Children's Day, when many things are free to children all day long. In some towns boys and girls are mayors-for-a-day and other high government officials, with adult consultants available but in the background.

To play Banosha Bendeshesha players divide and stand with hands joined, facing one another, in two rows about 25 feet apart. One row is Banosha and the other, Bendeshesha. To start, they shout, "Banosha! Bendeshesha!" Then the Banosha ask, "Which one will you take?" and the other answers with the name of one of the Banosha players, for instance, "We'll take Meira."

As soon as the player's name is called, she/he must run across and try to break through the opposite row by pushing and thrusting against the joined hands. If successful, the player then returns to her/his own side. Failure to make a breakthrough means the player must join the side and call out the name of another of her/his former side's players to join it, too. Sides alternate in calling out names. Winner is the side with most players left within a given time, or the game may be played until one side has all the players.

For the usual holiday party, all should be given white paper chef's hats to wear, for it is said that these hats were first worn by cooks in the Turkish monasteries. They were the same shape as the priests' hats, but were white instead of black.

GAMES FOR TRUNG THU   Trung Thu was brought to Vietnam by the Chinese and is a children's festival celebrated at the autumnal equinox, the fifteenth day of the eighth month of the lunar, or moon, calendar used by the Chinese and other Eastern countries, but around September 15-21 according to the solar, or sun, calendar used by European, American, and other countries of the Western world.

Girls enjoy Hago Asobi, or Shuttlecock Play, in which they try to see how long, using two long, slender sticks, they can keep a shuttlecock in the air. Boys like kicking a ball (*tz'uk kuk*) in a casual kind of football. (See Part I for informal soccer.)

Both boys and girls have fun with Biting the Carp's Tail. They form a line and hold onto the back of the one in front, making the carp or fish. The ones in front are the head; the ones at the end, the tail. The head keeps swinging around to try to catch hold of the tail and hang onto the last player, i.e., "bite the carp's tail." The tail tries to avoid being bitten. A long line affords the most fun in this game.

FLAG GAMES These are just the thing for celebrating United Nations Day, October 24, for that is the birthday of the United Nations. It was born on October 24, 1945, when the necessary number of nations approved the UN Charter, and the date became the official birthday. It is celebrated in most of the countries of the world. An important part of the UN is UNICEF, which works to help children of all nations who lack opportunities to grow up strong and healthy. Although each member nation of the UN has its own independence day, its birthday celebration as a nation—July 4 for the United States; July 14, Bastille Day, for France, are instances—October 24 is a birthday for children in all lands and of all peoples to celebrate with parades and parties and games.

Visitors to United Nations Headquarters in New York City never fail to carry on a sort of informal contest that could be called "Identifying the Flags Flying on United Nations Plaza." These are the flags of the nations of the UN, and few visitors can name all their flags correctly. A UN booklet shows the flags in color and their placement on the poles edging the plaza between Forty-third and Forty-fifth Street. It also contains interesting facts on flags, such as that the Dannebrog, the red and white flag of Denmark, which dates from the early thirteenth century, is the oldest flag now in existence.

BORDERS This is a popular game for an All Nations Party, especially a party focused on the children and youth of the neighborhood or community. Usually each family brings one dish to the feast that is a speciality of a nation that is part of the family background. Families get together in advance to plan the dishes and the menu.

In preparation for playing Borders, flags in color of all member nations of the United Nations are pasted on 3 x 5-inch file cards and names of their nations printed on them. Also needed is an up-to-date map, clearly showing the different nations.

Players, usually a group of a dozen or more, sit on the floor, ground, or steps. One of them acts as dealer and distributes the cards as far as they will go. Objective of the game is to get the most sets of bordering nations.

Players examine their hands of national flag cards and ask for the "borders," that is, the neighboring nation that they need to make a set of "borderers," a set of two nations that have one border in common.

For example, if a player holds the flag of Cambodia, he may ask for that of Laos or Thailand. Whoever has the flag called for must give it to him. The player then puts the borderers down in front of him and has "one set" to his credit.

Play continues clockwise, each player asking for a flag he wants to make a set. Winner is the player who has the most sets when it is no longer possible for the players holding flag cards to make bordering combinations.

In the case of island nations, any one of the nations across the coastal waters is considered a borderer.

It is well to appoint a Geographical Referee, with the map, at the beginning of the game to settle any disputes and to locate quickly the countries, if necessary, on the map to show what country bounds on what other country.

FLAG-KITE-FLYING CONTESTS These are popular in Japan. Such contests are sometimes held in Korea, China, Burma, Laos, Thailand, and Vietnam. The kites are simple, almost square, and painted to represent the flags of different nations. For kite-flying contests see Part III.

RAIL-SPLITTING CONTESTS The most celebrated of all days from ancient times were birthdays, usually those of the royal family. Public figures and the great ones in a country's history and legend are honored in modern times with birthdays on which there may be parades, but are always games for children. Rail-splitting contests were always held on Abraham Lincoln's Birthday, February 12, as part of the day's celebrations until the United States became highly urbanized and no longer used rail fences. The rails were split from logs in the rural contests, and the boy or man who could split a log fastest ordinarily received a prize of some kind. Sometimes rail-splitters divided into teams and even erected a rail fence for a farm family that needed it badly.

A game derived from the rail-building is played with two piles of sticks of the same length—half of them colored green, the other half yellow. One pile is placed at each end of an area divided into two equal parts by a line. Players form two teams; each team appoints a Guard for the "rails" and a Fence Rider.

Objective of the game is taking "rails" from opponent's pile and by laying them end to end along the middle division line, preventing the opponent from crossing over and taking any rails from one's own pile.

The Guards stand close to the piles and try to keep opponents from seizing any sticks. Fence Riders stand, one at each end of the division line, to see that rails laid on the line are not disturbed and that no opposing player leaps over the "rail fence." Any players caught become Guards of the opposing team. As the sides continue to build the fence, the passageway gets narrower and narrower and harder for players to dodge through. When the division line is completely fenced, the winning team is determined by the number of sticks taken from the opposing team.

KHOKAD   This is one of the games played during the Sound and Light Show given in celebration of the birthday on October 2 of Mahatma Gandhi, who never had a birthday party until he was an old man and had long been a great leader. He helped India win independence through nonviolent means. Youth of the 1960s were attracted to India from all over the world by sitar music, meditation, and Yoga, which were an integral part of the observance of the birthday of India's leader in nonviolence and advocate of handcraft industries.

For Khokad, a large group of children form Sitters and Standers. Each side chooses a captain. Sitters squat down in a line about three feet apart, with every other one facing in the opposite direction.

The captain of the Sitters begins the game by going around the line several times; then shouting, "All standing beware!", he dashes up the line and around, trying to touch with his outstretched hand any Standers who have not been quick enough to dart out and back and avoid being touched, no matter on which side the captain runs.

The captain must touch the head of the squatting player at the end of the line when he reaches it, although he does not have to go around on the other side, but may come back on the same side. As soon as one side is put out, roles are changed, and game continues. A captain may at any time he wishes, call upon any one of his players to take his place as captain.

KERMESS   This event honors Pieter Breughel the Elder, the great Flemish artist, who was born early in September, it is believed, in a village near Breda and lived in Brussels, Belgium, over 400 years ago. He painted everyday people doing everyday things, enjoying a feast, dancing, and having fun at a kermess, or country fair. And he painted children at play. During the kermess in his honor, many children's games which he depicted in his paintings are played. They are well-known games, most of them still played throughout the world and most of them included in this book. Here are the names of a few: Leapfrog, Blindman's Buff, Hide-and-Seek, Circle and Plain Tag, Pom Pom Pull Away, Knucklebones and Jackstones, Catch (simple ball game), Hoop Racing, Bandy Ball or Shinny, Spinning Tops, and Walking on Stilts. Games on stilts are played by skilled stilt walkers. Children simply try to walk on them to see who can walk farthest without touching the ground with the foot.

Since Breughel painted many proverbs and popular sayings, children like to act them out during the kermess. Here are some:

It's no use crying over spilt milk.
Big fish eat little fish.
While it is still good weather, mend the roof.
Actions speak louder than words.
Clothes don't make the man.
Don't cross the stream (or bridge) until you come to it.
If you want dinner, don't insult the cook.
A tyrant who goes to sleep seldom wakes.
Eggs that fight with stones aways get broken.
Dividing an orange doesn't change the taste.

Games for
Special Secular and
Religious Occasions

AMONG COMMON TWENTIETH-CENTURY sights are processions, noisy or solemn, called "marches." Reciting invocations, singing and chanting, marchers directed people's attention to every aspect of public concern. In this there is a resemblance to the rogations of the times of the consuls and, later, tribunes, the People's Protectors of Rome whose duty it was to ask the people (*populum rogare*) their will on a proposed decree or law, or to conduct an inquiry or make a survey with respect to their proposal of a law or a decree for passage by the people.

If, for instance, a senator was found guilty of misappropriating government monies and it was decreed that he be condemned to death, the people could veto the decree, and demand a lighter sentence.

Rogations belonged to a time when the public of Rome had not "cast off its cares." They were common at a time when "the people . . . bestowed commands, consulships, legions, and all else . . ." and young and old participated in games and did not long "eagerly for just two things—bread and circuses."

It was a time, too, when a tribune who had been elected a Protector of the People, or even a senator, would not find it beneath his dignity, when he was inquiring round, to visit a boy's college—a boy's elementary school, actually—and take part in a few games and contests, particularly if he had enjoyed them when he was a school boy.

Here are several boys' college games from the times in Rome when there were classes every day in reading, writing, and arithmetic, from dawn to noon without a break, with a few holidays in the summer and a few others at market times.

TRIGON   This is a ball game for three. On a playing area indoors or out about 40 feet square, place three bags such as are used in sandlot baseball, at the points of a triangle. Players stand at the points and throw a rubber ball (instead of the Roman leather or wooden one) as fast as possible clockwise or counterclockwise from one to the other, catching with one hand but throwing with the other. As soon as a player misses, he is out and another player takes his place.

Winner is the individual who stays in the game longest. If players are divided into three teams, then a scorekeeper keeps track of players who remain longest in the game, and winning team is that having more players who outlast those of either of the other two.

NUCIS   Players may use their nuts (*nucis*) or marbles. As many as wish may play, so long as there is a sufficient supply of nuts or marbles. Each player should have ten or twelve.

A ring about four inches in diameter is made on floor or ground, and each player puts three or more marbles into it, so that a pile is made. The more players, the more marbles and the higher the pile.

Several toelines are drawn at different distances from the ring, corresponding to the different arm's length of the players.

Players in turn stand straight, toeing their particular line, and, stretching out an arm (the other must be held close to side), let a nut (or marble) drop into the ring with the objective of having it fall onto the others and stay on the pile, or, at least, remain in the ring. Failure to do this costs the player the nut, which he puts in the ring, and ends his turn. Any nuts that he disturbs when he lets the nut fall so they fall from the pile or are knocked out of the ring, cost the same number from the player's own hoard, which he must place carefully on the pile together with those he displaced.

Winner is the player with most nuts after all have taken turns.

QUINQUE-QUINQUE   The Romans called this game for two "Five-Five," because it was played in the yard of a Roman boys' school on five lines scratched on the ground and with five stones (called men) and a die, i.e., one of a pair of dice.

At the start each player sets up his stones on the line directly in front of him, his Base Line. Objective of the game is losing stones as quickly as possible to the opposing player. All play is fast. This is no game for slowpokes.

Players toss for first play. Then players take turns casting the die. If 1, 2, 3, or 4 turns up, a player moves one or more men the indicated number of squares toward his opponent's Base Line, trying to lose stones (men) to his opponent and avoid having to take any of his opponent's stones. He must take any of his opponent's stones on the line—

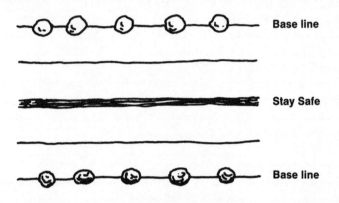

all except those on the Stay Safe line in the middle—upon which any of his stones come to rest at a cast of the die.

A player must move on every cast of the die if a proper number turns up. Any of his stones that reach his opponent's Base Line must be returned to his own Base Line and play continued.

Stones cannot remain on Stay Safe for more than one cast of the die.

Winner is player who first has lost all his men or who has fewer men when the board is cleared.

FOOT RACE WITH HURDLES   For a Roman foot race, set up two posts about 25-30 feet apart. Place three or more low hurdles (weighted cartons can be used) at intervals about an oval-shaped course (the *circus*), laid just outside the posts.

Two race at a time and the winner is first to complete the course twice. Runners may be divided into teams, and two race at a time for their teams. Team with most winners, of course, wins.

BEATING THE BOUNDS   Rogation Week in Saxon times in England was often called Gang (for *"going"*) Days because those were the days people went all about the parish with wands in their hands for blessing the fruits of the field and, at the same time, marking the boundaries. Men, women, and children walked in procession, chanting litanies.

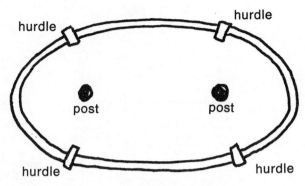

Course for Foot Race with Hurdles

Modern children, accustomed to using maps of all kinds, including maps of their towns and cities, have to draw on their imaginations to believe there ever was a time when maps were few and readers fewer, and children were "thrown into ponds or rivers, forced to climb over the roofs of houses that straddled the boundary line, rolled into briar hedges or bumped on boundary stones" to make them remember every important point of the parish boundaries. In any dispute later, they had good reason to remember the bounds exactly.

Beating the Bounds was done on Rogation Days—the Monday, Tuesday, and Wednesday before Ascension Day in the calendar of the Christian Church.

After the children had the boundary marks all too painfully impressed upon them, there was a feast of cakes and sweetmeats and the children were given money and other presents.

The custom gradually changed and the children, instead of being beaten, carried branches or willow wands with which they beat the boundary marks, and it all became a kind of learning game with the feasting afterwards as before. It is still a post-Easter event in some places in Britain.

A walking tour in town or city, or a hike at camp, at any time can incorporate beating the bounds. If not actually beating them, at least noting them carefully, with enjoyment for all.

WITTI DANDU This game is played during the fair and carnival following the several days of religious ceremonies celebrating the birthday of Krishna in India, where most of the people are Hindus. Krishna is god of youth and protector of children everywhere.

Two or more can play Witti Dandu. All that is needed are a *dandu* (a dowel 1 inch in diameter and 24 or so inches long, notched near one

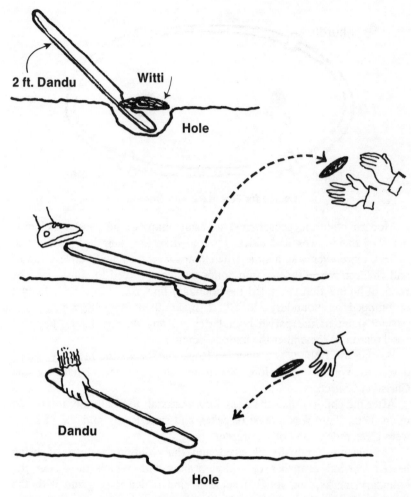

2 ft. Dandu   Witti

Hole

Dandu

Hole

end) and the *witti* (another dowel 7-8 inches long with both ends pointed).

The *dandu* is placed in a hole dug in the ground, the depth of the notch. The *witti* is placed across the hole. A player stamps on the *dandu*, catching the *witti* in the notch of the *dandu* and making it fly up. Another player runs to catch it and, if he succeeds, he tosses it toward the hole, while the first player attempts to prevent its getting in or near the hole by hitting it with the *dandu*.

Whenever the *witti* falls within half a foot of the hole, the first player is out and gives his place to the second player, who in turn is replaced by a third player.

Points are given for catching the *witti* on the fly and in pitching the *witti* in the hole or within half a foot of it. Player with most points after an agreed-upon number of turns at play is the winner of the game.

Since it takes considerable practice and skill to stamp on the *dandu* and catch the *witti*, players may choose to hold the *dandu,* catch the *witti* in the notch, and toss it up.

LEAPFROG TAG   After children in Burma have been to see shadow plays with paper figures that dance and act out stories of gods and goddesses, of heroes and demons, on a Buddhist holiday, then it's game time. In Burma, Thailand, and other countries of the peninsular region of Southeast Asia, and the islands of Java and Ceylon, where most people are Buddhists, there are many holidays devoted to Buddha, who lived and preached in India well over 500 years before the birth of Christ. His teachings spread over a great part of the East. Stories of his life reveal his great love for children and delight in them.

To play Leapfrog Tag all but two children form a circle, facing center, and stand bent over, hands on knees, in leapfrog manner. The two players—Runner and Chaser—race around the outside of the circle, the Chaser trying to catch the Runner. Runner may leap over any player, but when he stops before a player, that player must run. The former Runner then bends over and takes his place in the circle. A Chaser who tags a Runner becomes the Runner, and the former Runner joins the leapfrog circle. The new Runner may leap several "frogs" before stopping in front of one who least expects it and who then becomes the Chaser. This ruse makes for a livelier game.

RING THE TENT PEGS   Traces remain in this game of the days in the lands of the Moslems when raiders would storm an enemy camp before dawn and spear the tent pegs as they rode past at full gallop. The tents would collapse on the defenders and, as a result, the attackers had great advantage in the battle that followed.

Teams of adults hold contests at peg-spearing in which men on horseback ride full tilt at a big peg driven in the ground and attempt to impale it on a long lance.

But it's the children who play the game of Ring the Tent Pegs, after the holy month of Ramadan* observed by followers of Islam, the religion instituted by Mohammed in Arabia about the year 700 of the Christian era. There are often different Islamic holiday celebrations where most of the world's Moslems live in northern and eastern parts of Africa and the western and southern parts of Asia, but many of the same games.

---

* The month varies.

For Ring the Tent Pegs, nine pegs are driven in the ground 5-6 feet apart, in a big circle. Armed with nine rubber rings, players in turn dash round the circle, trying to ring the pegs. Players receive one point a peg for ringing. Number of points for game is set at the start. Teams may play in competition, alternating runners. (See Part IV for a variant, Down Come the Tents.)

Play with hoops is also popular among some Moslem children at holiday time. (See Part VI for games with hoops.)

CLAPSTICK BLIND-MAN'S BUFF This is a game for the celebration of the Lunar New Year by the Chinese on Taiwan and in Hong Kong. Overseas on mainland China, it is often referred to as the Spring Festival. People of Southeast Asia, such as the Vietnamese, call it the Tet festival. These peoples of the East use the lunar, or moon, calendar instead of the solar, or sun, calendar of Western peoples. The Lunar New Year falls between January 21 and February 19 of the solar calendar.

For Clapstick Blind-Man's Buff a small group of six or seven is best. Every player except the Blind Man has two sticks that make a loud noise when clapped together. Before the start of the game, players select places for themselves within a radius of 15-20 feet. The player chosen to be the Blind Man takes a moment or so to make sure he knows the location of the various spots. Then he is blindfolded and given a handkerchief with which to tag the players.

Two players must always be in motion, running to exchange places and clapping their sticks as they run. Players, before starting to run, signal those with whom they want to exchange spots, in order to avoid collision and confusion.

A touch of the Blind Man's handkerchief is all that is needed to tag a player, who then becomes the next Blind Man.

JUMPING JACKS Girls play this traditional Lunar New Year's game in Korea. They place a short board across a block of wood a few inches high, to make a seesaw. The two jump on the ends alternately, bouncing one another high in the air. It takes practice to do this, but it is lots of fun. Watchers familiar with English literature for children are reminded of Kate Greenaway's poem, *"The Little Jumping Girls,"* who jumped, jumped, jumped morning, noon, and night, and jumped from this town to that, over the sea and over the moon.

Other popular games for the Lunar New Year are Jumping Rope (see Part VI for games with ropes), Marbles (See Part IV for marble games), and just playing with balloons as all children play whether it be Lunar New Year of the East or Solar New Year of the West.

KICK BALL   This game is a favorite on January 1 in Haiti, for it is both New Year's Day and Independence Day. It is celebrated as the day when the slaves of Haiti turned their country into the first Negro republic.

Kick Ball is played like One Old Cat baseball (see Part III for ball games) except that the ball (a soccer ball or one about that size) and sometimes a big gourd is kicked instead of thrown. There are two bases, and one player rolls the ball with an underhand toss easily along the ground toward the base where the kicker stands. He rolls it so that the kicker can kick it. While the kicker is running from one base to the other and back, he may be tagged. In tagging, the ball is rolled at the player to touch his feet or legs below the knee.

NOODLEHEAD AND PARODY GAMES FOR PURIM   The Feast of Purim is celebrated on the fourteenth of Adar, the last month of the Jewish year, which is based on a lunisolar calendar, dating from the year 3761 before the birth of Christ. That puts the feast sometime in February or March of the Gregorian calendar in common use today.

Purim is the only Jewish festival which does not have an ambient sadness or sombre aspect, but is instead a time of gladness and merrymaking. It celebrates a victory over enemies that took place almost 500 years before Christ was born. Children's games are particularly important, for the day from earliest times centered upon children.

There are noodleheads all around the world because in most parts of the world there are people. So goes a folk saying from the Guianas in South America. Nearly all peoples have their special kind of noodleheads and stories about them. Among the ancient Greeks, Boeotia was the land of fools. In Germany there are the Schildburgers and in England there are several villages famous in folk tales for their noodleheads. The most famous, however, is the village of Gotham in Nottingham, with its Wise Men of Gotham. *Merrie Tales of the Mad Men of Gotham* was the title of one of the first collections, and it contains stories about the absurd tasks the Wise Men were always engaged in. They joined hands around a bush in which a bird was singing in order to shut it in and keep it singing all year. They put to sea in a sieve. They tried drowning an eel. They took their cheeses to market by rolling them downhill.

Also world-famous is Chelm, the legendary Jewish town which is entirely populated by noodleheads. They, like the Wise Men of Gotham, engage in absurd tasks, such as attempting to push a mountain out of the middle of their town because they are tired of having to climb it every time they want to get to the other side. They set a barrel of water to capture the moon when it shows its full round face in it.

It is in the ancient tradition of the happy holiday of **Purim** for children to engage in gay and comic play, such as the noodlehead story game of Then What Did You Do?

Before starting the game, a Word Scorer and a Timekeeper, preferably with a stopwatch, are appointed. The remaining players form two teams and sit facing one another.

Teams toss a coin for first to begin. First player on the team winning the toss starts talking as fast as he can about some absurd adventure or task. The Word Scorer keeps track of the number of words the talker uses. As soon as the talker slows down, showing signs of drying up, the Timekeeper calls time and, turning to the first player on the opposite team, asks, "Then what did *you* do?" That talker carries on until he, too, begins grinding to a halt; then Timekeeper calls time. Word Scorer counts the words of each talker and announces the result when Timekeeper calls time. Winning team is that with most words after all have talked.

Talkers may repeat words, but they may not repeat just one word or phrase over and over again. They must keep the narrative going. The best way is to pick a folk saying or proverb and build an absurd story on it.

For example, there is the tale of the Swedish lumberjack in the Michigan woods who was running from a bear when he came to a river. He jumped in and began swimming. Suddenly he glanced up and saw a wolverine on the opposite bank. The lumberjack stopped and treaded water while he thought what to do. In a moment he started to laugh, and he laughed and laughed and laughed. He had remembered hearing his grandmother say, "To live long, laugh a lot."

Here are some Jewish sayings that suggest themselves for the fast talkers:

A job is fine but it interferes with your time.
When a fool goes to bathe, he forgets to wash his face.
One chops the wood and the other does the grunting.
If the horse had anything to say he would speak up.

And here are some tasks for which the fast talkers can fast-talk hard and absurd solutions:

Breaking the traffic bottleneck.
How we got rid of the noise of the nearby airfield.
Keeping an eye out for trouble.
Cutting capers.
Killing time while waiting for your plane at the airport.

What we did about the pothole in our street.

How to stop people from feeding animals at the zoo and making
them sick.

How to avoid and treat sunburn.

How we used the weather forecast to plan our holiday weekend.

Rainmaking in a period of drought or prevention of rain during
floods.

Tying knots for fastening a boat to a horizontal rail; hitches for
hanging things from vertical poles; bowlines for slinging hammocks and lowering things from a height.

How to make Hamantaschen (Haman's Pockets in Germany)
and Orecchie d'Aman (Haman's Ears in Italy) and other
Purim delicacies.

Survival tactics while wandering in the north woods.

Purim-Spiele were at one time regularly performed at Tannhausen
in Germany. These were parodies or comic parallels of well-known
plays, legends, and myths; take-offs on tales of heroes, and just about
anything that lent itself to mockery in a dramatic way. Although the
parodies made fun of things, they were not without point and they did
not use parody merely for the sake of holding something up to ridicule.

This folk-drama of Jews is connected with Purim and had its beginnings when children masqueraded on the two-day feast and also
performed plays which they improvised on the story of Esther. Her
triumph over Haman and his plot against the Jews is related in the
Book of Esther in the Old Testament of the Bible.

Some young people may be familiar with the *Battle of Frogs and
Mice,* which makes fun of the old heroic epics, and with *Don Quixote de
La Mancha,* Cervantes' world-famous novel which parodies the grandi-
ose style of medieval romances with their knights in shining armor,
riding on white horses, and lovely maidens leaning out tower windows,
tossing down flowers.

But all young people and children who look at television are well
acquainted with commercials parodying upset stomach, nervous head-
aches, coughers, personal grooming habits, housecleaning, and on and
on. They are just as well acquainted with the television series that parodies the spy story, the Western, the science of space, earth sciences, and
science fiction; and the *Arabian Nights,* those tales of flying carpets, and
of genii in bottles fished out of the sea or a genie who appears out of a
lamp when it is rubbed.

For With Alice and Mother Goose in Wonderland, a Purim-Spiele
game, everyone is given two slips of paper and a pencil, and asked to

write a question associated with Lewis Carroll's *Alice's Adventures in Wonderland* and *Through the Looking-Glass* on one slip of paper; and, on the other, the name of a character in or a line from one of the Mother Goose rhymes.

Two big bowls are placed on a table, one labeled "Alice" and the other, "Mother Goose." As soon as a player has finished writing, he puts his slips into the proper bowls.

At the end of ten minutes, time is called and the slips in each bowl thoroughly stirred. The bowls are passed round and each player picks a slip from the Alice bowl and one from the Mother Goose bowl. Players are given a minute in which to think of the answer suggested by the name or line on the Mother Goose slip to the question on the Alice slip.

For instance, a player draws from the Alice bowl, "What happened to the dormouse at the Mad Hatter's tea party?" From the Mother Goose bowl, his slip has the words, "three blind mice." The player then has a perfectly good explanation for what happened: his relatives, the three blind mice, got lost and came knocking at the door and the dormouse had to leave the party and take them home. Although the dormouse is not a mouse, he does belong to the rodent family, and mice are therefore relatives.

Or, in another instance, a player has from the Alice bowl, "What was the last part of the Cheshire Cat to disappear?" and from Mother Goose, "Mary, Mary quite contrary." Putting them together, the player comes up with this answer, "Contrary Mary chased the Cheshire Cat so hard and long that nothing was left of him but his grin."

Instead of the books suggested here for the game, players may choose any two they all know. Here are some pairs players have used with much success:

> *Aesop's Fables* and *The Wind in the Willows* (Kenneth Grahame)
> *Fables of La Fontaine* and *Tale of Peter Rabbit* (Beatrix Potter)
> *Tales from Grimm* and *The Jungle Book* (Rudyard Kipling)
> *Adventures of Pinocchio* (Carlo Collodi) and *Adventures of Tom Sawyer* (Mark Twain)
> *Stories from Hans Christian Andersen* and *The Hobbit* (J. R. Tolkien)

RIDDLE CONTESTS   Play with words, word battles, contests about words, word-making, puns, riddles, riddle contests and stories, and other wordy fun are included in logomachy, which goes back beyond history. Bards in days gone by entertained with logomachy at feasts in castle and hall.

In fact, according to legend, Odin, the Norse god, disguised as a wandering old man with one eye and a hat drawn down over his face, propounded riddles for King Heidrek the Wise of Iceland. The riddles of *gestumblindi* (the blind stranger) they are called, and most subjects of the riddles are from the world of nature.

Here are some samples:

The Blind Stranger: What is it that hurts mankind, hinders speech, yet inspires speech? This riddle ponder, O Prince Heidrek.

Heidrek: Your riddle is good, but I have guessed it. The answer is ale, for it dulls the wits of men; yet it makes them talkative and, at the same time, tangles their tongues and halts speech.

The Blind Stranger: I left home and went on a journey. I came upon a way that went all ways, for there was a way under and over and going in all directions. This riddle ponder, O Prince Heidrek.

Heidrek: Your riddle is good, but I have guessed it. The way was a bridge over a river which was the way under, and overhead were birds flying the air ways.

The Blind Stranger: What is very big, travels over land and sea swallowing all it meets, is more powerful than the sun, yet is afraid of the wind? This riddle ponder, O Prince Heidrek.

Heidrek: Your riddle is good, but I have guessed it. It is the fog, for it travels over the earth and sea, darkens the sun, yet is gone as soon as the wind blows.

Riddle contests were among the popular pastimes during the Christmas holidays at Bracebridge Hall in England, about which Washington Irving writes with great warmth and feeling in *The Sketch-Book*. In preparation for the contests, players collect as many riddles* as possible. They choose sides and take turns asking the riddles, with the side giving the most correct or acceptable answers, of course, the winner.

Here are some riddles with arithmetic:

Side A: Riddle me this (customary phrase when asking a riddle): There were four birds in a field. One flew west. How many were left?

Side B: Three.

---

* See the following books: *Arrow Book of Riddles*, New York: Scholastic Book Services, and *Perplexing Puzzles and Tantalizing Teasers*, by Martin Gardner, ill. by Laszlo Kubinyi, New York: Simon & Schuster, Inc., 1969. Consult school and public libraries for other books of riddles.

Side A: The correct answer is none. The other three flew north. Riddle me this: There are a boy and a dog and 50 sheep in a pasture. How many feet are there?

Side B: Two hundred and six.

Side A: No. The correct answer is two. The dog has paws and the sheep have hoofs. Riddle me this. If four crooks went to rob a place and three were caught, how many were left?

Side B: One.

Side A: No. The correct answer is none. One was a shepherd's crook that one of the crooks used to hook the booty.

Riddle contests can start with simple riddles and work up to the more difficult. Some examples of riddles of various nationalities follow:

Italian

Riddle: What floats on water, but does not get wet?

Answer: The sun, moon, and stars.

Spanish

Riddle: What can climb a mountain but has no feet, and still carries its house wherever it goes?

Answer: A snail.

French

Riddle: What is as big as an ox but weighs nothing?

Answer: Smoke.

Mexican

Riddle: What is it that when you are asleep at night is empty, but when you're awake by day is full of bones?

Answer: Your sandal.

WORD EXCHANGE   This is a good paper-and-pencil game for a Christmas puzzle party. Puzzle Parties at Christmastime were a tradition in nineteenth-century England, and letter puzzles based on the special characteristics of the language were played; among them were anagrams, acrostics, crossword puzzles, and scrambled letters.

To play the game, guests are given lists of pairs of words and told to change the one word to the other, one letter at a time, but in fewest possible steps. Give them a number of examples:

Change *boy* to *man*:   b-o-y; b-a-y; m-a-y; m-a-n.
Change *wet* to *dry*:   w-e-t; y-e-t; r-y-e; d-r-y.
Change *eye* to *lid*:   e-y-e; l-y-e; l-i-e; l-i-d.

Following is a list of word pairs that can be changed in a few steps:

Sad to Fun	Pig to Sty	Fat to Pig
Ring to Hand	Eye to Ear	Hail to Hale
Mole to Hill	Miss to Girl	Joy to Woe
Head to Hair	Cub to Fox	Hose to Line

SUM, ES, EST   This Christmastime rhyming game of Latin-English logomachy is fun for the young who like using their wits.

Players break up into three groups: Sum, Es, and Est. Objective of the game is best seen from the following examples:

> Sum: I am an acrobat.
> Es: You are a clown.
> Est: He is a fat old man
>   Who can't get up or down.

> Sum: I am a hippy.
> Es: You are a cat.
> Est: He is a guru
>   Sitting on a mat.

> Sum: I am a lioness.
> Es: You are a crocodile.
> Est: He is a computer
>   Responding to a dial.

The groups change around at intervals, for the Est group has the greatest demands made upon its combined wits. Each group always gives its designation each time, thus combining Latin with English. *Sum* = I am, *es* = you are, *est* = he is.

NOUNS OF AGGREGATION   This brain-teaser in logomachy for the Christmas holidays is based on free association of ideas. Players divide into two sides, with those on one side taking turns calling out the plural of nouns, and those on the other side replying with the first noun of aggregation that happens to pop into the head of any one of the team's players. Method of play is best obtained from examples:

> Team A: Debutantes.
> Team B: A *flurry* of debutantes.

Team A: Wrestlers.
Team B: A *brawn* of wrestlers.
Team A: Contortionists.
Team B: A *twist* of contortionists.
Team A: Coffee-drinkers.
Team B: A *break* of coffee-drinkers.
Team A: Surgeons.
Team B: A *cutlery* of surgeons.
Team A: Politicians.
Team B: A *verbiage* of politicians.

When Team B fails three times to come up with a noun of aggregation, Team A exchanges roles with B. Teams may play competitively when a scorekeeper is appointed to count the number of nouns of aggregation supplied by each team.

Winner has the greater number in two out of three times round.

PIÑATA   This is a Christmas party game in Spain and in most Latin American countries. A large earthen jar is decorated with brightly colored paper to resemble an animal, bird, fish, or funny or fierce mask. The piñata is filled with candies and little toys, and hung outdoors in the patio or in the house. Players in turn are blindfolded and given a stick with which to hit the jar and try to break it and release all the good things. In some countries the jar is hung with a pulley so that it can be raised and lowered as the players try to hit it.

In Nicaragua and a number of other Central and South American countries, the Christmas party guests are given a big stick and, in turn, spun round several times before being told to hit the piñata.

As soon as the jar is broken, all scramble quickly for the sweets and toys.

SLAA KATTEN AF TÖNDEN   The English name of this Danish game is Beat the Cat out of the Barrel. It is a game for Shrove Monday, before Ash Wednesday of Lent, and it corresponds to the Piñata for Christmas. A barrel is filled with apples, oranges, candy, and nuts and a cardboard cat placed on top of it. The barrel is hung outdoors from a low tree branch. One at a time, children beat on the barrel with a big stick. The one who beats the barrel down is "king of the cats." A paper crown is put on his head and he is given the paper cat. All scramble for the good things to eat.

Part IX

GAMES
BEST KNOWN
TO URBANITES

Typical
Street
Games

THE MAJORITY OF street games are open-space or country games which have been adapted to the congestion of the city. Many rural peoples take well to cities as do many of their games. Over half a millennium before the Christian era, Aristides told inhabitants of the Aegean island and city of Rhodes: "Not houses finely roofed or the stones of wall well-builded, nay nor canals and dockyards, make the city, but men able to use their opportunity."

People look to the city not only for the chance to work and earn a good living, but also for a social environment in which they can develop and their children can get an education.

Children, themselves, seize upon whatever opportunities for play the city has to offer and, using ingenuity and imagination, turn them to advantage. There is always an element of we-do-as-we-like in their made-up games on city streets. By inventing new ways to play games, children create interesting hybrids—mixtures of old and new.

STOOP BALL Not long ago, a man advertised in a New York City newspaper for a stoop that could be used for that citified ball game known as Stoop Ball. He wanted it for a playground in a neighborhood of stoopless modern apartment buildings. He felt the children were being deprived of the joys of stoop ball which he remembered so fondly from his boyhood. The man received a number of answers to his ad and finally got his stoop. One answer in particular intrigued him although he did not follow it up. The writer offered to "deliver the genuine article for the right price and no questions asked."

The high stoop was characteristic of Dutch houses. Settlers brought it with them from Holland and introduced it into the architecture of New Amsterdam. The stoop was the result of raising the "parlor" floor well above the street level, making a steep flight of from seven to fourteen steps necessary in order to reach the house entrance. The flight of steps, including the top step, was known to the Dutch as the *stoep,* pronounced "stoop" by the English. It was a distinguishing feature of New York City houses from Dutch days to well past the time of the brownstones—those houses whose fronts of reddish brown sandstone were a mark of a family's wealth in the middle of the nineteenth century.

Stoop Ball is a city street form of baseball. It is played with a small, high-bouncing rubber ball by two to four players on a side.

Portions of the street, windowless walls, and other unbreakable architectural features are designated "singles," "doubles," "triples," and "homers." A player on the first side up, throws the ball with as much force as possible against the edge of a step, with the objective of hitting some designated thing, usually the wall of the building across the street, without having it caught or struck by the fielders.

Sides change when the ball has been caught or struck back three times by the fielders of one side. This often varies. In one variation, any fielder who catches a ball bounced off a step pitches it back at the stoop. Almost every neighborhood makes up its own rules, so a set of rules any group of players agrees upon is acceptable.

STICKBALL   Played with an old broom handle and a small bouncy rubber ball, this is another street form of baseball. (Other elementary forms of baseball called One Old Cat, Scrub, Long Ball, and sometimes Stick Ball for open spaces are described in Part III under Traditional Ball Games.)

Bases are whatever is on the street—hydrants, lamp posts, playstreet stanchions, drain grids, and so on. From three to six usually make up a side. The rules of baseball are generally followed, although usually the pitcher pitches and catches, standing in front of the batter at home plate. The batter, when he makes a hit, runs as in baseball, but he may not steal bases. He can be put out by any method used in baseball. To insure a lively running game, the pitcher gives the batter the kind of ball he prefers.

PUNCH BALL This game has long been seen on the streets of cities wherever boys could get hold of an old football or soccer ball. Buildings on opposite sides of the street ordinarily serve as goals, although lines are sometimes drawn across it. What happens to be available is used, for the game is rather go-as-you-like, and a large or small number may play.

Sides line up as in football or soccer, and the captain of the side winning the toss puts the ball in play by punching it toward one of his players, who runs up to catch it. The game proceeds as in football or as in soccer, whichever the players have chosen at the start, with players hitting the ball with their fists, i.e., punching it, to advance it toward the goal. Players may catch the ball, pass it to others, but may not run with it.

A point is scored for his side each time a player punches the ball over his opponent's goal line, or in the case of a building as the goal, punches it so that it hits the wall. With few participants, goals are too easily made if the goal line is long, so it is limited, for instance, to certain parts of a building wall.

ASSOCIATION This is the name used on the streets of cities in the U.S.A., but it is a form of football that goes on anywhere youngsters know about football, no matter what they call it.

Two, three, four, or five are on a side. Children use anything at all that is about the size of a football—a homemade affair of coconut husks as in places in the South Pacific where American soldiers have played football or informal varieties of football, or a paper-and-rag-filled plastic bag left behind by some tourist, such as was seen kicked and run with by boys in an Old Jerusalem street.

The ball is thrown, sometimes kicked too, as in football, toward the goal. A player with the ball is immediately out if he is so much as touched with one hand by an opposing player.

In Recife, Brazil, the ball is kept in the air by kicking until the last player makes for the goal and carries it over for a touchdown. Brazil's variety of football is really rugby soccer and is popular everywhere in the country. Boys use the streets or any place available. There is one goal only. The game calls for great speed, dexterity, and ball control.

STREET MARBLES This game is simply Marbles (see Part IV for games with marbles) as it is played in streets around the world—New York City, Rome, around fountains of Marrakesh (Morocco); in the arcades of Bern (Switzerland), Caldas de Reyes (Spain), Telč (Czechoslovakia), Gubbio (Italy); the covered streets of Istanbul (Turkey) or staired walkways shaded by *toldos*, or canvas awnings, of Seville (Spain). The differences in ways of playing the same game are due in large part to what it is played on, for it is the surface that determines how they go. Thus, the game on a manhole cover of an American city is unlike that on cobblestones, or on the steps of staired walkways, although the games are all forms of Marbles.

For instance, the top of the biggest stone of a stony street, say, in Bursa, a hillside resort in Turkey, becomes the marbles "ring"; certain steps of staired ways in, say, Italian and Spanish hill towns, are given different values and a marble knocked off one step may cost the one whose marble is knocked four marbles, while being forced off another step would cost him only two or perhaps nothing if it falls on a "safe" step.

Manufactured marbles are nearly always used by English, German, French, American, and Canadian city children, while pebbles and little balls of clay, rolled by hand and baked in the sun, are quite commonly found among those of other nationalities. At Iraklion in Crete, the island of Mýkonos, and other places in Greece famous for ceramics, children find pieces or broken tiles and potsherds practical. By simulating the surface of the "ring" used in street play of different countries, children can have a tour of foreign cities the marbles way.

LES BOULES   This game of bowls is *the* game for men and boys of Provence, France. In *"La Place,"* any town's gathering place for males, there is always at least one game going on. But Les Boules is played anywhere in any space, for none is too small or too large for devoted *boulistes*. It is even played in roads and streets, disrupting traffic. A bowler hurling the large wooden ball at the jack (the small bowl which is the target) or players gathered about measuring the distance of their bowls from it, pay no attention to honking horns and shouting motorists.

One year when a thousand barge and tugboat crewmen went on strike, paralyzing the harbor of Marseilles, France's chief port and throughway to Africa and the East, they played games of Petanque, a variant of lawn bowls, on the sunny quais. Bowling was a great pastime while crews waited for the strike to be settled and a most effective way to seal off the wharfs.

A children's variety of Les Boules that can be played in any space, anywhere, requires only some wooden or hard rubber balls, or baseballs —one for each player and one to serve as the jack.

When more than two or three play, sides are chosen and players write their names on their bowls. It is best not to have more than four on a side. The jack should be given a bright color.

A rectangular space is drawn. Sides are called boundaries; one end is the throwing line and the other "the ditch." At some distance from the ditch, inside the rectangle, draw a circle. Individual players or teams draw lots for throwing (rolling) the jack to start the game. The jack must stop within the circle to be "put in play."

After the jack is in play, bowlers take turns (in team play, first one player from one side and then a player from the opposing side), each player with the objective of rolling his bowl so as to make it (1) stop nearer the jack than his opponent's, (2) protect a bowl near the jack, or (3) knock away a bowl that is in a better position than his own or that of a teammate.

There are points for bowl nearest to jack, touching jack, hitting it out of the circle, and knocking it beyond the ditch or out of bounds. Players agree upon points at start of game. Winner may be the player or team with most points at the end of a certain period of time, or the one winning most games, a game being so many points.

In true French Southerner's style, children should fire away at the jack, that is, roll the ball hard, straight at it.

In the older forms of the game, such as in the Provençal, a small bowl (ball), not a pin, was the "jack," and large bowls were rolled at it. For other varieties of Bowls see Part I, under Games Carried Throughout the World by Colonists and Settlers.

JUMPING OR SKIPPING ROPE   Children are forever fitting their games into their surroundings instead of trying to conquer their environment. Some games fit city surroundings without any change at all. For instance, jumping or skipping rope, like Hopscotch (see Part V), was an anytime anywhere pastime that suited street life. It has a history of waxing and waning popularity, but jump rope never entirely disappears, for it is useful as an exercise even when its games have left the sidewalks and playgrounds for a time. Rope-skipping works well in relay races and various kinds of competitions.

There are kinds of jumping rope which one child can enjoy in self-competition. Beginners usually hold the rope with one end in each hand, turn it over the head, and step over it while running or standing. Player continues until a foot (or the feet if standing and jumping with both feet) catches on the rope. Beginners go on to turning the rope and stepping over it while skipping to see how many times they can jump without missing. Then they go on to more complicated movements with rope and feet, such as crossing the arms as they do a skip-step before turning the rope over the head and skip-stepping over it.

Sometimes when skippers are testing their skill, they use this counting method:

> One and two
> Drops of dew.
> Three and four
> Shut the door.
> Five and six
> Pick up sticks.
> Seven and eight
> Don't be late.
> Nine and ten
> Start again (or, Big fat hen).

The jumping or skipping is done to chanting, and altogether it makes for good fun and good coordination. Half a dozen or more single jumpers in space large enough for turning ropes like to play Jump to the Leader (often called Do as the Old Ox in Front of You in northern Italian cities, such as Ferrara or Milan). The leader stands in front, back to the group, and jumps to a chant which may be traditional or made up on the spur of the moment—maybe just three or four words snatched from current events; for instance, "We jump for peace."

As soon as the leader misses a step or catches the rope on his foot, a new leader takes his place, usually the jumper immediately behind him. The former leader goes to the back of the group, and jumpers shift so that one of them stands directly behind the new leader.

Three, playing together, use a long rope. Two turn while the other jumps or skips as many times as possible without missing. Upon a misstep, jumper exchanges places with one of the rope-turners.

Skillful jumpers often use two ropes. Two swing the two long strands in sweeping arcs, turning them alternately, while another jumps. The jumper must get into the rhythm of the swing by rocking to and fro before jumping in, and jumping or skipping over each strand in turn. The ropes may be swung inwards or outwards.

Children vary the ways of swinging the rope and of jumping and skipping, and some of the more common are Rocking the Boat, Running Through, and Fried Eggs.

Rocking the Boat consists of swinging the rope back and forth.

Jumpers hop over it upon each swing. Those who have acquired skill sometimes bounce a ball while jumping, or whirl around at each jump.

In Running Through, as two turn the rope, the skippers go through one after the other, following the leader who jumps once the first time, twice the second time, and so on until a misstep is made. All those who make missteps, drop out of the game. Winner is the last jumper.

In Fried Eggs, two turn the rope, another runs in and skips to the rhyme:

> Get out the pan
> And the butter.
> Put them on the fire.
> Get out the eggs.
> Put them in the pan.
> And you'll have fried eggs
> Or I'm a liar.

Then skipper begins to count—1, 2, 3, and so on—as other skippers run in and start jumping. When the rope becomes crowded, first skipper cries, "Scrambled eggs!" and the two rope-turners swing the rope faster and faster, until all skippers have tripped. Often, "Salt, pepper, vinegar, mustard, *hot!*" is said as rope-turners increase the speed of their swinging.

A chant recited by three skippers, as each begins to skip rope, goes like this:

> 1st skipper: Ham and eggs! Ham and eggs!
> I like mine fried
> Nice and brown.
> 2nd skipper: Ham and eggs! Ham and eggs!
> Flip mine over,
> Upside down.
> 3rd skipper: Ham and eggs! Ham and eggs!
> Beat my eggs with a beater.
> Scramble 'em! Scramble 'em! Scramble 'em!

Rope-turners increase swing speed on each "scramble."

Children like to use their names and those of their playmates in Jump Rope Rhyme-ins, and here are some examples from the streets and playgrounds of some American cities:

Joe, Joe, stubbed his toe
On his way to Kokomo.

Sarah, Sarah is a terror.
I'd do anything on a dare-er.

Pete, Pete took a seat
In the plane for Martinique.

Polly, Polly is so jolly.
She has a cat and dolly.

Sid, Sid, look what he did!
Got in the ashcan and shut the lid.

Joan, Joan threw a stone.
She'll throw another if you don't leave her alone.

John, John gets up at dawn,
Because he has to mow the lawn.

Sam, Sam is a lamb.
Until he gets in a jam—then *wham!*

In these Jump Rope Rhyme-ins, the first line is always chanted by the rope-turners or nonskippers at the time. Rope-turners continue to swing until they and/or others have thought up a rhyme for the name of the next skipper in the line. As soon as he hears his name, the skipper runs in and skips until he thinks of a rhyming line to take him out. Much liberty, of course, is taken with rhyme and meter, as in this: "George, George is awfully large, / Because he sits and eats all day on a barge," as well as in some of the other rhyme-ins and rhyme-outs above.

Crawfish, the shellfish which resembles a lobster but has no claws, is a favorite food in New Orleans, and its name the subject of a favorite chant for skipping rope.

Two turn the rope and do the saying. Others run in one after the other and skip first on one foot, then on the other, before running out. The rope-turners say:

> Kiskadee!* Kiskadee!
> Save a crawfish head for me.
> Look around the fishermen's beds,
> You'll see nothing but crawfish heads.

---

*Probably a corruption of *qu'est-ce que dit?* (what does he say?)

Rope-turners after a while suddenly switch to:

> Don't cost pesos, don't cost cents.
> Now you have to climb the fence.

They shout the words "climb the fence" and raise the rope gradually as skippers try to clear it, jumping higher and higher, until no one can make it, and the game is over.

In cities along the Texas-Mexican border, rope-turners are heard to say:

> Brown as a coffee-berry,
> Red as a bean.
> That's the prettiest color,
> I've ever seen.

> Yellow as a daisy,
> Black as ink.
> That's the prettiest color,
> I do think.

> Orange as a pumpkin,
> Green as grass,
> Keep on jumping
> As long as you last.

Other names given to Jumping Rope are *El Reloj* (The Clock), in Peru and other South American countries; *Tobi-Koshi* (Jumping Over) in the south of Japan; *Tsuna Tobi* (Rope Jumping), around Canton, China.

With two or more ropes turning, teams compete in relays.

CONKERS This is one of the games played with nuts or pebbles, both of which lend themselves to games that can be played anywhere and, therefore, are often seen in city places. (For more games of this type see Part IV, under Beans, Peas, and Marbles as Universal Playthings.)

Conkers, typical boys' language for "conquerors," is an old game with many different names, but it used always to be played with chestnuts or hazelnuts in English, Scottish, and American cities.

Two or more can play, each playing with his own supply of nuts or all sharing a big bag of them.

A ring is drawn and each player puts one or two nuts (number depending upon whether there are few or many players) into the ring. A string is put through a nut, and players take turns whirling it and trying to strike the nuts and either crack them or knock them out of the ring. A player is entitled to all those he cracks and knocks out.

Sometimes the nuts are heaped up within a ring, and a nut is thrown at the heap to knock them out of the ring.

PEBBLE TOSS   A game of chance for two, this demands quick thinking and a quick eye for form. A handful of pebbles is tossed on the ground or pavement. One player quickly scoops up some of them. The other with a glance at those left tries to estimate how many there are. He must take no more than a second or two. Enough time to count them is never permitted.

As soon as he thinks he knows, he tells his opponent, "Toss down one," "two," or "three," or "Don't toss down any." If the player has estimated correctly, the pebbles that are now on the ground should be an exact multiple of 4 (2 × 4, 3 × 4, 4 × 4, etc.) and he wins. If he has estimated incorrectly, the number of pebbles will not be such a multiple, and he loses.

STOW THE JARS OF OIL AND WINE   This is a seaside resort game derived from underwater archeology. Uncovering the wrecks of ships in the Aegean Sea, teams of divers and scientists have been able to study them and their cargo. In a recent expedition, scientists discovered the hulks of Byzantine and Roman merchantmen among the rocks about Yassi Ada, a Turkish offshore island, not far from Bodrum (Halicarnassus). After many seasons of work below and topside, they were able to make detailed drawings and renderings of a Byzantine merchant ship, showing how she appeared over twelve centuries ago and how her gear and cargo of jars of wine were stowed aboard. Although modern vessels have their cargoes stowed efficiently in compartments, their stowage is no more compact and space-saving than that of ancient merchant ships plying the Mediterranean.

To play the stowage game, only a pile of pebbles or little shells is needed. Two to four can participate, playing as individuals or partners. The outline of a ship's deck, looking down on it from above, is drawn on the sand, and players sit around it.

They take turns putting pebbles or shells within the outline. Objective of the game is the placing of as many as possible in it, without having one pebble or shell touch another or the deck lines. A player must place each close to one other or others, but without having them touch or without touching the neighboring pebbles himself. A touch

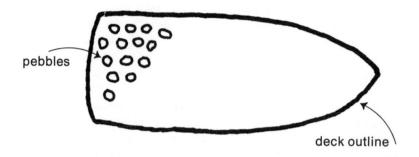

and he is out of the game. Winner is the player who remains after the others are out whether the deck is filled or not.

Children who play the game a great deal acquire dexterity, spatial judgment, and an eye for size, and can crowd an amazing number of pebbles into a small outline and have none of them touch.

For an on-going game for everyone, however, particularly those who have little skill at "squeezing in," a player is not required to drop out if he touches a stone, but simply loses his turn and keeps the pebble, called a "touch stone." When the deck is covered and no more pebbles can be squeezed in, the game is over and the player with fewest touch stones is declared winner.

SNATCH THE CHEESE The game is always played any place there is something high on which to place the "cheese," represented by a small block, a little bag of sand, or anything that a player can jump up, snatch, and run with. The top of a big rock or post in a park or playground, a window ledge above a sidewalk, or the like, is the high spot.

Players divide into teams, usually six to eight on a side with one team trying to snatch the cheese and the other trying to prevent it. Members of the team defending the cheese, cross their arms, stand a few feet from the cheese, ready to "bump" away would-be snatchers. They must use shoulders only in defending the cheese.

Opponents may push past defenders to get at the cheese, but they must not attempt to knock anyone over or hit or kick. Snatching team need not all go out at once, but may send out one or two at a time, diverting the attention of defenders from the main body of snatchers.

Sides are changed after one team makes three or four snatches, which constitute a turn. The team winning three turns out of five is the winner of the game. Players need guile and the planning of strategy rather than muscle to win at Snatch the Cheese.

Games from
Medieval England
And Europe

THE ONLY PLAY which church and king advocated for all able-bodied men and boys in England, Scotland, and France during medieval times was Roving, the play-word for what was actually archery practice. All other play, games, and pastimes were frowned upon, especially if engaged in by the lower classes. Games and sports were objected to in particular because they tended to discourage the practice of archery, upon which the military might of a country depended in those days.

King Edward III of England wrote to the Sheriffs of London that "skill at shooting with arrows was almost totally laid aside for the purpose of various useless and unlawful games" and he commanded the Sheriffs to put a stop to "such idle practices." Cities, towns, and villages were the chief culprits. There were city neighborhood contests, uptown vs. downtown events, and whole villages competing against one another in football and other ball games.

London merchants, for instance, were constantly complaining to the king about football. As city people and merchants to boot, they stood in little awe of the king and practically demanded that he do something about the great noise and disturbances in the streets caused by people "hustling [i.e., pushing, shoving, jostling, etc.] over big balls."

So King Edward passed a law against playing the sort of free-for-all then called football in the streets of London.

In France, king and state were just as adamant with regard to *soule,* the French wild kind of football.

After Edward, King Richard II went further and passed a law prohibiting "all playing at tennis, football, and other games called corts [various ball games played in courts], dice, casting of the stone, kayles [a kind of ninepins or skittles], and other such importune games."

ROVING While "utterly crying down" the idle practice of games unrelated to military skills, kings "cried up" Roving. A skilled "rover" was also a skilled archer, a chess-piece of power in the continual wars of the Middle Ages, those chess games played with real men by the various monarchs, barons, and ecclesiarchs.

Municipalities set up and maintained "butts and pricks," where citizens practiced shooting. The butts were the mounds of earth, sod, or hard-packed hay or straw upon which "pricks," or targets, were set. Actually, the prick was the mark or spot, that is, the bull's-eye, in the center of the target.

On fine days, city dwellers and townsmen, with arrow-filled quivers on their backs and bows in hand, wandered about suburbs and countryside, shooting at any target they fancied. Sometimes there were prizes awarded, but usually it was the glory of being accounted an expert marksman that mattered, just as in more recent times, gun-carrying fighting men display good marksmanship medals on their chests.

Today for boys and girls, roving a target course set up at camp or in any large space offers much fun and an opportunity to gain muscular coordination and skill in measuring distance. Targets are small, round pieces of paper affixed to barrels, posts, trees, rocks, or real or simulated haycocks and corn shocks. Each target location should be given a name by the boy and girl Rovers: for example, Daniel Boone's Oak, Green Giant's Corn Shock, Meteorite, Plymouth Rock, Pike's Peak, Rabbit Hill, Indian Mesa, Cliffs of Dover, or any name that appeals to them.

Targets must be shot at from different distances; each target has the proper distance clearly marked and the place to stand from which to shoot designated. Players rove from one target to another as in the Middle Ages.

Target-shooters use rubber-tipped arrows in their bows and carry a piece of colored chalk or crayon with which to rub the tips as one does a billiard cue before each shot, so that the marks of shots are unmistakable. Shooters also carry score cards with their names and those of the targets on them.

Each target needs a Scorekeeper, who punches with a punch the score cards of those who hit the target from the proper distance away.

Those who lay out the course also make up a set of rules for awarding good marksmanship and championship buttons.

ROBIN HOOD ROVING TOURNEY This is an adaptation of medieval Roving and a popular mid-thirteenth-century games tourney for family and friends called Round Table. The name is in part from Robin Hood, the legendary English hero with whom the common people have identified for centuries. Whoever Robin Hood was, he probably played often at Roving during his early youth, for, according to one tale, he was a townsman well known for his archery when he finally rebelled against the Establishment and took to the woods with his *meyné* (men) to harass the high and mighty.

The Round Table was a "social occasion, accompanied by various games," most of them games of skill having to do with vaulting, stone and lance casting, dart shooting, tilting at targets, and the like. It was a recreational tournament in protest by aristocrats and the upper classes against the violence, mayhem, and butchery that accompanied the tournaments—in truth, ordeals of battle—of previous generations. The Good King Arthur and his Knights of the Round Table, where there was neither head nor foot so all were of like rank, had tried to cool men's war fever by introducing gentler modes of existence and injecting *douceur de la vie* (the sweetness of life) into the gory hand-to-hand conflicts of the tournaments.

The roving tourney for today's children affords a progressive course of events of skill that can be arranged within the abilities of the 7-11's and/or 10-14's at camp or in a large recreational area somewhere. It must be large enough to allow contestants to rove, in other words, walk slowly, some distance to get from one event to the other. This also prevents jamming up as contestants take turns in the different events. The series finds good use at fairs and carnivals held by groups or organizations in schools, churches, and recreation centers in the community, neighborhood, or housing development, in celebration of a holiday, community action program, or as part of a fund-raising campaign.

Eight or ten activities are sufficient for the tourney, although more may be added if it is desirable. Each event must be manned by a Scorekeeper with a punch for punching the score cards of contestants. For timing events which have a time element, Scorekeepers should have stopwatches; but egg timers—inexpensive sandglasses—will serve very well.

Each contestant is given a score card (a quantity of these should be made up in advance), on which the events are listed with their value in points and a "yes" or "no" box-check for medals. Contestant writes his own name at the top of the card.

Here are ten typical events taken from the thirteenth century and after, references to which appeared in diaries, journals, statutes, and various documents of the times. Each event is worth the number of points indicated, but those who arrange the tourney may set whatever points and rules for play they think most suitable. Suggested prizes are homemade gold medals (gold seals on cardboard backing) lettered with the name of the event. A certain number of gold medals entitles a contestant to a Grand Prize. A certain number of points entitles a contestant to a Championship Prize. The number in each case should be decided upon when the tourney is being arranged. Prizes should be simple and of little intrinsic value; it's the doing well while having fun that counts.

EVENT 1.   SKIP STONES.   Squares of old carpet are laid out irregularly and at different distances apart to represent stepping stones across a stream. Contestants must leap lightly, i.e., skip in the old sense of the word, with both feet from one stone to another without missing.

Points: 5, which also entitles contestant to gold medal.

This event may be made more difficult for contestants of greater ability by having them use a pole and vault from one stepping stone to another for the same number of points.

EVENT 2.   CASTING THE STONE.   For the big stone disk or water-rounded cobble used in the old days, substitute a wooden plate such as is used for picnics or barbecues. Contestant tosses it underhand from a toeline to goal lines at different distances away. Distances are gauged by ability of the average contestant.

Before tossing the "stone," the contestant must tell the Scorekeeper the goal line for which he is trying. If he makes it, he gets another try at another line, and can continue until he misses.

Points: nearest line, 3; next line, 5; farthest line, 10. Points needed for medal: at least 3.

EVENT 3.   DART SHOOTING.   A dart board having a bull's-eye and three concentric circles, is set up. Contestant is given three suction-type, rubber-tipped darts, allowing him three tries at the board.

Points: bull's-eye, 20; circle nearest bull's-eye, 15; next, 10; last, 5. In the three tries, a contestant must make 20 or more to be entitled to a medal.

EVENT 4. LANCE CASTING.   The lance is a wooden pole or shaft about five feet long. Objective of the event is the throwing of the lance, that is, casting it, a certain number of feet from a toeline. The number of feet required depends upon the average age and ability of the casters taking part in the event.

To throw or cast the lance, the contestant grips it, fingers up, in the middle and holds it shoulder high, rocking it back and forth several times to get into the rhythm of casting, then letting go with a big thrust. Contestant must cast the lance the required number of feet at least once in three tries.

Points: 10 for each successful cast. At least one successful cast is needed for contestant to be entitled to medal.

EVENT 5. JOUSTING.   Among the Knights of the Round Table of the thirteenth century this consisted of two knights on horseback tilting at each other with blunted weapons, usually lances, in an attempt to unhorse one another. Children of the period imitated their elders in jousting games. In one game, their horses were barrels, which they sat astride while they thrust at each other with poles. In another, two contestants rode a hogshead, one at each end, and tried to unseat one another by pushing in a kind of hand-to-hand struggle.

Today's jousters in the ten years and older group sit astride skateboards or scooters. They face each other, their hands grasping the ends of long sticks or poles, the other ends of which are well cushioned, resembling giant-size cotton-tipped medical swabs.

Objective of the contest is the unseating of one jouster by the other within two minutes; if neither player succeeds, the contest is declared a draw. Jousters must not strike out or jab with the pole, but must push and thrust with it, using one hand only.

Points: for unseating opponent, 20; for draw, each contestant, 5.

For the under-ten contestants, the event is set up somewhat differently. The two challengers are given hobbyhorses—sticks with horses' heads (jigsawed out of wood or cut from linoleum), which they straddle.

A 20-foot-long, 10-foot-wide rectangle is drawn to represent the tiltyard, and a tilt cloth—a piece of canvas about 2 feet high—is stretched down the middle, the length of the rectangle.

Challengers with well-cushioned long poles, which they hold under their right or left arms (both must use either right or left) and grasp with one hand, approach each other from opposite ends of the tiltyard. When they are within pole's-length of each other, they attempt to push one another outside the sideline, as they pass.

After each encounter, challengers ride on to the end of the tiltyard, quickly turn around (hence the word "tournament"), and approach each other again from opposite ends of the yard on the other side of the tilt cloth. They must keep clear of the tilt cloth at all times. (A wooden center-fence may be used instead of the canvas, as in the later Round Tables, if it's more practical.) Time allotted for each encounter, 3 minutes.

Points: 5 for each time a contestant pushes opponent out-of-bounds within the 3 minutes allowed. A draw is declared if neither challenger is pushed out-of-bounds on both encounters. For challenger to be entitled to a medal, at least 5 points are required.

For the youngest who want to play, or if it is thought desirable to avoid person-to-person competition, set up a Tilting-at-the-Ring event in which the contestant, armed with a stick, runs toward a big, hanging ring and attempts to unhook it as he runs past. Hooking the ring on the merry-go-round is a survival of Tilting-at-the-Ring of five or six hundred years ago.

To win, the contestant must unhook the ring in 3 attempts.

Points: 10 for each successful attempt. At least 10 points are needed for a medal.

EVENT 6. BEAR WRESTLING. Two challenge each other to "bear wrestling." Scorekeeper gives each one a padded jacket with hood, and challengers stand on the circumference of a circle about 8 feet in diameter, and fold their arms. When the Scorekeeper blows a whistle, each challenger starts hopping on one leg toward the other.

The wrestling consists of trying to push and shove each other out of the circle, while hopping on one leg and using upper arms and shoulders only. The clumsier they appear, the better, for any spectators should enjoy watching.

This is an event that gives the young ones a chance to do what they like best doing—pushing and shoving—yet at the same time it is a game with the free-wheeling they enjoy.

Time allowed for the wrestling bout: 2 minutes.

Points: 5 for each time one challenger pushes the other out of the circle. No points for either if both step outside or quit hopping on one leg. Points required for medal: 5 or more.

EVENT 7. PUFF-THE-ARROW TARGET SHOOTING. A cardboard circle about a yard in diameter and painted green, is set up, with the bottom about three feet from the ground. Six to eight small circles cut out of yellow paper are pasted on it in irregular fashion. Half of the circles are numbered 10, the other half, 5.

Each contestant is given a tube—a roll made of a piece of 8½ x 11-inch paper held by adhesive tape—and an arrowhead cut from tissue paper. (In the medieval contest, a needle stuck in a tuft of wool was used. A bobby pin holding a piece of wool yarn would be a safe substitute.)

Objective is the hitting of one of the circles with a feather-light arrow blown through the paper tube, from a line three feet away.

Contestant is given four puffs, whether he succeeds or not.

Points: sum of circles touched by contestant's arrow in each successful puff. A referee is needed to call out the values of the circles hit. To be entitled to a medal, contestant must have at least 10 points.

EVENT 8.   QUARTERSTAFF CONTEST.   When Robin Hood of Sherwood Forest was about twenty years old, he met the stalwart seven-footer of the old English ballad, the John Little of "Robin Hood and Little John." (After joining the band, he was renamed or had his names switched around, as it were, to Little John, by Robin and the other men.)

The two met in the woods on a long narrow bridge and neither would give way. Each refused to let the other pass and they got into a fight over it. And Little John gave Robin Hood a good thrashing and "tumbled him in the brook."

In one version, the two engaged in fisticuffs; in another, they used quarterstaffs. The quarterstaff was a long, stout staff, a common weapon in those days. It came by its name because it was wielded with one hand in the middle and the other a quarter of the way from the end.

In accordance with Round Table custom, the wild character of the quarterstaff contest was gentled; then the use of quarterstaffs, clubs, and the like in Round Table tourneys finally was outlawed, and harmless things substituted.

For today's quarterstaff event, two opponents sit, face to face on the ground, one on each side of a line. They press the soles of their bare or shod feet together. The Scorekeeper hands each opponent a plastic hoop or an old bicycle tire.

Contestant's objective is putting the hoop or tire over the head and around shoulders of his opponent and pulling him across the center line. This must be done while keeping his feet pressed against those of his opponent. Time allowed: 2 minutes.

Points: hoop over opponent's head, 10; and another 10 for pulling opponent across center line. To win medal 10 points are needed

EVENT 9. CURIOUS COMBAT OF MOCK-KING AND COURT-CLOWN. As
the murderous and war-provoking elements of the tournaments were
gradually changed by law and social opinion, they began to be a min-
gling of pageant and sports meet. For example, a tournament held in
Windsor Park in England was called Jousts of Peace. And, in the combat
with swords, for example, the mocking, merry, clowning jousters carried
swords whose blades were limber whalebone and silver-painted parchment. Their bucklers, or shields, were of thin wood. They wore helms,
that is, helmets, of soft leather. They pantomimed a fierce hand-to-hand
combat—sword and buckler play—for the fun of the thing and the
amusement of royal, noble, and common spectators.

This Round Table event can be played in the same way today by
boys and girls by making it a Chefs' Combat. The Scorekeeper hands
the two challengers paper chefs' hats for helms; padded mitts for right
hands, instead of the knight's tough leather gloves or gauntlets, a cardboard chef's knife instead of a whalebone and parchment sword, for
each challenger; and a paper plate with a strap for the left hand made of
a piece of elastic stapled to the back as a substitute for the buckler of
thin wood. The buckler was a small shield, usually round, with a leather
or metal strap through which the knight put his left hand to hold it and
parry blows, rather than to protect his body. Contestant uses paper plate
in the same way.

Challenger's objective is the disarming of opponent, that is, causing
him to drop his weapon, or rendering it useless as a result of receiving
parries of buckler. Time allotted: 2 minutes.

Points: 20.

EVENT 10. CAROUSEL. At first, this popular French game was
played by cavaliers on horseback who pelted each other with balls
until one or the other was driven from the field. Then, later, it became
a sort of procession and free-for-all in which players pranced about in
costume and pelted one another in an attempt to drive as many from the
field as possible. This was followed by a *ballet d'action,* which was a
danced pantomime based on a folktale, legend, chronicle, fable, or
allegory.

In this last event for the children's tourney, the Scorekeeper waits
until there are four to eight ready to play. Then he hands half the number tissue-paper balls, and tells them to stand back to back. The other
players are "seconds" and must pick up the balls after they are thrown.

Contestants, upon the Scorekeeper's signal, take eight steps away
from each other. Turning around quickly, they throw the paper balls at

each other until one is hit. The seconds pick up and return balls to the contestants. Time allotted: 1 minute.

Seconds are ball-throwers when the next group of the same number has gathered and is ready to take part in Carousel.

Points: 20 for a hit. One hit entitles contestant to medal.

After the last event, tournament players add up their score cards; they are honor-bound to do it honestly and correctly like golfers in tournament play. They then present the cards to the Tournament Officials at the designated place for their gold medals and any other awards and prizes.

It can all end, as in the old days, with feasting—the serving of refreshments.

Bridge Cities
And
Their Bridge Games

THERE ARE QUITE a few cities that can be described as bridge cities: Venice with its 450 bridges; Amsterdam, Venice's rival in number; Rome, Paris, Tokyo, Leningrad, Stockholm, Shanghai, Osaka; San Francisco, Chicago, New Orleans, and New York.

Probably best known as "the city of bridges" is Venice, although most bridges there seem more like elevated crossings over street-canals than what one thinks of as actual bridges. The Rialto over the 100-foot-wide Grand Canal is an exception and was at one time the great merchandise mart of the Mediterranean.

Two cities have namesake bridge games with which they are always identified: London, England, and Avignon, France. These two singing dramatic games—London Bridge and Sur le Pont d'Avignon—have been played for centuries, went through many changes, and still exist like a hardy evergreen.

LONDON BRIDGE Today there are dozens of bridges over the Thames River, but for hundreds of years there was only one bridge across it—the one in the game. And in 1967 London sold her old bridge to the United States. It not only had been sinking into the Thames, but it was also becoming a great traffic bottleneck. A California firm, which was building Lake Havasu City, Arizona, as a recreational and light industry city, bought the bridge and gouged out a mile-long channel in the desert for a waterway for it.

This bridge is not the original London Bridge, for the first was undoubtedly a Roman structure, built of wood perhaps, at the time of the Conquest of Britain in A.D. 43. Three others, at least, followed the first at the same place. The one bought from the City of London was officially opened in 1831. The first London Bridge game is a lot older than that.

Among the many different chants or songs accompanying the game, is a particularly poetic and historically descriptive example from *Nursery Rhymes of England*, edited by James O. Halliwell in 1842, and, as he wrote, "Collected principally from Oral Tradition."

> London Bridge is broken down,*
> Dance o'er my lady lee,
> London Bridge is broken down,
> With a gay lady.†

> How shall we build it up again?
> Dance o'er my lady lee.
> How shall we build it up again?
> With a gay lady.

In all the succeeding stanzas, the second and fourth lines remain the same. In all stanzas but the last, the first and third lines are identical; following are the words for these first and third lines: "Build it up with silver and gold," "Silver and gold will be stole away," "Build it up again with iron and steel," "Iron and steel will bend and bow," "Build it up with wood and clay," "Wood and clay will wash away." The rhyme concludes with the following stanza:

> Build it up with stone so strong,
> Dance o'er my lady lee.
> Huzza!‡ 'twill last for ages long,
> With a gay lady.

---

* Usually "falling down" in the U.S.A., in both the first and third lines.
† Usually "my fair lady" in the U.S.A.
‡ Hurrah! in American English.

Ways of playing at least equal the number of different rhymes, but here is a version that has been popular for a long time in America.

Two children are chosen by the players to be Tower Guards, and they stand facing each other, several feet apart. (They are often called Prison Guards, or just Guards.) Other players form a line and walk between them chanting or singing the first verse to some tune. At the finish, Tower Guards join right hand to left hand, and raise arms, to make a single arch. Players pass under the arch, singing second verse. The Guards then raise both arms to form double arch, and players' line goes through to accompaniment of third verse. Tower Guards then take up the fourth verse and as they finish it, they lower the arch and enclose one of the players and take him/her away to London Tower. They continue singing and letting the arch fall on players and taking them away to the Tower until all players have been put in it.

As soon as the last player is brought to the Tower, all, including the last, break out, and the Tower Guards must catch two quickly to take their places.

SUR LE PONT D'AVIGNON   This is another singing, dramatic game always associated with a city and its bridge. Music and literature flourished in the prosperous wine and garden produce country of southern France, where Avignon, "the freeist, happiest city of the time" (twelfth century), was situated. Here the Rhone River divided into two channels, with the Isle of Barthelasse between them. Here, in the twelfth century, Petit-Benoit and his fellow monks, who called themselves, *Freres du Pont* (Brothers of the Bridge), accomplished a marvelous engineering feat: from Petit-Benoit's design, they built the longest bridge of stone masonry ever constructed.

The lighthearted Avignonais used it to cross to the Isle of Barthelasse, where they danced their gay *farandoles*. Never did they dance on the bridge, even before many of its stone arches were swept away during a great storm. *"Sur le Pont d'Avignon, / Tout le monde danse, danse,"* goes the French children's song, denying the fact, but it and the game belong to the late seventeenth or early eighteenth century, long after the bridge at Avignon lay in ruins.

Following is one way of playing the singing dramatic game. The group of boys and girls may be small or large, but there should be an even number of boys and of girls, if they take turns acting out the different verses. If all sing and act, the number does not matter. French and English versions follow.

French	English

French

Sur le Pont d'Avignon,
Tout le monde danse, danse.
Sur le Pont d'Avignon,
*Tout le monde danse en rond.**

Les beaux messieurs font comm' ça,
Et puis encore comm' ça.†

Sur le Pont d'Avignon,
Tout le monde danse, danse,
Sur le Pont d'Avignon,
*Tout le monde danse en rond.**

Les belles filles font comm' ça,
Et puis encore comm' ça.‡

Sur le Pont d'Avignon,
Tout le monde danse, danse,
Sur le Pont d'Avignon,
*Tout le monde danse en rond.**

Les petit chats font comm' ça,
Et puis encore comm' ça.§

Sur le Pont d'Avignon,
Toute le monde danse, danse.
Sur le Pont d'Avignon,
*Tout le monde danse en rond.**

Les petites bergères font comm' ça,
Et puis encore comm' ça.||

Sur le Pont d'Avignon,
Tout le monde danse, danse.
Sur le Pont d'Avignon,
*Tout le monde danse en rond.**

English

On the bridge of Avignon,
Everybody dances, dances.
On the bridge of Avignon,
Everybody dances round and round.

The handsome men do like this,
And again like this.

On the bridge of Avignon,
Everybody dances, dances.
On the bridge of Avignon,
Everybody dances round and round.

The pretty girls do like this,
And again like this.

On the bridge of Avignon,
Everybody dances, dances.
On the bridge of Avignon,
Everybody dances round and round.

The little cats do like this,
And again like this.

On the bridge of Avignon,
Everybody dances, dances.
On the bridge of Avignon,
Everybody dances round and round.

The little shepherdesses do like this,
And again like this.

On the bridge of Avignon,
Everybody dances, dances.
On the bridge of Avignon,
Everybody dances round and round.

---

* Children skip around and around, hands joined, each time they sing this stanza.

† During this verse, children bow twice with hands held as in dancing minuet.

‡ During this verse, children curtsy low twice.

§ During this verse, all make "paws" of hands and stroke whiskers.

|| During this verse, children pretend to wring out whey from curds in cheese bag.

Elles font un gros fromage,	They make a big cheese,
Et puis encore comm' ça.#	And again like this.

Sur le Pont d'Avignon,	On the bridge of Avignon,
Tout le monde danse, danse.	Everybody dances, dances.
Sur le Pont d'Avignon,	On the bridge of Avignon,
*Tout le monde danse en rond.**	Everybody dances round and round.

Sur le Pont d'Avignon,	On the bridge of Avignon,
Tout le monde danse, danse.	Everybody dances, dances.
Qu'il fait bon danser, danser	How good it is to dance, dance
*Sur le Pont d'Avignon.***	On the bridge of Avignon.

LONDON BRIDGE TILTING   This was a game invented by the boys of the city, which called for "shooting the bridge." This meant that they armed themselves with wooden staves ("lances"), took a boat or barge, and rowed it up or down the Thames. As they raced past the target, which they had placed on one of the arches, they tried to splinter their lances against the target.

It is doubtful that this old London game will ever be played under the arches of old London Bridge in its new home at Lake Havasu City, Arizona, where it was transported from London, piece by piece and stone by stone, beginning in 1968. But an archway or open doorway can serve young lancers as a run-through for the game of Dart in the Basket.

Hang a wicker basket in a door or archway, just high enough for the children to touch standing on tiptoe. Each player before the start of the game is given several sheets of 8½ x 11-inch paper with which to make airplanes—the simplest folded kind children are always launching. Player then writes his name on each plane-dart. When all are ready, they take turns running through the doorway, attempting to toss a dart into the basket, which has been set swinging back and forth.

All misses must be left where they have fallen. When players have used up their darts, the game is over. Points may be given for each dart put in the basket.

For a party, the swinging basket can be filled with candies and fruits,

---

During this verse, children smack the air with the right hand as though patting a cheese dry with a butter or cheese paddle.

* Children skip around and around, hands joined, each time they sing this stanza.
** Just before this last verse, all the children whirl around several times, then stop and stand in a circle. During the verse, all join hands and go skipping around in a circle, gradually one at a time letting go hands and whirling off by oneself, singing, *"Qu'il fait bon danser, danser / Sur le Pont d'Avignon."*)

and children can race through, trying to tilt at it with the tips of their fingers and make it tip out its good things. All scramble for them.

This is a variety of the Spanish and Latin American *piñata,* a hanging jar filled with good things to eat. Children take turns or try all together to break the jar, so candies come tumbling down, and all rush to get them (see Part VIII for holiday versions).

GIUOCO DEL PONTE   City dwellers and suburbanites played this game on the Ponte di Mezzo in Pisa, Italy. The bridge was in the center of the city, and contestants, wearing helmets and carrying shields, gathered at the river—the city group on one side, the suburban on the other. A signal was given and they rushed onto the bridge with the objective of holding it for their side. The game was rough, but safety measures included the protective helmets and shields, and a strict rule of "no hitting below the belt." The fight was followed by feasting.

For children who would like to play the Pisan bridge game, use a play street or a lined-out space for the span. Sides are chosen for City and Suburb, and one player is selected to be Bridgemaster. This player stands in the middle of the "bridge" and calls out commands.

At the start, City and Suburb take their places at opposite ends of the bridge. When all are ready, the Bridgemaster calls out either "Go, City!" or "Go, Suburb!" whereupon the group called must march up to the middle of the bridge and wait until the Bridgemaster shouts, "Turn them back!" If City-ites have marched up to the middle, that is the cue for Suburbanites to dart forward and try to catch as many City-ites as possible before they can return to the safety of their own bridgehead.

The Bridgemaster can then (1) command Suburbanites to return with their captives, who are now themselves Suburbanites, to their own end of the bridge, or (2) can command the City-ites to "Rush the bridge!" and try to retake those who have been captured; or (3) command both City and Suburb to return to their own bridgeheads, the Suburbanites taking their captives. Then the Bridgemaster can command the latter to march to the middle of the bridge and the remaining City-ites to "Turn them back!"

Objective of the game is the attempt to capture all the members of one group by the other group, so that one side does "hold the bridge."

In order to make a capture, a player must tag an opponent, crying out at the same time, "I turn you back!" Tagger then grasps his captive's arm and the two stand, waiting for the Bridgemaster's next command.

In this game much depends upon the skill and imagination that the Bridgemaster brings to the game. He must try to keep the game going at a lively pace, giving first one side, then the other the advantage in his commands, so that the struggle for the bridge is well balanced between City and Suburb. Therefore, before a player is selected to take that part, it should be made clear to him that what is needed is not just a series of commands for the sake of commands, but commands that involve strategy to the end that the game is fun for all.

Venice, Italy, has a bridge named Ponte dei Pugni, that is, Boxing or Fist-Fighting Bridge, where groups carried on combat like that on the bridge in Pisa. City bridges lend themselves to the contest type of games. In this they are like roads. For other contests see Part V.

TOLL BRIDGE   This is a variety of Hill Dill or Pom Pom Pull Away in which Toll Taker is the name given It. Toll Taker assumes his place in the middle of the play area—the bridge—and the others line up seven or eight yards away, facing him. The same distance away from the Toll Taker's back is the other end of the bridge.

When the Toll Taker calls out, "Cross the bridge!" players dash for the opposite end, while the Toll Taker tries to tag as many as he can. All tagged must join him in calling for crossing the bridge and in tagging. The last one the Toll Takers tag is the next Toll Taker.

Counting-out Rhymes
To Find
Who Will Be "It"

THERE ARE SO many games that require either the drawing of straws or "counting out" for determining who goes first, who is to be It and the like that it's always good to have a few more, just in case players are tired of those they have been using. Although those over ten may think counting out "babyish" they often resort to it. These from different countries offer a taste of the beauty of languages. There are no ugly languages, say the poets of the world.

English

Hoyda, hoyda,
Butterkin, butterkin,
Buttered fish,
Potato knish,
Make a wish.
You're the dish.

Zeenty, peenty, hither, heathery
Bumfy, leery, over, Dover
Saw the king of Hetzel Pretzel
Jumping over Jerusalem dyke.
Brown trout,
Pike, whitefish, yellow carp.
Airie, lurie, you're *out*.

Portuguese

Um, dois, três, quatro,	One, two, three, four,
Cavalo, galinha, vaca, gato,	Horse, hen, cow, cat,
O senhor é um pássaro? Nao!	Sir, are you a bird? No!
A senhora é um pato? Nao!	Ma'am, are you a duck? No!
O senhor (a senhora), é um ganso!	Sir (Ma'am) you are a *goose!*

Estonian *

Laula, laula	Sing, sing,
Uks, kaks, kolm, neli,	One, two, three, four,
Laula	Sing
Uksteise ees't	One after the other
Uks, kaks, kolm, neli,	One, two, three, four,
Laululind.	Songbird.

Spanish

Cafe con leche	Coffee with milk,
Leche con cafe,	Milk with coffee,
Leche, cafe.	Milk, coffee.
Uno, dos, tres, cuatro,	One, two, three, four,
¡Vamos!	Let's go!

French

Poule, poule sur le mur	Chick, chick on the wall
Picote, picote du pain dur.	Pecks, pecks at some hard bread.
Poule qui picote, picoti, picota	Chick that pecks, pecks here, pecks there
Lève deux ailes et saute au bas.	Lifts its two wings and jumps down.

West Indian (from Jamaica)

Makes no difference
What you eat,
Whether rice or greens or meat;
All the flavor sure is lost
Unless you have some pepper sauce.
Pep-per—*pepper!*

---

* Estonia is one of the fourteen national minorities of the U.S.S.R. Its language is rich in folktale and folk poetry.

Bibliography

Antey, John W. *Sing and Learn.* New York: John Day Co., 1965.

Armstrong, Alan. *Maori Action Songs.* San Francisco: Tri-Ocean Inc., 1960.

———. *Maori Games and Hakas.* San Francisco: Tri-Ocean Inc., 1964.

Arrow Book of Riddles. New York: Scholastic Book Services.

Beaver, Edmund. *Travel Games* (rev. ed.). Fergus Falls, Minn.: Beavers.

Bell, Robert C. *Board and Table Games from Many Civilizations.* New York: Oxford University Press, 1960.

Bett, Henry. *Games of Children, Their Origin and History.* Detroit: Singing Tree Press, 1929.

Boys' Clubs of America. *Games to Build* (rev. ed.). New York: Boys' Clubs of America, 1962.

Bruegel, Peter, the Elder. *Children's Games.* Edited by Paul Portmann. New York: Taplinger Publishing Co., 1964.

Chase, Richard. *Old Songs and Singing Games.* New York: Dover Publications, Inc.: 1968.

Culin, Stewart. *Games of the Orient.* Rutland, Vt.: Charles E. Tuttle, 1958.

Douglas, Norman. *London Street Games* (2d ed.). Detroit: Singing Tree Press, 1968.

Eisenberg, Larry. *Fun and Festival from the United States and Canada.* New York: Friendship Press, 1956.

Elder, J. D. *Song Games of Trinidad and Tobago.* Austin: University of Texas Press, 1964.

Falkener, Edward. *Games Ancient and Oriental and How to Play Them* (1st ed.). 1892. Reprint. New York: Dover Publications, Inc., 1961.

Farina, Albert, *et al. Growth Through Play.* Englewood Cliffs, N.J.: Prentice-Hall, Inc.: 1959.

Fisher, Aileen. *Holiday Programs for Boys and Girls* (gr. 2-6). Boston: Plays, Inc., 1953.

Fisher, Aileen, and Rabe, O. *United Nations Plays and Programs* (gr. 6-10). Boston: Plays, Inc., 1954.

Freeman, Ruth. *Yesterday's Games.* Watkins Glen, N.Y.: Century House.

Gardner, Martin. *Perplexing Puzzles and Tantalizing Teasers.* Illustrated by Laszlo Kubinyi. New York: Simon & Schuster, Inc.: 1969.

Gomme, Alice B., ed. *Traditional Games of England, Scotland, and Ireland.* 2 vols. 1894-8. Reprint. New York: Dover Publications, Inc.

Gwinn, Alice E., and Hibbard, Esther L. *Fun and Festival from Japan.* New York: Friendship Press, 1956.

Haddon, Kathleen. *String Games for Beginners.* Cambridge, England: W. Heffer & Sons, 1967.

Hallock, Constance M. *Fun and Festival from Southeast Asia.* New York: Friendship Press, 1956.

Harbin, Elvin O. *Games of Many Nations.* Nashville: Abingdon Press, 1954.

Hartwick, Harry. *The Amazing Maze.* Illustrated by Reynold Ruffins and Simms Taback. New York: E. P. Dutton & Co., 1969.

Hole, Christian. *English Sports and Pastimes.* Freeport, N.Y.: Books for Libraries, Inc., 1949.

Huizinga, Johan. *Homo Ludens: A Study of the Play Element in Culture.* Boston: Beacon Press Inc., 1955.

Hummel, Margaret G. *Fun and Festival from China.* New York: Friendship Press, 1956.

Hunt, Sarah E. *Games and Sports the World Around* (3d ed.). New York: Ronald Press Co., 1964.

Hunt, Sarah E., and Cain, Ethel. *Games the World Around* (1st ed.). New York: A. S. Barnes and Co., Inc., 1930.

Ickis, Marguerite. *Book of Games and Entertainment the World Over.* New York: Dodd, Mead & Co., 1968.

International Council on Health, Physical Education and Recreation. *ICHPER Book of Worldwide Games and Dances* (gr. 1-6). Washington, D.C.: International Council on Health, Physical Education and Recreation, 1967.

Jayne, Caroline Furness. *String Figures and How to Make Them, A Study of Cat's Cradle in Many Lands.* 1906. Reprint. New York: Dover Publications, Inc., 1962.

Keene, F. W. *Travel Fun Book.* New York: McGraw-Hill Book Co.

Mead, Margaret. *People and Places* (1st ed.). Cleveland: World Publishing Co., 1959; New York: Bantam Books (pap.), 1969.

Millen, Nina, ed. *Children's Games from Many Lands* (rev. ed.). New York: Friendship Press, 1965.

Morrison, Lillian, comp. *Sprints and Distances; Sports in Poetry and the Poetry in Sport.* Illustrated by Clare and John Ross. New York: Thomas Y. Crowell Co., 1965.

Newell, William W. *Games and Songs of American Children* (2d ed.). 1903. Reprint. New York: Dover Publications, Inc., 1962.

Opie, Iona and Peter. *The Lore and Language of Schoolchildren.* London: Oxford University Press, 1959.

————. *The Oxford Dictionary of Nursery Rhymes.* London: Oxford University Press, 1951.

Potter, Charles F., comp. *More Tongue Tanglers and a Rigmarole* (gr. 3-5). Illustrated by William Wiesner. Cleveland: World Publishing Co., 1964.

Rohrbough, Katherine Ferris. *Fun and Festival Among America's Peoples.* New York: Friendship Press, 1956.

Sebeok, Thomas A., and Brester, Paul G., eds. *Games.* Studies in Cheremis, vol. 6. Bloomington: Indiana University Press, 1958.

Shepherd, Walter. *Mazes and Labyrinths, a Book of Puzzles* (2d rev. ed.). New York: Dover Publications, Inc.: 1961.

Spicer, Dorothy Gladys. *Folk Party Fun.* New York: Association Press, 1954.

Stern, Theodore. *Rubber-Ball Games of the Americas.* Seattle: University of Washington Press, 1949.

Sutherland, Efua. *Playtime in Africa* (gr. 1-5). New York: Atheneum Publishers, 1962.

U.S. Committee for UNICEF. *Hi Neighbor* (gr. 2-6). 8 vols. New York: Hastings House Publishers, Inc., 1961.

Wagner, Guy, and Gillolev, L. *Social Studies Games.* Darien, Conn.: Teachers Publishing Corp., 1964.

Wagner, Guy, and Hosier, M. *Language Games*. Darien, Conn.: Teachers Publishing Corp., 1963.

Webster, David. *Crossroad Puzzlers*. Garden City, N.Y.: Doubleday & Co. for Natural History Press.

———. *Scottish Highland Games*. New York: William Collins, Sons & Co., Ltd.

Wells, Irene, and Bothwell, Jean. *Fun and Festival from India, Pakistan, and Ceylon*. New York: Friendship Press, 1956.

Wright, Rose H. *Fun and Festival from Africa*. New York: Friendship Press, 1956.